FROM THE INSIDE

Ruth Wyner now works with the Dialogue Trust on prisoner
rehabilitation and prison reform. She lives in Cambridge.

'*From the Inside* tells a judicial and a very personal story…
through direct observation and painful experience'
Times Higher Education Supplement

'Intelligent and informative' *The Big Issue*

'Wyner's outrage at being jailed – for doing her job – is pulsatingly
present throughout the book. I, for one, can only wonder what
went so badly wrong with our judicial system that a bright, feisty,
committed, compassionate social worker could end up doing a
longer sentence than the woman in her next cell who'd
killed her boyfriend'
Anne Garvey, *Jewish Chronicle*

'While Wyner's book is an impassioned plea for prison reform
and clarity in the law… its strength lies in her description
of life in women's prisons and its human costs'
Times Educational Supplement

Ruth Wyner

Aurum

CRI

First published in Great Britain
2003 by Aurum Press Ltd
25 Bedford Avenue, London WC1B 3AT

This paperback edition first published 2004

All characters from prison are composites.
Names have been changed to preserve confidentiality.

A catalogue record for this book is available
from the British Library.

ISBN 1 85410 970 7

10 9 8 7 6 5 4 3 2 1
2008 2007 2006 2005 2004

Design by Ken Wilson
Typeset in Minion by M Rules
Printed by Bookmarque, Croydon, Surrey

contents

For my family, especially my mother, Anna;
Gordon, Joel and Rachel; Angela, Jim, Nick and Alexis;
Harold, Mary, Max and Deborah; Betty and Gillian.

'Punishment must be exacted even if it does not fall upon the guilty.'
SIGMUND FREUD, 1923

'People took such awful chances with chemicals and their bodies because they wanted the quality of their lives to improve. They lived in ugly places where there were only ugly things to do. They didn't own doodly-squat, so they couldn't improve their surroundings. So they did their best to make their insides beautiful instead.'
KURT VONNEGUT JR, *Breakfast of Champions*, 1973

'Miscarriages of justice can happen to anyone, at any time, for any offence.'
MICHAEL MANSFIELD QC, *Presumed Guilty*, 1993

acknowledgements

I owe a debt to Sally Cline, without whom this book would not have seen the light of day, and to Andrew Franklin at Profile Books, who got me started.

My good friends Jenny Fox and Libby Smith: what a very long time it has been for us. To Denis Hayes, who never lost sight of what he knew and believed despite the personal cost. Whatever it takes, Den. And Jenny Mace, who read through reams of early manuscript without complaint. To Chris and Marion Roberts for helping see me through the trial, and Andrew Mount: you did too. Pete and Lindsey McGaffin: I picture you marching with young Laura Mae. To Sarah, Iris Hunter, Colin and Stephanie Shaw for their help and friendship, and to Agi Lloyd: your wisdom permeates this book. Also Cambridge Group Work, the Association of Therapeutic Communities, everyone at 1a Stockwell Street, and the staff and my fellow students at the Turvey Institute for Group Analytic Psychotherapy: you are all just great.

Never forgetting the Wintercomfort trustees, especially Sarah Barrow, who as chair held firm despite massive pressure (no – not the brandy!), Katie Knapton, who so helpfully shared a secret, and George Reid, my great protector at St John's College bursary; thanks to the staff there too. Henry Rothschild, Wintercomfort's founder, it was such a comfort that you stood by me, and Nicky Padfield, my learned lawyer friend, how I value your good-humoured good sense. And remembering the staff and the clientele at Wintercomfort who lived through those difficult times; it was grossly unfair on you all.

This book has only been possible with the help of the Cambridge Two campaign: the organizers and activists, the people who so generously contributed to the Support and Fghting Funds, those who signed and collected petitions, wrote to me in prison and wrote to the powers that be: I owe you guys, lots. Most especially I must thank Alexander Masters: you were an inspired campaign chairman.

Lastly to those women who shared my time inside: your strength was my strength. And to all the other victims of miscarriages of justice, mostly little known: I wish you strength too.

one

Jonathan Haworth was a new judge out to make his mark. Sitting on high in red and purple robes, grey wig perched on his head, he wiped his moustache and appeared to lick his lips as he appraised the hapless pair in the dock before him. He told us to stand. This was the moment I had been dreading but had been unable to imagine, it held such a terror for me. Haworth had reportedly been heard boasting at a lawyers' party that he was going to send John and me to jail. I could hardly believe it. Now it was really happening. I hauled myself to my feet and gripped the rail in front of me.

'You will go to prison for five years.'

My vision blurred; I felt sick from the inside and worked hard to remain upright. It was worse than I had thought possible. I glanced at my husband but looked away again quickly, struggling to control myself, fearful of total collapse. A detective sergeant who had been involved in the case, and who had not looked at me once throughout the seven-week trial, now fixed me with a fierce eyeball-to-eyeball stare. He had got a result and was savouring the moment, sending waves of hatred my way – hatred that at root seemed to have nothing at all to do with me.

John got four years. The judge continued to spin words around the courtroom until a crescendo of anger from the crowded public gallery drowned him out.

'Disgraceful!'

'Disgusting!'

'How dare you!'

A drug addict who had used our projects stood up and called out: 'I'd be dead if it wasn't for these people,' then stormed out of the courtroom. More shouting; someone wept. Everybody looked confused, apart from the police, who had got what they wanted.

Our lawyers had presented the mitigation in an attempt to keep our sentences to the minimum: the barristers bobbing up and down, anxiously flapping their black gowns like winged protagonists. They need not have bothered. I heard that Haworth had come to court with his eight pages of sentencing remarks already typed up for the press. He had been against us from the start. British justice had, for me, been transformed into surreal farce.

'Take them down,' ordered the judge. There was a round of supportive applause as John and I were led to the cells below. I managed to turn briefly for a last look and a wave at those familiar faces I would not be seeing for a very long time. Walking down the narrow wooden steps, I felt I was walking away from my whole life: family, children, work, home. Everything.

The legal team came to see us, shocked by the judge's pronouncements. They vowed to fight on and told me that after we had left the court, my normally restrained twenty-three-year-old son, Joel, had, amid the general mêlée, got himself arrested for walking up to Haworth, staring him in the eye and declaring him to be 'Scum!'

'The judge made him apologize,' said my barrister, 'but he did it in such a way that we all knew he didn't mean it.'

Then I got a distraught five minutes with my deeply loyal son and my husband, Gordon. My daughter, Rachel, aged sixteen, was at school, unable to face coming to court with us. How on earth would Gordon break this to her? We spoke through a pane of toughened glass in a grimy room that contained a few bare wooden tables and chairs. These were to be the parameters of my new life: dirty, unpleasant surroundings. We said our farewells and pledged our love, holding back the tears, being strong for each other.

Our families gone, John and I had a two-hour wait. We hardly spoke, were shrouded in despair.

'We'll have to get used to this waiting around.' I said. 'There'll be a whole lot more of it in prison.'

□ □ □

Prison: I had never expected to end up there. How could a civilized society do such a thing to me? And to my family, my husband and two children? Perhaps that is a question every prisoner asks at some point, but I think I had special reasons for it to come to mind.

Homelessness is an unusual trade. I had been a hard-working practitioner since the end of the 1970s, when I ran shifts single-handed at a rough night shelter in Norwich. The disused church building had housed up to forty-five raucous, desperate, frequently drunk, often seriously mentally ill, usually disturbed and distressed men, plus five women in equal disarray. I had slipped into the job by accident and my move into management some years later seemed equally accidental. I was committed to the work and prepared to push things forward. It was not a popular job but it suited me.

So why did people want to send me to prison? I had made some enemies among those who were disgusted by my clientele, those whose sympathies did not extend to people visibly suffering from failure and misfortune. It is not always easy to see the human being within the dirty wrappings of old clothes. But why was there such resentment for people like me, those for whom helping the homeless had, accidentally or otherwise, become their profession?

I was neither saint nor sinner; I was just earning my living in the best way I knew how. Even so, I ended up being hauled through the British courts and thrown into jail in a wave of hysteria and a blaze of publicity that struck fear into managers of homelessness projects throughout the country.

The charge was that John and I had allowed heroin to be traded at a day centre for the homeless, one of five projects run by Wintercomfort, a local Cambridge charity of which I was the director. This was despite the fact that we adhered to accepted good practice. Despite the fact that we had drawn up a tough new drugs policy. And despite the fact that we had agonized about the burgeoning problem of drugs among the homeless at our weekly staff meetings, our monthly board meetings and the six-weekly advisory-group meetings attended at our invitation by the police, who, incidentally, had never once warned us that we could be breaking the law.

We had provided our day-centre services for heroin users, among others, at the behest of the local authorities: health, housing and social services. Some of our 300 clientele had conducted heroin deals behind our backs in the outside courtyard of the day centre and we were deemed to have known. It was as if we had been found guilty by association.

The only way I could make sense of my prosecution was to accept that it was political: people wanted to put a stop to me developing and raising funds for homelessness projects in Cambridge. They wanted to shut me up. Now they had. I was locked up, and locked out of the world.

□ □ □

It was early evening: too late for us to go to our respective jails, which meant that we would spend the night in police cells, something I reckoned would give a measure of satisfaction to the Cambridge cops, though I knew some of them were embarrassed by our prosecution. I would do my best to retain my dignity. The guards came for us and my whole body flinched as they snapped on the heavy silver handcuffs, one half on to my wrist, the other half on to theirs. I was led out of the Guildhall and hustled into the back of a waiting police van. The last thing I saw before the doors slammed shut was Cambridge's newly erected Christmas tree dripping with warm golden lights, the wet streets shimmering with reflections as shoppers hurried home laden with their purchases. I felt a powerful and primal urge to run; only the handcuffs held me back.

The drive to the police station was all too short. I greedily drank in the view through the van's back window, my last look at these familiar streets. We were bundled into the cells. I had been there once before, when I was arrested eighteen months previously and held for nine hours. Those windowless rooms were about 8 feet square and each had a rock-solid bench along one wall, with an extra bit of space round the corner for the open toilet. There was no washbasin and the floors were stone-cold. A frosted skylight in the ceiling let in a little natural light. You could be viewed through a hatch in the heavy door that was banged shut behind me. Keys rattled in the lock. No words were spoken. I sat on the bench, stunned, and looked at my watch. It was 7 p.m. Alone and isolated, I felt like a nothing, a nobody, just a weak, pink, pathetic creature, loathsome and worthless. My feet were icy. They had taken my shoes away.

The evening wore slowly on. I was given a polystyrene cup of strong, sweet tea, which I gratefully forced down my throat, plus a microwaved meal, which I could not begin to swallow. A few tears squeezed their way out from time to time as I perched on the bench, swathed in the two thin blankets I had been given. There seemed to be no heating. As the night wore on, I lay down but did not sleep. Thoughts swirled in my head, punctuated by more bouts of weeping.

Punishment and pain: that was what it was all about. I needed to protect myself so that it did not hurt as much, so that I could emerge intact and hold on to that precious soul part of me, which I needed to hide away, to keep safe from the barbarism to come. Abuse, I knew, was inherent in the prison system, and being a middle-class professional woman, I was no ordinary prisoner. I could get it worse.

I was reminded of kids' games where you get caught by the other side: cowboys and Indians; cops and robbers. But this time it was for real: grown-up, frightening and brutal. How could they take me away from my family? I belonged there with them, with Gordon and Joel and Rachel. That was my place, that was where I was needed. The horror and shame of abandoning my daughter tormented me; at sixteen, she was standing on the threshold of womanhood and she needed her mother.

December the seventeenth 1999, the verge of a bright new millennium; but I saw only gloom and despondency ahead. It was hard to fight off the feelings of failure, feelings that I must somehow deserve this, that I was as wicked as the idiot judge seemed to believe. How could anyone even suggest that we had allowed heroin to be sold at the day centre when we had spent so much time and energy trying to combat the problem? The jury had believed it, that was what counted, and the local evening paper had leapt upon the story.

I was the same person as I always had been, I told myself. Waves of misery spun me through the night as the cell light blazed continuously. They would not turn it off. There was no relief to be found anywhere.

□ □ □

I had been arrested in May 1998 and, after a nine-hour stint of interrogation and incarceration in police cells, was accused of knowingly allowing heroin to be sold on our premises, known as the Bus, contrary to Section 8 of the Misuse of Drugs Act 1971. John, the manager of the Bus, got similar treatment the following week. The trial, eighteen months later, had lasted seven weeks. I'd had to drag myself the 40 miles up to King's Lynn Crown Court every day, that being the prosecution's choice of venue. Someone told me it had the highest conviction rate of any Crown Court in the land.

At the time, people said we were convicted for doing our jobs. Everyone, including the prosecution, accepted that we had not benefited or profited in any way from our so-called crime. But Wintercomfort was vulnerable, being a small but outspoken local charity. I became its director in January 1995, having already spent fifteen years working in homelessness in East Anglia. At that time, Cambridge had one of the worst homelessness problems outside London. It still does.

The homeless and the rootless are inevitably attracted to well-known and well-heeled places that sound familiar, like Brighton, Bath, London of course, and Oxford and Cambridge. On top of that, Cambridgeshire had become by the mid-1990s the fastest-growing county in England: business was booming. Unfortunately, house-building did not keep up. Council stock was limited and house prices in the private sector soared. Whatever accommodation was available for rent soon got snapped up by professionals coming in, or, as landlords' second choice, by the 15,000 students who descended on the city every year. The homeless hardly got a look in. Oxford was lucky in that one of its graduates had set about developing quality services for the homeless in the city back in the 1970s. The response in Cambridge was much slower and less adventurous.

It was also a time when heroin addiction was becoming endemic in the homeless population. People in distress are inevitably attracted to substances that ease their pain and, if they are sleeping on the streets, also numb their bodies to the cold and the discomfort. Alcohol was always an attractive option, and continues to be so, but the appearance of heroin in large amounts along with a general lowering of the age of the homeless meant that the conventional image of the alcoholic old tramp was increasingly replaced by more youthful but still decrepit shambling figures: heroin addicts, shunned by the community and by many of the local homelessness projects and the statutory agencies as well.

Heroin: the most effective painkiller known to mankind. As well as easing the pain of street living – the aches in your bones, chest and skin problems, and deep tiredness from long stretches without a good night's sleep – it counters mental anguish to great effect. When you have had a hit, everything in your world seems absolutely fine. There is no stress or tension, only relief.

A major difficulty for health workers is that heroin also effectively disguises the symptoms of mental illness. Psychiatric problems have always been a feature of homelessness. That multiplied hugely with the closure of the large mental hospitals in the 1970s and 1980s and the advent of care in the community. Decent accommodation was not always available to former in-patients and support in the community was often not properly in place. People would drift and end up on the streets or in night shelters. The shelter I had worked at in Norwich began itself to feel like a psychiatric ward, except that staffing was minimal and most of the residents were not on any medication for their condition. Homelessness workers grew to understand that heroin addicts, and alcoholics too, were frequently self-medicating for their condition, either because nothing else was available to them or because the drugs prescribed by doctors had intolerable side effects. The picture was a complex one. For many people, rattled by the sight of the homeless living outside social norms, it was easy to condemn.

When I got to Cambridge, I worked urgently to raise funds for the city's unmet needs and to raise awareness of the local situation. Wintercomfort trustees told me to 'shout it from the rooftops'. So I spoke up, got Wintercomfort and homelessness into the local papers, on to television and radio news, and developed a high personal profile in the city. Ironically, the *Cambridge Evening News* quoted me in two separate stories warning about the increasing problem of heroin use among the homeless at the very same time that the police were gathering the evidence that led to my arrest.

'Drug addiction is becoming more of a problem than alcohol for the city's homeless, a charity boss has warned' ran the *Evening News* headline on 12 March 1998. Then, on 2 April, the paper quoted me as saying: 'There has been an enormously worrying increase [in heroin use] and it's become so much easier to get hold of the drug … It is making our work harder because people have an additional difficulty to deal with.'

I was anxious to protect my clients and my projects but did not realize how urgently I needed to protect myself too.

□ □ □

The Bus was an open-door day centre, which meant that people could come and go at will, unless banned by the staff. Bans were imposed for violence and for infringements of our drugs and alcohol policies. The project was funded by social services, along with the health and housing authorities, with a remit to encourage those unable or unwilling to engage with services to come and use them in an informal setting. People with drug problems who were homeless or at risk of becoming so were among those we were expected to target. We offered help with the basics, such as food, clothing and washing facilities, along with access to a GP, mental health nurses and drug and alcohol workers. People were given advice and support to help them gain and maintain accommodation, and every afternoon we ran discussion groups or activity sessions.

We developed what we thought was a good and trusting relationship with our liaison police officers, the beat bobby and the sector inspector, through formal and informal meetings as well as the advisory group. My barrister argued in court that the police owed a duty of care to those they advised. We were certainly never advised that we risked breaking the law, but this argument was not acknowledged.

So while one arm of the law was reassuring us that we were working within our remit, the other arm was running a surveillance operation that led to our arrests. A secret eye-in-the-sky camera trained on to our courtyard caught some of our clientele engaged in exchanges that looked like drug dealing. Two undercover policemen were subsequently sent into the day centre twelve times and, after asking around among our downtrodden project users, were able to buy £10 deals of heroin on nine of those occasions. As a result, eight of our 300 clients were arrested and sent to prison for dealing.

We were happy that they had been caught, but not happy to hear the police describe them as 'major drug dealers'. We saw them as small-time addicts, homeless and ex-homeless, out to make a hit for themselves. Selling £10 deals in the courtyard of a homeless day centre, while reprehensible, is hardly big-time dealing.

My arrest came as a complete shock. No one consciously expected it. But, looking back, it was as if I had picked up on something in the ether. That morning I had woken at 3 a.m. and, unable to settle again, was at Wintercomfort by 4.30 a.m. where an enormous pile of outstanding paperwork languished in my office. Fortified by strong coffee, I spent the next five hours wading through everything until my desk was cleared. I joined the Bus staff supervision at 9.30 a.m., was arrested an hour later and held in the police cells until 8 o'clock that night. That was my first experience of the cells. They had not changed since then, but my status had changed. Then I was a respected charity director. Now I was being imprisoned as a convicted criminal. It seemed a cruel and inexplicable transformation. I had no idea how devastating it would prove to be.

I was arrested shortly after the police had asked us to give them the names of those we had banned from the project for drugs: drug use as well as dealing or suspected dealing. We were not warned we could be breaking the law if we did not comply. The request was made prior to the arrests of the dealers, so we had no knowledge of the covert police operation or of the situation that it uncovered. We explained that we could not give out names because of Wintercomfort's confidentiality policy, a standard policy that I had written on coming into the post. The police had seemed satisfied with that. Astonishingly, in court the trial judge told the jury that the very act of writing such a policy could be seen as demonstrating an unwillingness to help the police. Like most of our colleagues in the sector, we had understood it to be good practice to offer a confidential service to our clientele.

Three of the convicted drug dealers gave evidence against us at our trial, tempted by the prospect of days out of prison as their reward, fish and chip dinners, inter-prison visits, and other inducements. Of these three, two tried to correct matters in court. One of them said she had only given her original statement under pressure from the police and that all the drug addicts on the Bus had in fact hidden their activities from the staff.

'The police told me they'd look after me, take me back to Cambridge, and that I had a lot better chance of parole if I gave a statement,' she said at the trial. 'I just told them what they wanted to hear.'

The second dealer agreed with everything suggested to him in the witness box, whether from the prosecution or the defence, having been warned by the police that he could be prosecuted for perjury if he changed his evidence.

The third, one Timothy Pocket, stuck to his story: that he openly sold vast amounts of heroin on the Bus, which we knew to be an impossibility with our impoverished client group. As for selling the drugs openly, the police surveillance camera showed that deals were never done in front of staff. In court, staff were continually criticized for walking past dealers, but they did not know who the dealers were. On the videos, we saw our local beat bobby walking past the dealers too; he did not know who they were either.

Pocket was a fluent witness, too fluent, but he made a serious mistake: he repeatedly said he came into the Bus to deal at 9 a.m., but the project never opened before 11 a.m. Even so, his evidence was seized upon by the judge, who said he found this man with twenty-six years of criminality behind him 'a convincing witness'. It was crucial to our convictions. But Pocket's evidence had been given under inducement: he had asked for a reduction in his prison category, which would make his life behind bars considerably easier, and he got it. He was also given cigarettes, paper and food, and I was not surprised when, of all the eight convicted dealers, Pocket got parole and was let out of prison early, as was his girlfriend. Apparently his deals were not limited to those involving drugs.

My defence solicitor visited some of the other imprisoned addicts. They said they had explained to the police that I had strengthened the no-drugs procedures on the Bus and that I had certainly not turned a blind eye. One complained that the police continued to pressurize him to give evidence against me after turning off their tape. To his credit, he resisted. Looking back, I regretted not calling these others as defence witnesses to counteract the false picture given by Pocket, though I doubted whether it would have made any difference to the end result.

We did not get information about or transcripts of these police interview tapes, and my barrister was convinced that the prosecution had plenty of other material that could have been useful to us but was not disclosed as it should have been. For instance, we heard that police had contacted other homelessness establishments, asking to see their drugs policies. When they found out that Wintercomfort's was superior to most, and was in fact used by the National Day Centre Project as a model policy for its members, they quickly backtracked.

This illustrates what many consider to be a defect of the British justice system. In my case, the police made an arrest and, based on an assumption of guilt, carried out an investigation, collecting evidence that fitted their picture but discarding that which did not. They were unwilling to disclose discarded evidence because it would not have helped their case. If I had been in France, for instance, an independent person would have carried out the investigation once the police had made the arrest, and that person would have sought the truth, rather than the basis for a conviction.

I knew that some people in Cambridge were aggressively unsympathetic to the plight of the homeless and I had become identified with the cause. They were roused in particular by my attempts to set up a controversial new hostel in the city. Concerned about the numbers of people still sleeping rough, many of them clearly vulnerable, I initially helped a local church group establish a night shelter in the basement of their church building. It was very cramped and understandably received only temporary planning permission, for a period of three years, so I set about finding adequate permanent premises. With business booming in Cambridge, nothing seemed to be available to us, until someone suggested that we use a large space under what was known as the Elizabeth Way road bridge. This was one site that no one else wanted. It seemed ideal.

In September 1997 I submitted a planning application to Cambridge City Council. I also put in an application to the National Lottery Charities Board for half the building costs. We could raise the other half on appeal.

It was as if I had set light to a tinderbox. There was massive protest against the planning application from people who lived on a small estate of privately owned houses around the corner from the Elizabeth Way bridge. The flames were eagerly stoked by one or two individuals who terrified their neighbours with stories of how the shelter's clientele would be a threat to women and children and to the overall safety and security of their lives, scandalously demonizing the homeless. The aim of their campaign was to discredit Wintercomfort and me, and to blame our provision of services for attracting homeless people into the city. Some of the local councillors jumped on the bandwagon. Others refused to be tempted.

One of the first written objections to the planning application came from the police, who largely based their arguments on the project causing an increase in people's fear of crime. They then turned their minds to running the covert surveillance operation of the Bus project, setting a secret camera into a roof tile in a building over the road and training it on our courtyard area. After a couple of months, in March 1998, the police took a break to decide what to do next. During this period, two important decisions were made involving Wintercomfort: full planning permission for the new Elizabeth Way shelter was granted, and £400,000 was awarded towards the project by the National Lottery Charities Board, their largest-ever grant in the Eastern region. We were ecstatic, but our triumph was short-lived. Shortly afterwards, the police recommended the covert surveillance and sent in their two undercover officers to try to purchase heroin. They arrested eight people and charged them with selling £10 deals, and then they arrested me. Needless to say, the Elizabeth Way project foundered and the lottery money was lost to us. Cambridge continued to have one of the worst street homelessness problems in the country.

After I had been charged I was restricted by bail conditions, set by the police, which made life particularly difficult. I was not allowed to go into Wintercomfort's premises or to contact the twelve members of staff who had been on site when I was arrested. They had been interviewed by the police and were designated as prosecution witnesses. So I set up camp in the bursary of St John's College and from there ran Wintercomfort, carefully circumventing those twelve staff I was not allowed to contact. St John's is one of the grandest of the Cambridge University colleges and the bursary staff were enormously kind, but for me the place was a gilded cage.

We wanted to get the bail conditions lifted and were granted a hearing at the High Court. I had taken on Karim Khalil as my barrister and the first time I spoke to him was on the phone: he was at the High Court and telephoned me at the bursary.

'I'm about to go in to see the judge,' he said, sounding quite rattled, 'but the Charity Commission has just rung me here. They say that if we succeed in getting the bail conditions removed they'll suspend you and John.' The Charity Commission had powers to suspend us if the Wintercomfort trustees would not do so and if they had good cause. We wondered why they were so keen on this step and how they had known our case was coming up in court. Who had told them?

'We could win over the bail conditions, but it would be a Pyrrhic victory,' Karim continued. 'What do you want me to do?'

'We'll have to withdraw,' I replied.

'OK,' Karim agreed, 'but I'll still try to get the one lifted that prevents contact between you and John.'

In that he was successful. We were, after all, being tried together. How on earth could we develop our case if we couldn't communicate? But the action by the Charity Commission was highly questionable. 'Perverting the course of justice,' someone suggested. 'And contempt of court.'

The very next day, despite our withdrawal from the High Court hearing, the Charity Commission suspended us anyway. We simply could not win. Now I was in limbo: the professional had become the outcast. It felt as though I had lost everything. I had no idea that things were going to get a whole lot worse. I carried on going to the bursary, needing to have somewhere to be, and in the evenings retreated early to my bed, clinging to my sanity. Reality becomes precarious without its usual fixed points.

I brought in a consultant to look after Wintercomfort. Unfortunately, she proved to be good at spending money but not at raising it. Our financial reserves were decimated and Wintercomfort came close to collapse. After five months, the trustees managed to get the suspensions lifted through an appeal to the Attorney General's office and I managed to raise some emergency funding to see us through.

So I continued, on bail, for the full eighteen months. Then, at the beginning of my trial, the prosecution decided to drop the staff witnesses. They did not want to call them after all. It seemed as though interviewing my staff, designating them as prosecution witnesses and then drawing up bail conditions to prevent me from contacting those prosecution witnesses had been a ploy to stop me working. I feared that the police really were out to fit me up.

Exactly what were they up to? While we were on bail, the Cambridge police were central to the development of a series of local meetings on homelessness, hostels and heroin with an aim of producing written guidelines for practitioners, which looked likely to be published prior to my trial. That felt dangerous. The first meeting was held the day after my arrest. John and I managed to make it to the second one, about a month later. I remember the manager of the local drugs project stating that there was no legal responsibility to inform police. Assistant Chief Constable David Winsor responded: 'You don't have to tell the police but you have no protection if you don't.' People visibly winced. During one of the breaks, a police inspector told me: 'Situations often have their martyrs.' Perhaps that made it all right for him, but it did not make it all right for me. It felt like an attitude rooted in the Dark Ages.

The police seemed desperate to prevent me from attending these meetings, and spent two hours at the bursary trying to persuade my trustees to force me to withdraw. In the end they succeeded, but we sent another representative, a barrister who managed to stall the publication of guidelines long enough to allow Release, the national drugs charity, to produce definitive ones of their own: *Drug Use on Premises: Guidelines for Direct Access Services*. The guidelines were desperately needed. Project managers throughout the country were stunned by the events at Wintercomfort and were anxious about their safety after what had happened to John and me. A lot were now less willing to take on addicts, which hardly fitted the government's much-vaunted policies of countering social exclusion.

'We've just got to the point of developing best practice for working with homeless drug addicts,' someone from the National Homeless Alliance said, 'the need to stabilize them before moving towards detox and rehab. This case has shot all that to pieces.'

Even prison governors found our situation confusing. Roy Woolford, governor of Parc prison, told the *Independent*: 'If these people are guilty, then prison governors should be brought to book because, technically, with the level of drug taking there demonstrably is in prison, we are failing too.'

I wondered what I would find in the jail I was sent to.

two

I was doing a little yoga on the cold cell floor when they came for me at 9 a.m. The discipline of it was bringing me back to myself a little and I felt annoyed at the interruption. But my life was no longer my own. As I was taken out of the cell I saw a washbasin and asked to use it. They let me splash my face and hands. Though I had brought some clean clothes, I was not allowed to change into them. It seemed as if they were trying to turn me into something dirty.

At the reception desk I was double-handcuffed up, on both wrists and then to the guard. A copper shot me a sardonic look and I involuntarily felt a wave of hatred in response. It wiped away the urge to weep. John came out too and we were taken into the sweatbox (prison transport van). We were each locked into one of the six tiny cubicles. They had hard plastic seats, no seat belts and barely room to move at all. Already it felt hot, stuffy and airless. The handcuffs came off once I was safely secured inside.

As we got underway Cambridge swept past looking beautiful, bathed in the reddish gold of the morning sunlight. I feasted on the countryside; it was like a last supper. All too soon we were overtaken by a grey wall of cloud. After a couple of hours, we stopped at Luton and dropped John off – he was en route to Bedford prison. We wished each other luck. My transport then had to pick up two women from the local court. I was left in a cell with them for a while. Both were heroin addicts. One was on remand and the other, Leanne, was complaining about her eighteen-month sentence for heroin supply. Like many addicts, Leanne's reddened and pockmarked face was evidence of her damaging lifestyle.

'It weren't commercial,' she said. In other words, she had got the heroin to share with friends. I managed to blurt out my tale. My compatriots were shocked and proffered puffs of their fags. Although I had not smoked for ten years, I gratefully accepted.

Bound for Holloway, we were handcuffed up again and boxed back into the van. The other two cracked jokes, which lifted my spirits a little, but I felt uncomfortably dirty, sweaty and sordid, bumping around in the privacy of my cubicle. More tears overtook me. At Holloway prison our transport slowed down to creep past the gates and through a long narrow entrance that spread out into a courtyard. We had only just arrived and already I felt hemmed in. No handcuffs this time: the prison fences were enough.

The prison officer at reception checked and logged my belongings. I must have looked rough. She allowed me to buy a couple of phone cards with what was termed my 'private cash'.

'I should only let you have one phone card, but seeing as it's your first time, you can have two,' she said, adding: 'It's not so bad when you get used to it. See, this girl here came in only yesterday and look at her now.' She pointed to a young woman pushing a mop who could do little but smile at this obvious misrepresentation.

I had the first of many strip-searches to come. This was a terror for me. I thought they would poke around inside my private orifices. To my enormous relief they did not. I got looked up and down and turned around, but was allowed to keep the top or bottom half of my body covered at any one time – an embarrassment nonetheless but a lot better than I had feared.

Then I got locked in a room with six fellow prisoners being booked in with me. Five of them were heroin users and the sixth was on remand for stabbing her violent boyfriend when they had both been drunk. All these women were young enough to be my daughters. The room was large but bare: hard tables and stacked-up chairs, a two-way mirror covering one of the walls so that the officers could see us, but we could not see them. I idly read the notices on the noticeboard, then sat on one of the chairs with my feet up on another. The hours of waiting were endless, and the waves of depression continued. We managed to chat a little, the addicts suffering variously from their withdrawals. I got some inedible sandwiches and a drink of water for my lunch but food seemed unimportant. What was there to keep well for? Anyway, I did not feel hungry, was still deeply traumatized.

Each of us was taken out for a swift health check. The nurse's kindness upset me, though I was grateful for it, and I desperately held back my tears while she gave me a pep talk: 'See it like going to boarding school. There are other women your age in here. You just need to find one friend.' The doctor's evident distaste and ill humour were somehow more palatable.

By 4.30 p.m. I was processed and on D3, the intake wing. Marching through the prison, the décor of it seemed designed to depress; everything was shabby and rundown. I was allocated a place in one of the four-person dorms. To my disappointment, the beds were no better than the one in the police cell and my mattress was badly stained. My locker was smashed in at the back. All the furniture was hard and unrelenting, the lighting dim and the atmosphere heavy.

The wing was built around a corridor, which formed a square with the cells, the staff office, the dining room and the two bathrooms and one shower opening off it. D3 was set in the part of the prison that used to be a hospital, I was told. Another place of pain but also a place of care. The heavy cell door clanged shut behind me; the sound of the keys in the lock was quickly becoming familiar.

'When you get out, you'll automatically jump when you hear a rattle of keys,' Martine, one of my cellmates, knowingly informed me. She was tiny – 5-foot-nothing tall and barely 6 stone in weight – but fiercely determined. Strong white teeth dominated her shrunken face and with her tiny skinny frame she resembled a starving child. Martine was on remand for shoplifting.

'Banged up at Christmas, for fuck's sake,' she complained. 'Some bastard ripped off my dole cheque. I was only trying to get some food for me and my kid.' An old hand at prison, Martine was the only one of the five addicts I checked in with who had decided not to opt for the prison hospital drug detox.

'They give you nothing that's any help,' she declared, 'and it's twenty-four seven bang-up, surrounded by complete nutters, believe me.' Leanne, my pockmarked friend from the transport, had gone there. I wondered how she would get on.

Martine's defiance felt like a protection for me as well as for her, but she had her own ordeal to come. It started on the first night when she was cold-turkeying badly, tossing and turning and unable to keep still, her legs thrashing the thin blankets into an indiscriminate pile. In the morning she looked weak and pale, her face reflecting the green colour of our worn bedding. She wanted to talk and told me a bit about her chaotic life, how she had been living with her little boy in a bed-and-breakfast, and had two 6-foot black guys on the go.

'I'm good in the sack,' laughed this tiny wench, going on to give me some unrequested details of her energetic love-making. She also talked about her upbringing, the difficulties she'd had. Her eyes started to swim, but it was only when she spoke of her small son that the tears flowed.

Another bed in the cell was occupied by a beautiful but doleful black American imprisoned for drugs importation, who spent most of her time pretending to read but was really staring at a photograph of her own little boy. We also had the boyfriend-stabber, who would not stop talking. She drove Martine and me to distraction. When you are locked in a cell with someone, there is no escape – except for the American, who got a wing-cleaner's job and was moved out to better quarters. Her bed was taken by an ordinary-looking woman in her late fifties who had stolen £1000 from her employers, the Post Office. She was rigid with fear at being in prison. She had paid the money back and her incarceration would cost the state considerably more than she had stolen in the first place. I wondered why she had not been given a community-service order.

The next to go was the boyfriend-stabber, off to court. At first her bed was filled by a Jamaican woman who was in for importing cocaine and spoke a fast patois that I could hardly understand. Martine had it off to a tee. She had mixed with Jamaicans, she told me proudly, and so could translate. The Jamaican woman had three kids at home and said she took the cocaine on her first-ever trip abroad because she had been told her thirteen-year-old son would be killed if she did not comply. The son was now in hiding with his grandmother.

She painted a frightening picture of Jamaica: of a rule of terror, extreme poverty, and people living in basic shacks. But at heart there was a degree of real civilization. She explained that if someone was hungry they were fed by whoever happened to be around, and if they were homeless they were invited to stay. Our modern British society can hardly boast that level of humanity.

An oddly deluded woman followed the Jamaican; she claimed to be half Russian, which she might well have been, and reckoned she knew the absolute truth, which she most definitely did not, but she drove us mad trying to impart it. From what I could gather, she was in prison for doing the same to a judge, who would not accept a psychiatrist's advice that this woman simply was not well.

These were my fellow sufferers, and I soon learned to join Martine in referring to the prison officers as screws. They were our jailers, and most of them seemed to feel that they had the right to demean their charges as well as lock them up, to inflict further punishment by being gruff and high-handed. I found them fearsome and had not yet come to understand their anxiety, their need to keep us inmates down and in our place, to avoid being destroyed by the huge sea of angst that this dreadful prison created and had to contain.

'Miss, miss, sir, sir,' Martine would shout through the hatch in our door, holding a thin roll-up she had made out of scraps of tobacco. 'Have you got a light, please, miss, please, sir.' Anything for a bit of activity, to lighten the crushing boredom of bang-up.

At Holloway the cells were piled five storeys high and contained a degradation that was previously beyond my imagination. It was as if you ceased to be a person when you got to prison, were not of any import at all. We were just part of the institution's bureaucracy, which in itself was utterly confusing. Everything had to be applied for and waited for, had to fit into the system, whatever that was. Finding out what you were entitled to was difficult enough. Knowing how to get it was the next hurdle. When we were not locked in our cells, I often saw people queuing up, doing things with a purpose, but I did not understand what was going on and no one bothered to tell me. I guess they reckoned I had plenty of time to find out.

My defence systems were struggling to cope with the trauma, the omnipresent anxiety and overwhelming depression. The purpose of this was to punish me, I reminded myself constantly. It was not personal; I was in a system, and had to toughen up. I felt completely disempowered. I did not belong to myself anymore, was merely an object of state custody.

Yoga continued to help. I did a little in the early morning while the others slept and Martine thrashed, finding a space on the floor between my bed and the barred window. A few quiet and concentrated movements – again it was as if I got something of my person back; it brought me into myself, made me feel that I was real, solid, and still there.

Generally, sleep eluded me during the five days I spent at Holloway. I got only fifteen minutes of outside exercise in that time. 'Isn't there some sort of law about getting daily exercise outside?' I wondered aloud. Wearily, the others assured me that there was.

One day, outside exercise was cancelled because it was supposedly too cold outside. We were allowed to walk along the corridor outside the cells for half an hour instead. The sun was shining, bright and strong, and I resented some impersonal authority making decisions for me about whether or not it was too cold to go out, as if I were a child. I could hear seagulls crying to each other and opened a window in the cell to see them whirling about. These windows were made up of strips of smoked glass through which you could not see properly, separated by built-in bars. You could open every other strip and this offered a peculiarly jagged view of the outside world. At this time of year it was too cold to leave them open for long.

Then I heard a blackbird sing. Peering through a window strip I spotted it perched in a tree below, blithely unaware of the value of its freedom. I now understood the acute symbolism that birds had always held for prisoners.

□ □ □

The prison day was dreary. You were woken at 6.30 a.m. by the screws clanking down the corridor and shouting to us through the hatches to get up. Usually no one stirred. I would do my yoga, if I was not already at it, and then get back into my hard bed. The screws returned at 7.30 a.m.

'Come on, ladies, you should be up and dressed.' We were let out for breakfast in the dining room down the corridor: two slices of stale bread, marge and cereal. On Sunday we got a hard-boiled egg with bread. I made up a sandwich, but eating it seemed to increase the hunger. The night before we were issued with tea-bags and sachets of whitener and sugar, so that we could make something resembling a cup of tea at mealtimes, using hot water from large plastic jugs. Everything was plastic: the plates, the cups and the cutlery.

There was lock-up from around 8.15 a.m. to nearly midday. Once a girl from my cell was taken to 'education'. I was envious, always dying to get out. Gym was sometimes a possibility but sessions seemed to be cancelled more often than not. I managed to get there once and chose to swim madly about in the pool, which was Holloway's pride and joy. My loosened tears mixed with the chlorinated water.

Lunch consisted of a stale sandwich, undrinkable soup, crisps and an orange, and, like all the meals, was a hurried, joyless affair. More bang-up followed, from 12.30 p.m. till dinner at 5 p.m., a hot meal but barely edible. It was best to stuff it down fast, if you could manage to eat it at all, so that you did not taste the food or feel its texture in your mouth. I rarely ate more than a few forkfuls.

Food could not be sent in, but you could buy snacks at the prison canteen once a week, as well as fruit, coffee, tobacco, stationery, toiletries, precious phone cards (at specific times we could make but not take phone calls) and batteries for a radio or Walkman. Everyone had a limit on their weekly spend, regardless of how much money they got sent in. Mine started at £10. At Holloway I got taken to the canteen once, escorted along confusing corridors into a room which had colourful murals on the walls. Tears sprang up from nowhere when I saw them, a little bit of cheeriness in this arid place. I paced around struggling to control myself and the emotion eventually subsided. I am not a person who usually weeps easily and every time it happened I could not bear to let anyone see me, feeling it was a sign of embarrassing weakness.

When my turn at the counter came, I bought a double phone card, shampoo, chocolate, oranges and apples. It came to £10. I did not buy tobacco, then realized immediately that I should have done as I had become a smoker again. A major worry was my Walkman, my one item of luxury, my own special and personal treasure. Inmates were allowed only one set of batteries in Holloway; apparently, lots of them together can be used to make bombs. I resolved to carefully ration the playing of my tapes and to stick to the radio where possible, as it used less power. I kept the Walkman in my bumbag, which the screws had allowed me to keep, along with my stamps and phone cards – the things of worth in here that I was frightened might be nicked. Even so, I could not help noticing that bits of the chocolate kept disappearing from my locker. I suspected Martine, but said nothing. She was better than I was at scrounging tobacco and shared whatever she could get hold of.

Following the screw back from the canteen shop to the cell, I realized I had developed a prison persona: hands in pockets, a slow uncaring walk, shoulders hunched, scowling and grumpy; a woman of few words but always a curse at the ready. It had happened in just two or three days. There I was, Wyner, prison number EH 6524: scared but not going to show it; ready for anything but behaving as if I didn't give a shit. My defences were up, and I knew I needed them, but also I feared that the real 'me' had been destroyed. Would I ever get her back again?

□ □ □

Some evenings we had 'free association' for a couple of hours, which meant we could wander around the wing, chat to other people, watch

TV, read a newspaper, shower, or use the phone, all a great relief after the long hours in the cell. I watched people wandering aimlessly about, most looking disorientated, confused and deeply unhappy, but there were attempts at geniality too. I found a phone and managed to ring home using one of my phone cards. It gave us a lift to be able to speak, to feel we could maintain a little contact, that I had not completely disappeared. But the units on the phone card got used up fast and we did not dare speak for too long.

Then I heard someone exclaim: 'Five years! For a first offence too.' I was being talked about. A trio came up and got me into conversation. One of them pulled out yesterday's *Independent* and there I was: a half-page article with a full-blown picture of me. The *Independent* was available on the wing along with the usual tabloids. I was pleased at the coverage but did not want fame, least of all in here, and played it down as best I could.

One of the three told me she used to help out at a London day centre; she had wondered if she would meet me in prison, and now she had. She was like a vulnerable child, softly-spoken and frightened, in for making false 999 calls. She was one of the few inmates to get a single cell, presumably because of her obvious frailty.

'It's very lonely in there,' she complained. 'The time goes really slow.' Later I discovered that she had regular cell checks during lock-ups, with a screw taking a quick look through the hatch. Suicide watch. It seemed unutterably cruel to lock someone away and then continually check to make sure that they endured what for them felt unendurable. But the alternative did not bear thinking about.

During lock-up in the evening we were offered hot water for making cups of tea. It was brought round by one of the inmate 'workers', who seemed to me to work twelve-hour days for £7 a week. They opened the hatch in the cell door and you handed your plastic cup through to them. On my first experience of this my heart went to my throat: such a stark image of our deprivation. After a few days, I seemed hardened to it. Was the shock subsiding? Was I already becoming institutionalized? The grim despair of this place was everywhere, on the faces of the women, inherent in the routines. Part of the very fabric, like me.

□ □ □

I was called to see the allocations officer and elected to go to Highpoint prison in Suffolk. It was only forty-five minutes' drive from my home in Cambridge, and proximity to the family was my priority.

They did come to visit me at Holloway once. Newly convicted prisoners got a visit with a 'hand-in' of allowed belongings within forty-eight hours of being incarcerated. Gordon brought me a bag I had left ready-packed at home. It was my first prison visit. Grim with anxiety, I got marched with a group of other inmates to the visits hall downstairs, where I was frisked, searched and the things in my pockets were taken off me. We all waited in a side room.

At last I was called to a table to be with my special three: Joel, Rachel and my husband Gordon, my life companion for over twenty-five years. Embracing was allowed only at the start and end of the visit. For the rest of the time we could hold hands so long as our hands remained above the table. My daughter and I wept together and I whispered in her ear: 'It's the shock, my darling. It'll pass, we'll be OK,' though I hardly believed it myself. There was so much to say; it felt good to be with them, but after half an hour we had to finish. Letting them go was deeply painful. We could have no more visits for a fortnight.

Things seemed peculiar and unreal when I got back on to the wing. That small taste of my life outside had disorientated me. I chatted to the 999 phone caller and rebalanced a little. Lock-up was soon, at 5.30 p.m. that day. I tried to ring my mother. The phone was permanently engaged. But I did manage to call my sister, who sounded bright and delighted to hear from me. She said she wanted to join the fight to get me out so I gave her a number to ring in Cambridge, and asked her to contact mum and let her know I would ring the next day. I explained that my phone cards were limited and that I wanted to save the double one for Christmas.

When I had finished, I was hassled by two girls who had seen me at the phone.

'Just one unit. Please,' they begged, very young-looking, very desperate. I gave them a card that had just one unit left on it and left them to fight over who should use it.

Back in the cell I wrote two letters: one to the people at work, wanting to reassure them, and the other to the family, saying how much their visit had helped me, how great they were. Then I read a book, extracts from Irish writing given to me by a friend from outside. I chose a piece entitled *Homesickness*. It was the first time during my incarceration that I had been able to read, to focus on the words. I found myself feeling quite contented, enjoying the story I had chosen. Was it real pleasure? Or was it the feeling you got when the acute discomfort of shock started to lift?

□ □ □

The transport to Highpoint got cancelled twice. On the second occasion they needed my bed on D3, so for what thankfully turned out to be my last night at Holloway I was moved upstairs, to a wing for convicted prisoners. I reckoned I had been put in the noisiest cell in the prison. My new cellmates had just got their weekly canteen, which meant they had new batteries for their radios. One was on full blast and a black girl who looked no more than seventeen cavorted frantically to the music. Another woman, very pretty and in her thirties, doing four years for armed robbery, lay on her bed sweating out a bad dose of flu. My third cellmate had a pile of cardboard envelope folders and I asked her shyly if she could spare one. Later in the evening she did. I sorted out my papers and put them in it. I stuck my photos of my family on to the noticeboard above my bed, in true prison fashion: with toothpaste.

I still could not eat much. On this wing prisoners picked up their meals from the dining room and, for some reason, ate them in the cells. Perhaps the dining room was too small. That evening I managed to down some rice and an orange. The rock cakes we were given were too hard to get your teeth into, so I picked out the raisins to nibble.

I felt upset by the move; I had started to settle a little on D3, but here I was surrounded by strange faces and rough, hard speech. The people seemed tougher than those on the intake wing, and I felt they were eyeing me up suspiciously. With the constant loud music drumming into my head, I found myself struggling with new streams of tearfulness. I tried hiding in the cell's toilet to weep, but it did not help. The armed robber, who was called Jules, noticed and heaved her sweating body over to give me a sympathetic hug.

'Don't worry, we all get it when we first come in. Comes in waves, doesn't it?' and she offered me a fag. It was reassuring to know that my reactions were normal, that I was the same as the rest.

I did get some outside exercise that day. Waiting to go with a group of other inmates, I felt their eyes upon me as they chatted among themselves and I tried to look elsewhere.

'She notices everything, you know,' said one. I felt embarrassed, did not know what to say, and my fear of antagonizing them left me completely tongue-tied. Once we got outside my legs urged me into a fast walk, round and round the small square courtyard that was my exercise yard, with the screws posted at each corner. The others mostly strolled or hung around to chat.

'Ruth!' A shout from a window. It was Leanne, her pockmarked face peering out from a window in the hospital block.

'How are you doin'?'

'OK. And you?'

'Oh, all right.' But she looked wan.

In the evening we had a visit from a screw, who whispered to Jules through the hatch: 'I'll bring you something later on, some cake if I can get it.' But at 11 p.m. the news came back.

'Those bloody bitches wouldn't let me bring it in.' This screw had already shown me a little extra kindness. Coming to wake the boyfriend-stabber early for court when I was on D3, and seeing that I was already up, this officer stretched the rules to give me hot water for a cup of tea. I was not really allowed any until breakfast. It was a small gift that was a blessing, as were people like that in a place like this. Unfortunately, this officer, known throughout the prison for good-heartedness, was one of a kind; an isolated harbinger of humanity, a faint beacon of hope in this landscape of desolation.

The next morning my three cellmates were taken off to I knew not where – I could never figure out what was going on at Holloway – and I heard an unearthly yell drifting across the outside courtyard from one of the other blocks: 'RUTH! ROOOTH WYYYYNERRR!'

A feature of Holloway was the way women shouted to each other from their cell windows. It was constant in the evenings, sometimes well into the night: eerie disembodied voices searching for connection. Again it came, insistently: 'ROOOTH WYYYYNERRR!' It was my friend Martine.

'MAAARRTIIINE!' I shrieked back through the gap in the window.

'WAVE SO I CAN SEEEE YOOOO!' she yelled.

I waved and she did too: a tiny arm far away.

'ARE YOU GOING TO THE GYYYYYM?'

'CAN'T. I'M GETTING SHIIIIPPED OOOOUT!'

'GOOOOD LUUUCK! KEEEP UP THE FIIIIGHT!'

'YOOOO TOOO. TAKE IT EEEEEASY!'

'BYE!'

'BYEEE!'

Martine had been my tutor. She had showed me the ropes: how far you can go with the screws, hustling them to relieve the gruelling tension and tedium of lock-up; and how to keep yourself closed and tight so that the place did not get to you too badly. In return, I had helped her through her detox, sitting by her bed while she talked and wept. She had said how surprised she was that we got on so well, coming from such different backgrounds, and had thanked me for helping her through the cold turkey. I had told her, truthfully, that she had done well.

I waited alone in the cell, impatient for the sweatbox that would ship me out to another place of torment. I felt the inactivity of prison would destroy me, as would the lack of agency. I was used to making decisions for other people as well as for myself, as a charity director, running projects and heading staff teams, overseeing budgets and leading on new developments, often having to deal with angry opposition to them. In Cambridge I had got to be quite a well-known, if rather controversial, figure. But homelessness was a controversial area, and now I had been beaten down, reduced to nothing, as a result of my endeavours.

Maybe it would be better at Highpoint, I thought. Though prison was always prison. It seemed surreal: my arrest; the long months on bail while I struggled to keep Wintercomfort afloat; the pantomime of the trial; and now jail. Did I really deserve this?

I had been outspoken during my time working in homelessness, certainly more outspoken than most of my colleagues, speaking up on behalf of those I was entrusted to serve. That was my job. Was it also my crime? To speak up for the destitute and the dispossessed in our midst, people from all walks of life who had lost hope for the future. I had got to know these people, those who lived like shadows, seen by many as a stain on our communities, as lower and lesser, undeserving of our aid.

Now, locked away, I had become one of those shadows myself.

three

I have arrived at HMP Highpoint after a gruelling two-hour journey in the sweatbox. It was dark when we got here and I could only see vague outlines of high gates and fences as we passed through. A thunderous pain was pounding against my skull. The nurse who checked us out on arrival told me my blood pressure was up.

'Not surprising, after what you've been through,' she said.

It was too late to have our belongings sorted so we were given a prison nightdress and toiletries and taken on to our wing. There were four others with me. One, designated a suicide risk, went to the prison hospital. That surprised me; she had seemed quite ordinary and cheerful. The others were: Billie, a bright Liverpudlian who had got so hot in the sweatbox that she had stripped down to her bra; Nancy, a short, hugely overweight and excitable woman who seemed to tell everyone, in the first few minutes of conversation, that she was sexually abused as a child; and Pearl, a tall black Londoner who became my first roommate. They did not like to call them cells here, I was told, despite the omnipresent bars and the heavy iron of the spur gates.

We have our evening meal, actually walking outside from the unit to the canteen, through gates in fences that have been left unlocked to let us pass, carrying our allocation of plastic plate, bowl and cutlery. It looks like we will get outside here a bit more than we did at

Holloway. Screws stood guard as we ate. The food was a little better than at Holloway. Then we headed back, keeping to the narrow concrete paths because the grass was sodden and muddy.

Now I am waiting near the unit's front gate to get across with the medication run. I am on a low dose of a mild antidepressant, which I take at night. It helps drive away some of the insomnia. But most of all I am desperate to get something for my thunderous headache which is driving me wild. The screw comes up to open the gate and there is a surge forward. Eventually, I realize why: the screw will only take twelve at a time. Nancy and I are left behind, looking disconsolate. The screw looks at the sorrowful Nancy.

'OK, you come along then.'

'What about me?' I demand. My need for painkillers is urgent. But I am ignored and left behind.

This is the trigger that breaks me. I stomp up to the cell and have a good weep, but need to get myself back together for the second medication run. I fling myself under the shower. It is cold but does not extinguish my fury. When the screw gets back, I am waiting for her by the gate, full of it.

'You didn't have to leave me behind,' I rail, 'I've a terrible headache, I need painkillers.' I am staring into her eyes, incensed. She stares back, sizing me up. I know that physically I am no match for her but I am beyond reason or fear.

'Well, you'll just have to wait,' she says, and it is a mercy that she chooses to walk off. A few minutes later another screw takes me and a couple of other stragglers to get our medication. I manage to persuade a reluctant nurse to give me three 200mg Ibuprofen pills and swallow two straight off. They take the edge off the bursting pain in my head and I feel vaguely human again.

□ □ □

I am in the room with twenty-four-year-old Pearl, who is being very sweet to me, flashing her large white perfect teeth as she smiles and offers me anything she can. She undoubtedly feels a bit anxious, being naturally loud and boisterous and now having to share, at close quarters in this small space, with a forty-nine-year-old white woman who is fighting an overwhelming depression.

We have got our belongings from reception and have packed them away. Here, in this prison, we have the luxury of a lockable locker and our own cell-door key. During some of the day we can wander around the unit, which is on two floors. Because there is plenty of spare space right now we have all got upstairs rooms – a good thing. Downstairs is known as Skid Row: a claustrophobic corridor with just six double rooms and one toilet and shower behind the spur gate. I discover that lock-up at Highpoint allows us some freedom: we have access to all the rooms on our spur, and to the washroom, which means we can socialize and wash or take a shower whenever we like.

I do not feel like socializing. Apart from our shared humanity, I feel I have little in common with anybody at the moment. All I want is my own space. Nancy feels the same. Her incessant chattering has been replaced by an urgent anxiety that she blinks out to me through her thick round specs. I find her neediness a drain on my own scarce resources and regret that I cannot give her the friendship she wants right now.

The landscape of the prison is a bleak one: various buildings all separated by 25-foot metal fences topped with rolls of vicious-looking razor wire. There are three units, squat flat-roofed over-crowded buildings each separated by this fencing, which is everywhere you look. My unit is N3, room number 36. Gates in the fences are left open or locked, depending on the status of movement within the establishment. It is all strictly organized. Security is the priority; paranoia is the norm.

At least there is a little grass around. I can see a few bare trees. Huge black crows fly among them, as big as ducks – they must do well off the detritus of this place – plus a flock of birds I do not recognize. They have a distinctive high-pitched call. The birds hold a fascination for me, as at Holloway. I jealously watch them swoop over the fences.

This morning I was left locked outside the unit after I had come back from reception. The screws did not see me walk past their window and I did not hassle them. I relished the opportunity for a few extra moments outside – all the time I yearn to be outside. I hardly felt the bitter cold, was mesmerized by the black silhouettes of the crows moving against the wintry blue of the sweeping East Anglian sky. Relishing the space around and above me, it felt good to be closer to home.

Now that I am back in my room, I am tormented by feelings that I have let down my kids, my family; that they are suffering because of me. It is Christmas Eve. I have stuck their photos on my locker door with a few scraps of masking tape that I found at Holloway and carefully stowed away. When I spoke to Gordon on the phone last night, he told me of the campaign that was gathering: sixty people came to the first meeting. While naturally enormously grateful, I feel I have let them down too, putting them to this trouble. As if it was all my fault.

'Don't be so daft,' Gordon says. 'Everyone wants to help.' But I feel so helpless.

Memories of the outside torment me. The empty life I am leading lets them crowd in, rich and vivid, people and places. I can conjure them up at will, but I get little enjoyment from it. Home and holidays, cities and countryside, work colleagues and friends. All there in extraordinary detail. It is as if the lack of stimulation here causes other parts of the mind to become more active.

But I have found a place to get a little privacy: a small lounge that seems to be rarely used. It has a line of chairs that are softer to lie on than my prison bed and the window faces out to the sunset. I am sleeping very badly at night, and when the spur gate is unlocked I like to relax prone on these chairs, or gaze through the window at the sunset, willing it to last. Beauty is a rare find in prison. I wonder if the other inmates yearn like me. My observations of them tell me that they do. I am not so different.

Occasionally I listen to the radio on my Walkman, though the reception is very bad here. I try to hear the news but its value seems to be diminishing. What does it matter to me, in prison? Classical music soothes, though sometimes it brings forth my tears. One time I caught a pop song my daughter used to listen to and wept without relief.

Ah, I have a cup of coffee, my first since my sentencing a week ago. Another inmate has given me the makings, only instant stuff but coffee it is, and I use water from the washroom taps, not yet having managed to fathom the secrets of the unit's hot water. We do not get it given out at mealtimes like at Holloway, and to furnish yourself with a flask you have to buy one from the prison canteen at £7.99 a throw, nearly a week's spending allowance. No, I have not found the hot-water urn but I do know there is one, somewhere. We have not been given tea-bags either. Nothing has been explained; it never is.

□ □ □

My mood lifts a little. Because it is Christmas Eve, the normal transfer of our personal money from Holloway has been delayed and we have not been able to buy phone cards. So the screws offer a bit of festive spirit in the form of a free five-minute phone call home. One of them sits opposite me as I dial. How good it is to hear the family, sounding fine, just like themselves, not destroyed.

Then I see that the post is in. I have thirteen letters, which means the others in the queue have a long wait, but they take it in good heart: 'You're popular.' The screws open each letter in front of me, checking for illicit enclosures and tearing the stamps off the envelopes, I assume in case drugs are stored underneath. I take my haul to my room. The cards and letters buoy me up. Gordon has sent a cutting of a hugely supportive article in the *Observer* by Nick Cohen and has written with more detailed news of the campaign. Peter Bottomley MP has tabled four questions in Parliament and a benefit gig is a possibility, maybe with some big names. My sister and brother-in-law are travelling to Cambridge for campaign meetings, revisiting old territory as they originally met as students at university there. My good friend Libby comes to the meetings too, driving up from the south coast. The support is incredible; it gives me a real lift, though I am aware that my mood is unstable and that the depression will no doubt return.

Naomi, my mother's friend, has sent me an Indian blessing that I have not heard for some thirty years:

May the long time sun shine on you
And all love surround you
And the pure light within you
Guide you all the way home.

I write it out carefully on a piece of plain A4 paper in nice lettering and with my best pen. Using my trusty toothpaste I stick the home-made poster in the middle of one of my two large noticeboards, both of which are already spotted with old toothpaste marks.

'What's that?' asks Pearl. I read it out to her, for her, and she looks pleased. Then Pearl sighs, slips her radio on and settles down on her bed to read her Bible, mouthing and muttering the words as she traces them with her forefinger. I can hardly bear to think of the time that I have ahead.

□ □ □

My third day at Highpoint and it is Christmas Day. As usual I have slept badly, awake from 2 a.m. to 5 a.m., aware of the hardness of the bed. I could not turn on the light as it would have disturbed the slumbering Pearl. Sleep finally comes for me and I have two dreams. The first one is a variation on my usual dream theme in here of abandonment, of being ignored by my loved ones and becoming engulfed in terror and distress. In the second dream I am on my own in a cell and John, my co-defendant, is being escorted into the one next door. He is bloodied and bandaged, as if he has been beaten up, and in a way I suppose we both have.

I try to shower the emotion out of my body. Everyone is up and about wishing each other a happy Christmas. Today we get a morning treat: instead of our usual breakfast in the cell of cereal and a dried-up croissant, we can go to the dining room for egg, bacon, sausages and tomatoes or baked beans. I am basically a vegetarian, and a Jew to boot, but have never been able to throw off my penchant for bacon. What we are offered here is fatty and greasy but it tastes like pure succulence and I scrounge a second slice from a girl who has left hers.

As at Holloway, meals are rushed affairs, eaten under the omnipresent eyes of the screws. The dining room is cavernous and draughty and the atmosphere muted. Finding a non-threatening table to sit at vexes me as I do not know many faces. Sitting alone would be uncomfortable, and possibly dangerous. I gaze at the mass of women, all of us social outcasts. Around half are black; they are the noisiest and most demonstrative of us all and mostly, but not always, sit separately from the white women. On one occasion I joined Pearl and her Jamaican friends but could feel the discomfort from these otherwise friendly women, as if I had crossed an invisible line. For my Christmas breakfast I sit with Nancy and some other people I recognize from the unit. Conversation is pretty cursory and it is impossible to relax.

When I first came to prison, I found it difficult to understand anything said by anyone, black or white. They all spoke hard and fast, missing off bits of words and using slang I did not know, often to the sound of beating music from radios turned up much too loud. It all assaulted my ears and the words slipped by me. Now I pick the words out better and fall in with the lingo, swear and curse and jibe with everyone else.

I take the short walk back from the dining room, the day bright and sunny, the sky clear blue. It is not too cold and the waning moon is setting. I gratefully allow the freshness of the day to wash over me. The wind is blowing hard but no longer howling through the fences as it often does here during the night. With regret, I re-enter the unit.

At last I have found the hot-water urn: it is in the downstairs laundry room alongside the washing machines and dryers. I make a cup of tea to wash down my special breakfast, using the real milk I got issued with for cereal but did not use. A decent cuppa: what a delight! For much of my time in prison I have felt thirsty or hungry, but this morning I am pretty much satisfied.

I stand in the hallway sipping my brew, leaning casually against a wall, when a woman with long fair hair catches my eye. It is Angela, one of the eight people convicted of dealing £10 wraps of heroin at my day centre. Like most of them, she got four years. Her partner,

Timothy Pocket, was the one who came to court to give the most damning evidence against John and me, saying he had dealt thousands of pounds worth of gear at Wintercomfort. We knew it was not true, given the impoverishment of our client group, but the jury had no concept of this and the judge's attitude did not help.

'I heard you'd arrived here,' Angela says, giving me a broad smile. 'It's terrible, what's happened to you and John.' she continues. 'I wrote to Tim when I heard and gave him a good telling-off for what he did.' The smile is disconcerting, her speech too sickly sweet. I ask if she is still with Tim and she says she is. I know I cannot trust this woman but am in no position to act on that. Angela has been in here longer than I have; she has her mates and the privilege of a single room, is no doubt well in with the screws. I accept her apparent concern with good grace and head off for the telephones.

First I ring my mother, using up eight precious phone-card units, but I am as glad of the contact as she is.

'Happy Christmas, mum,' I say, and can sense her biting back the tears. But she is reassured that I am fine and still sound like the daughter she knows.

'My Christmas present is being here rather than Holloway,' I say, and tell her that we can get out a little more, that I am coping. I also tell her how vivid my visual memory has become, because I want her to know that I remember and think about the family. But she picks up on what that represents, the emptiness of this environment, the sheer deprivation, and anxiously starts: 'Oh dear —' Quickly, I move the conversation on.

Now it is time to ring home.

'Dad missed you this morning,' says my Rachel, my brave girl. And she tells me how she loves the leather coat I got for her Christmas present before I was sentenced, says it looks really good, and the silly woollen hat as well. Then she starts to cry.

'Don't cry, dove,' I say, working hard to hold myself together for her. 'I think of you all the while. What are you having for your Christmas lunch?' She is able to talk again. A sad Christmas; the police, that judge, bringing such sadness, unnecessary sadness, into our lives.

Phone calls over, I join the line of women going to the Church of England service, partly because the singing will do me good and partly for the walk in the open air to the prison chapel. It is a new building, clean, airy and colourful, in contrast to the rest of the jail. The Bishop of Dulwich is coming. One of the chaplains leads us in a few carols while we wait for the bishop to arrive from the men's side. This prison used to be for the men until they got a new one built. It is not without precedent that, as women, we got what was left over.

We sing heartily to get our feelings out. Women move here and there to embrace friends from other units. The bishop and the minister arrive to don their robes and everyone quietens down. There is complete decorum during the service. A few people from the outside have come to join us, with good intentions no doubt, but I resent their presence – somehow it feels voyeuristic. One woman has two small children with her; they are delightful but make me feel acutely sad. An inmate sings a doleful solo song that pierces into me.

When it is time for Communion, I go for a break and wait around the back, hidden from view, my exit from the chapel barred by the usual locked door. At the end they give out large bars of Toblerone. Someone comes to tell me to get one for myself. It feels patronizing but I know that the chocolate will give some comfort. Anyway, I can share it. Afterwards there is time for a cup of tea and some chat. I shake the bishop's hand and thank him for coming, surprised that my normal way of speaking is still there.

Back on the unit we wait to be let out for lunch. As usual, I enjoy the short walk outside, to the dining room, but the meal is a total disappointment: slices of what look like reconstituted turkey, rock-solid bread and Yorkshire puddings and undercooked roast potatoes. The Christmas pudding is like leather. I manage to chew a couple of mouthfuls from the middle of my slice. We get issued with thinly filled sandwiches for the evening, crisps and an apple. Lock-up will be early so the screws can get away.

After our disastrous Christmas lunch we are stuck on the unit, but the spur gates are left open so we can get to the TV room. The rest of last night's video is showing: a truly violent film which I nevertheless enjoy. It echoes something festering inside me.

Halfway through the film we get a call for evening medication, and we have to get it from the office rather than healthcare as the staff are wanting to get away. In there I see the screw I had confronted on my first day over the medication. She is a butch-looking woman in her forties with short grey hair and a string of earrings down one ear: Miss Morris, though I will not call her that, will not call her anything. A lot of the inmates just use 'Miss' or 'Sir' like Martine did, but I will resist it. The screws strike me as arrogant, offhand, and they do not have my respect. But I desperately fear their power and decide to make amends.

I go back to the office when medication is over. The nurses are just going. Deferentially, in my role as prisoner, I wait. Then I go up to Morris: 'Guess I owe you an apology for Thursday.' She briefly eyes me up and down, then says: 'Done. It *is* Christmas Day.' Returning quickly to the movie, I feel the damnable tears starting up and go to my room for an unstaunchable weep. What has brought this on? The memory of the incident? Or is it my powerlessness and lowliness as a prisoner of the state? It was my treatment in state custody that brought me to the end of my tether and here I am apologizing for it – so frightened of the situation that I apologize for something that is not my fault. It disgusts me. I feel deeply ashamed.

As a concession to Christmas there are a few bits of bedraggled tinsel around downstairs. I have to fight an urge to pull them down. And then we get a Christmas quiz. Miss Morris is joined by Miss Hardy, a younger officer with cropped hair and a distinctive rolling walk. I reckon these butch screws must like the uniform and the pre-dominantly female environment as well as the power buzz. We organize ourselves into teams of four. The winners get a pouch of tobacco and the losers have to eat a six-pack of mince pies there and then, leading to much hilarity. Morris has a loud, beefy laugh which echoes around the unit.

'At least she's enjoying herself,' says the woman sitting next to me.

Afterwards it is early bang-up so that our jailers can get away to enjoy their Christmases. The other women on my wing are becoming curious about my case and some of them ask me about it. I do my best to explain and show them the article from the *Independent*. I sneaked it out of Holloway. The response is outrage.

'Man, are you gonna win that appeal,' they predict with absolute certainty. Pearl enjoys the attention her roommate is attracting, and jumps on and off her bed, loudly predicting with the rest: 'Go for it, Ruth, you whop 'em good and proper.' Pearl must find it hard to contain that youthful energy, shut up in this dreary place.

Billie, the Scouser who came with us from Holloway, says that there are some people that you know are innocent, just by looking at them.

'You look like a careworker,' she says, and tells me about a stint she did working with the elderly for Jewish Care, how she really enjoyed it. Her way of asking.

'Yes,' I say, 'I am Jewish, but we don't really keep anything up.' There is a lot of categorizing in prison: you are black or white, Asian or whatever, a Londoner, a Northerner, as if we want to place each other, all of us strangers haphazardly thrown together. Perhaps it is a way of becoming more solid, of holding on to your identity, in this situation where just about everything in our lives has been forcibly wrenched away, putting our very selfhood at risk. Many of the inmates say they have not met a Jew before. I suspect that they have, without knowing it.

I gain strength from their support and sympathy. Five years is a long sentence. I have yet to meet anyone else doing as long, though I know there are others with eight-, ten- and twelve-year stretches, mostly for drug importation. Am I really such a menace to society? Such a bad person? They ask about John, my co-defendant, and I tell them he is in Bedford prison and very depressed.

'Women are stronger than men,' they say. I ask if men's prisons are harder than women's, but I'm told no, that is not so – the men stick together more.

'No way would the screws talk to the men the way they talk to us women,' says Billie. 'There'd be a riot.'

Pearl shuts down at around 9 p.m. after taking her night-time medication. It must be strong stuff; she becomes quiet and cut off very suddenly and if I did not know it was the tablets, I would be insulted. First she lays her head down, listening to her radio, and soon she is snoring. I am glad to be able to turn the radio off, though I can hear two others blaring away down the corridor. I tiptoe around the room as if Pearl was my sleeping child. Eventually, I sleep too, fitfully as ever and wake in the early hours. When I do get off again it is to the usual distressing dreams of being left out, left behind, while others languish in luxury.

□ □ □

We have got Christmas over and now it is New Year's Eve, the Millennium New Year – a special time of hope, but inevitably I feel low. The radios blare out as ever but annoy me more than usual. On Radio 1 they are doing a countdown to the great event, the new millennium: sixteen hours to go; fifteen hours, forty minutes and ten seconds; fifteen hours, thirty-five minutes and thirty seconds; it just goes on and on.

It is a Sunday and I decide to try to get to the gym; I have figured out that they usually come for us at 9 a.m. on weekends. I put on my tracksuit bottoms and a pair of Rachel's old tennis shoes that I have brought with me and wait downstairs by the gate. Fifteen minutes later (fourteen hours and forty-five minutes to go) I ask a screw and she says: 'No gym.' Fuck this place. I storm back upstairs. Pearl is not in the room and I do some yoga, trying to cut out the omnipresent radios (fourteen hours and thirty minutes to go). I am about to start some meditation when in comes Pearl. She gets something and is off again. I try once more. Pearl comes back again and goes. I start again. This time a screw comes in to do the daily check on the bars. It is hopeless. I give up.

If only I could block out this millennium stuff, the hype and the excitement. It is not for me, I am in mourning, for the loss of my family, my friends, my life. I go down for some hot water from the urn to make myself a treat: camomile tea. I have bought the tea-bags with my weekly spend from canteen. Going past the TV room I hear the millennium crap going on in there as well. I just cannot bear to watch it. This day feels long, and empty. There was to have been a millennium beauty contest during the afternoon but it has been cancelled, much to the disappointment of those who have been getting their costumes ready. We are told the prison is short-staffed because lots of the screws have the flu.

'Good,' I think to myself.

Back in the room with my camomile, I take out my book of Irish fiction. It is huge and heavy but I have happily lugged it around with me. We always have to carry our own stuff when we move; the screws do not help you. I pick out one of the stories. Pearl comes in and I cadge some tobacco. She has no cigarette papers, so I screw up my courage and go across the corridor to Janine, a stony-faced woman from Northern Ireland. She is listening to a tape of mournful Irish music.

'That's her brother singing,' says Billie. I express my appreciation of the music and ask: 'Is he in a band?' Janine gives me a withering look: 'No, he's in the Maze prison.' She lets me take a packet of fag papers that is half full and Pearl gratefully takes a share before she wanders off. I settle down to read the story, handling the book like a precious object.

I get through lunchtime bang-up and when the spur gate is opened up I stroll downstairs, still feeling low, to make another cup of tea. My name is on the whiteboard: I have a visit! I race into the office and hope that I am not too late, try to pull myself together: it will be the family. I am let out and a screw walks me across the compound to wait outside the door of the visits hall. After the usual frisking I am shown through. There they are, my special three. Huge hugs and kisses. We have an hour and a half. It goes fast.

They tell me how they managed over Christmas, that they loved the presents I got for them before I went to jail. I tell them how I am getting on. Are we putting a positive gloss over things for each other? Probably we are; I guess we need to. Gordon says the cats are sleeping on my side of the bed, keeping it warm for me. My special cat is constantly craving attention. Missing me. I miss her too. Rachel is going to the Millennium Party in the centre of Cambridge with her boyfriend. I say I hope she enjoys it and tell Joel to have one for me. He asks me to describe the prison layout, wanting to place me in my new surroundings.

When the visitors leave, we convicts have to wait, sitting at the tables in our red chairs. The visitors sat on the blue ones, which now seem painfully empty. The loss feels acute in these moments of waiting, waiting to get frisked again one by one, to get a strip-search if the screws deem it necessary, and to get locked up again. Back on the unit I am more restless than ever. The millennium hype is still dominating the TV. I try the video room. They are watching *The Railway Children*, a change from the usual gory violence. I catch the end, when the father is released from prison. This is too much. I get up to go.

At 7.30 p.m. we are back locked behind the spurs, early again so that the screws can go off and enjoy themselves. People make last-minute phone calls.

'You'll be sure to see them every day,' says one woman as I pass. Our children, oh, how we miss them, and how they must miss us. Thank goodness mine are pretty much grown. After being locked up we all get roll-checked as usual, have to be in our rooms to be accounted for by the screws. They spend a great deal of their time checking the roll and making sure that no one has run off. If only we could.

Then Grace comes to visit Pearl and me. She is a gorgeous creature, even more stunningly beautiful than Pearl, tall and slim with classic features, her head closely shaved. I call her Grace Jones, but she coyly dismisses the compliment with an idle wave. Like Pearl, Grace is from South London. After playing a few games of cards, the two of them begin a dialogue, centred around their adventures in Brixton. It flows as if choreographed. Stories dance out of the scrapes they have got into, usually at the hands of violent men. Pearl recounts how she knifed a guy who gave her two black eyes and then she got off in court for it. Grace tells us of the time someone nearly killed her with a hammer. Her relatives beat him up severely.

'And the police: man, they did not look into this case, did not look into it at all. They knew he was crazy, he'd done this before. I was six weeks on that life-support machine. My father, he went mad, but the police they did nothing.'

'Yeah!' Pearl and Grace touch fists before moving on to the next tall tale. Inevitably, I hear about the drugs. In prison I get to learn that when people talk about smoking a pipe they are referring to crack cocaine, not tobacco or marijuana. Pearl and Grace are giving me a glimpse of their world, which is almost completely hidden from mine. How, if you are born into this, can you ever escape from it? This is the world inhabited by their families, often large and close, and by their friends. It contains what they know.

Pearl shows me a letter from her solicitor and asks if I will write a letter to him for her.

'I'm owed some days,' she says. 'I need to get my days back.' Although she cannot write very well, Pearl is able to hold in her head a quite complex set of facts about the various occasions when she was kept in police custody, and she also understands the system by which those days can be claimed back. After careful reckoning, she believes she is owed eleven days, and that they should therefore come off her sentence. She has to explain it to me several times and we then write the letter, Pearl detailing what she needs to say point by point while I get it down, using her own words as much as I can. When I read it back she is satisfied. The evening drags on. I write my own letters and read a bit. Pearl goes to see Grace.

Normally, we all try to bed down early to make the time pass faster, but tonight is different: we want to see the New Year in, and the new century. Everyone seems a bit agitated. The radios blare out loudly. Most nights so far we have had water fights on the landing: people throwing bucketloads of it at each other, getting completely soaked, and then spending ages mopping the stuff up. Using play to drown their frustration. Pearl and I are glad to have avoided any involvement in it. But tonight the water is not flowing. The atmosphere is tense.

Bet comes in from next door. A desperately skinny middle-aged Londoner, she puffs at her fags as she gives me a long, sorry tale of how she had her own house with her husband, but after twenty-seven years of marriage he developed cancer and she lost him after nursing him through a long illness. Then she picked up with another man and together they got involved in heroin. She sold her house, the money disappeared, and somehow she got the blame when the man was beaten up over a dispute about dealing.

'I was supposed to have set it up but I didn't, you know. Really I didn't.' Bet is a fairly typical, ordinary-looking London woman. Who can say what the truth is?

'That man of mine was a mason,' she declares. 'Wore the same ring on his finger as the judge. My solicitor nearly wept when I was found guilty.' Who can say indeed?

Bet decides to write some of her own letters. After she has gone I feel very alone and look at the photos of the family stuck on to my cupboard, imagining what they are up to right now: Rachel will be raving it up with her boyfriend in Cambridge and Gordon and Joel will be together at home. Grace sticks her head round the door.

'What are you doing? Come an' join the party.'

Everyone is gathered on the central landings, all of us squeezed together behind the thick white bars of the spur gates. I have two sets of bars to the back of me and three in front, familiar faces behind them all. Someone puts Radio 1 on loud, and here it comes, the final countdown: 5, 4, 3, 2, 1. We all erupt, yelling, whistling, hugging and kissing, scenes being repeated throughout the country. The music rings out. A large black woman smashes a cake tin repeatedly against a wall, the noise reverberating. Then I am up on a chair, arms high, whooping and grooving with the rest.

'She's moshin'!' gasps Grace. Too right I am. I catch sight of a screw checking us out. As far as I am concerned, the bastard can look as much as he likes.

Fifteen minutes later everything has died down. I chat awhile to Annette, a Yorkshire lass doing four years, and then I am back in my room and, like most of the others, thinking about those on the outside, straining to pick up their thoughts on the ether.

The next morning we get a good report on our behaviour. But all was not well on House 2, the most chaotic of the three houses. We hear that there was a near-riot. Apparently, people tore radiators off the walls, flooding the place, threw buckets of slops over the screws, even piss and disinfectant, did whatever damage they could do. Some of the inmates got sent to the punishment block, or shipped out to different prisons. There are nickings and adjudications and even talk of criminal charges. Some start to the new millennium for them.

□ □ □

Annette is wanting to be my friend. In the morning she comes in to see if I have anything to eat – she has had no breakfast and is hungry. I give her a slice of lemon-curd cake I have left over from last night and in return she lets me smoke half her roll-up, doing 'twosies' as they call it in here. People are constantly sharing fags, food, whatever; we never seem to have enough of what we want, live with ever-present deprivation.

Then she lends me a little tobacco for later and I add it to the store of dog-ends I have in my jacket pocket. It is a colourful striped light wool jacket that really belongs to my daughter. I wear it constantly.

'Thank you,' I say to Annette.

'You're welcome,' she replies, like the ordinary Yorkshire lass that she is.

I hear Annette's story. She got her four-year sentence for selling a £10 deal of heroin to an undercover policeman.

'I'm not really a dealer,' she says. 'My boyfriend was the dealer, but he was out. So I gave the guy a bit out of my personal stash, thought I was doing him a favour.' She will do at least two years before she comes up for parole. Two years in this environment will toughen her up, might even make a real criminal of her.

We hear the rattle of keys and Miss Morris comes in.

'Just wanting to check your bars,' she says, and gives the ones at the window a push and a shake. These bars are 2 inches thick all round and I cannot imagine how anyone could possibly start to cut into them. Then she has a quick look round the cell and I wonder if there is a curiosity among the screws about this inmate who receives stacks of mail, gets into the newspapers, is not a run-of-the-mill criminal, but nevertheless muddles along well enough with her fellows.

With the intrusion over, Annette says: 'The screws have shitty lives outside.' This may or may not be true. But the thought helps.

□ □ □

Today I make it for my first session in the gym. There are only three other inmates there. Two spend their time necking in a corner of the hall. The instructor ignores them and shows me how to use the equipment, suggesting that I start with fifteen minutes each on the rowing, cycling and jogging machines. There are weights in there as well, but we leave them for now. I have never done this before. It feels good to push myself physically, to cream off some of the stress.

Afterwards we are walked back to our units. Back in the room, Pearl gives me a present of a card with a story written on it, about God being with you all the while.

'You are here for a reason,' she says. I myself do not believe in a personal external God. The only reason I can imagine for being imprisoned is to make it look as though Cambridge police are winning the 'war on drugs', to give them more leverage to turn my colleagues into police informers and to stop me from continually developing new projects for homeless people. But I thank Pearl for her gift and stick the card on the side of my locker.

'I know you, when you are at home, always rush rush rush,' Pearl persists. 'You are a woman who works, always working. When you get out of here you will have more time for your family, you'll appreciate them more and they'll appreciate you good too. Just you see.'

My Pearl surprises me. This young woman is perceptive.

□ □ □

During the evening lock-up Pearl chats to me about her family, her white teeth sparkling. We are both lying on our beds. I am knackered from the gym. Pearl is knackered from life, and too much TV. She says she gets on well with her dad but that her mum is always moaning, always cleaning the house.

'So that's where you get your house-proud nature from,' I josh. Every morning Pearl tidies the room and mops it, with disinfectant or bleach if she can get hold of any. Sometimes she makes my bed for me, if she judges that I have not done it well enough myself.

Pearl boasts that her parents have been together for twenty-seven years.

'It's a good thing too,' she says. 'I wouldn't let no other man come into my house and try to tell me what to do. I don't want my mother to go with no one except my dad.' I ask if she has a boyfriend outside.

'No,' she says, 'but lots of boys want to speak with me.'

'I'm not surprised,' I say. But Pearl has already started a family: she has a toddler being cared for by her mother, has photographs of the little girl on her locker and up on her noticeboard.

Pearl gets me to write another letter, this time to a boy in jail. She speaks fast and I write hurriedly to catch on paper not just what she says but also how she says it. She is satisfied. I willingly give her an envelope and a stamp in return for all the fags she has shared with me, doing twosies.

Today is the first day I have not wept. Despite being someone who does not normally weep easily, tears have been springing up from nowhere in here. Now it is subsiding. Feeling pleased, I try to settle on the bed. All down one side I ache, physically, from the hardness of the thin mattress. But I think the pain is beginning to ease off and hope I am becoming accustomed. I lie first on my good side, then on my back, and then my front. Nothing helps much. Even the pillow is hard.

Pearl is now deep in her drugged slumber, but the radio from the room opposite is louder than ever. Janine, the tough-looking Northern Irish woman, is blasting out the whole corridor. Pearl has warned me about Janine: 'I don't like to talk to them you know.' She tells me that they do the ouija board in the room.

'Bad vibes, huh?' I say.

'Yeah,' says Pearl. 'Bad vibes. Janine is the kind of person to be racist.' Janine looks to me like she could be violent, has a mean and hard way about her – though it might be a protective front. I have come across it so often in night shelter work. Janine gets Valium at healthcare, which seems quite unusual in here, and I presume that helps to keep her quietened down.

Eleven thirty, and the radio is still on very loud. I reckon Janine must turn it down soon. The rule is no loud music after eleven. Twelve midnight. Twelve thirty. Still the music blares out. I wonder what I can do; I cannot stand this night after night. I am tired, always tired. I could make a complaint in the office, picture myself doing it, but do not want to. People tell me some inmates put anonymous complaints in the postbox – it is one way to avoid repercussions. But I understand the general repulsion about crawling to the screws, grassing people up. The screws are our jailers. They are the common enemy. Only cowards cross the divide.

So I build up my courage and get up to speak to them. Janine is in her room with Billie and a few others.

'I'm sorry, but I just can't sleep. Do you think you could turn it down a bit? I'm ever so tired and, y'know, don't mind the radio on, but it is very late. It's about compromise, really.' Janine, looking rather surprised, wordlessly obliges.

'Thanks.' I say, and feel glad I did not go to the screws, that I have confronted it for myself. As I settle down I hear them saying the word 'compromise', tossing it around between them, as if it is a new concept that they have not come across before.

Sleep comes.

□ □ □

Another boring day, another noisy night. Marie, a stocky white woman with a squint and a body covered in tattoos, has the noisiest and most coarse laugh I have ever heard. She shares a room with Scouse Billie, who has just got a job in the kitchens.

'Darling, I'm home,' Billie screams on her return to the wing.

'Fuck off,' yells Marie.

'Where's my bleeding supper?' Billie demands. More loud cussing and then peals of laughter, Marie's strident and venomous. It reverberates around the corridors and is intensely annoying. A water fight breaks out in the bathroom and now they are banging on each others' doors, roaring with hilarity. I can hear three radios: Pearl's, Janine's and another from up the corridor, all tuned in to different stations. It is impossible to relax. And then, at last, a little blessed quietness. I try to read.

Nancy suddenly hurtles into our room and throws herself on to my bed. She is very red in the face and looks upset. Life is not easy for Nancy, sharing with Janine. Whatever she might say or do, Nancy will never be accepted as one of the crew. She looks and behaves differently: massively overweight, articulate, but much too chatty in her efforts to be accepted, Nancy does not know how to create her own space. She is just not cool. On top of that we have her stories about being sexually abused as a child, which wind everyone up, especially those who have suffered such abuse as well – and there are plenty of them in prison.

I ask Nancy what the matter is, but she will not speak – maybe because Pearl is there, I do not know. She looks very upset. Then she suddenly goes. I hear rushing about outside and Janine pokes her head through our door.

'Ruth, Ruth, where's Nancy?'

'I don't know,' I say. 'She's just gone.' They go up and down the corridor looking for her. I look as well. Everyone seems hyped up but they will not tell me what has happened.

Not long afterwards we hear the clank of keys and I look through to the gate. A screw calls me over for a private word. It is Miss Hardy, the young screw with the rolling walk.

'You're a friend of Nancy's. Do you know what's happened?' I tell her about Nancy being upset, but that she would not talk to me about it. We speak low so no one can hear.

'I think she's a bit paranoid,' I add. I turn to see Nancy cowering in someone else's room.

'She's a poor coper,' says Hardy. 'See if she'll speak to the Samaritans.' When I relay the message, Nancy insists that she will only talk to the screws. Another one appears and the two of them open the gate and take Nancy off, to the hospital wing we think. We can all see from the scars on her arm that Nancy has a history of cutting up – self-harming. There is a lot of that about in prison as well.

I go back to my corridor, where the atmosphere is electric.

'She's going to grass us up,' someone says, jittery as hell. I try to be reassuring, do not want Nancy to be scapegoated. Pearl takes me to one side. She has been investigating.

'It's that ouija board,' she tells me. 'They were all doin' it: Janine, Grace, Billie, Marie and Nancy, and some others. It said that Nancy was not in for theft like she told us, but that she was in for child abuse.' I remember Nancy saying that her co-defendant was in for child abuse as well as for theft.

'Well, if they're co-defendants, they'd both be charged with child abuse as well as theft,' says Pearl.

Grace says: 'Not necessarily,' but the suspicion had been planted and the ouija board confirmed it, despite Nancy's denials.

'Ouija might be evil, but it don't lie,' says Pearl. Now I realize why Nancy was so worried. Child abusers are loathed in jail and are at risk of being beaten up if the other inmates get to them. They have to be kept apart. For whatever reason, Nancy did not come back.

□ □ □

Pearl wants to play cards and gets the deck from Grace's room. She insists on playing black jack. Grace joins us for the game. As usual, Grace is skimpily dressed, this time in a very tight pair of hotpants and a minuscule crop top. Her head is newly shaved and she has spiced herself up with some make-up. The weather is freezing but in here it is as warm as toast, the heating almost too strong, pumped out by large white wall-mounted old radiators with their hot pipes encircling the room.

Our card-playing is highly competitive and gets quite noisy. Peaches must have heard us. She comes in from her room next door, a Jamaican woman, as massive as Grace is slim. Peaches steers herself ponderously through our door and flops on to Pearl's bed.

'I'm hungry,' she declares, puckering her full lips. I have just given Grace and Pearl my unwanted Penguin bar to share and have nothing else left.

'You only hungry because you can't be bothered to walk to the dining room,' Pearl scolds, as she gives Peaches a few slices of bread she has saved from supper. Peaches helps herself to an apple and gets stuck in, refusing my offer of some margarine.

'I don't wan' none of that stuff,' she says, then rolls her eyes skyward and laughs a deep, throaty laugh, mouth wide open, huge belly jiggling. I think she finds my presence in the room with three black women quite amusing.

Pearl and Grace get me back into the cards, while Peaches munches on and continues to eye me up. Then everybody is thirsty. Grace slides off to bring four oranges from her room. She slices and squeezes them into a plastic jug, adds sugar and water and the drink is ready. It is very refreshing. Laughter and jokes are flying fast now. Grace and Pearl are back into their shared dialogue and spontaneously flow together. Peaches picks it up and joins in, lapsing into pure patois, which encourages the other two further, all of them speaking fast and furious, dancing the half-familiar words around me and at intervals becoming overcome with hilarity.

Then the songs start. Grace and Pearl jump up and down enthusiastically as the three of them share ditties from their childhoods. They all know the songs, the semi-patois, a fast mass of words and rhythm that I can hardly decipher. But I can make it out a bit and exclaim: 'You're singing dirty songs.' They laugh at my feigned shock and sing some more, beating out the strong rhythms and relishing their joint remembrances. It gets louder and louder. They urge each other on as they search their memories for the comfort of the tunes that they grew up with, the ruder the better. Louder still, the wing is rocking with the sound of it. The hour hits midnight. We must be keeping everyone up.

We are for sure. Screams and shouting from outside the door of the room break through the hilarity: it is Billie, the little Scouser, out of her mind with fury. She bangs at the door, lifting the little flap that covers the small window in it, and we are all horrified at the sight of her: bright red in the face with anger, screeching at us, 'Bastards, cunts, animals!' Billie is raging with a deep fury that has been wrenched to the surface by these black women singing their childhood songs. We freeze at the unexpectedness of her reaction: such aggression from out of nowhere. I am worried someone will open the door and start a fight. But the others sit as aghast as I do, and, her furious harangue thankfully over, Billie retreats back to her room.

A long and noisy postmortem follows. The black women shout their abuse out into the corridor, but add a sensible let-out clause to their threats: 'No way do I want to go to the block for dissin' that cow.' Diss her good they could. Like me, Billie only reaches up to their shoulders. She would be no match for any of them.

'What she doin' attackin' the door?' says Grace. 'Boy is she gonna wake up with bruises on her arm.'

'Yeah,' says Pearl. 'We'll tell the screws, hey, we'll say we got some self-harmin' here, hurtin' herself like that, the stupid bitch. An' did you see her bangin' her head on that door? Her head!' Pearl shakes her own head in disbelief.

We certainly were much too loud, but have put up with noise from Billie and her mates for nights on end – screaming water fights and radios thundering out. Grace is particularly annoyed about being called a bastard.

'I ain't no bastard, my mother and father were married for sure when I was born.'

Pearl thinks Billie is racist.

'I don't like to be called an animal. Don't like that at all.'

They manage to talk their anger down and after half an hour they slope off to bed.

I dream about my dead maternal grandmother: that she is living in our basement, infirm and in her bed, and I feel guilty about not looking after her properly. Then there are two blackbirds in the room. They seem wounded so I throw a large white stone at one, trying to finish it off humanely, but it only serves to make the birds fly away. They are not as severely injured as I had thought.

In the morning I wake with fear in my stomach. The attack from Billie was fierce. She is well in with the other white women on the landing, including Janine. They are a tough lot, and the black women are either tall or broad or both, but I am small and white and not used to fighting. Will they take it out on me? Then Pearl comes to tell me that she has just hit Marie because Marie called her a black bitch, and that she has been to the screws to tell them what has happened and what went on with Billie last night. She has also told them that we have been kept awake for nights by the others shouting and laughing and doing the ouija board.

'They said they'd sort it out,' Pearl says. I wonder if they will.

At lunchtime I am called into the unit's office. Miss West, who is the only black screw I have seen in the place so far and the senior officer (SO) for this unit, takes me into a side room and asks me about Nancy. It looks as though Nancy has been making a range of allegations against Janine and Marie, among others. I refuse to be drawn in.

'Nancy was very anxious,' I say. 'I found Janine OK if you spoke to her decently.' West presses me for more but does not get it. I see the screws as the enemy, do not trust them an inch. They can do their dirty work without me.

When I get out, people quiz me about my private chat with the SO. I tell them what I said; I do not want to be seen as a grass, and anyway am not one, will not be one. I cannot see any reason to help these jailers, who treat me like shit, strut about as if they enjoy their power and seem happy to discomfort us all. I have a pretty long sentence to do and know where my allegiances lie.

After lunch we are herded behind the spur gates for lock-up. The three black women in the room preen themselves and each other. Grace plucks Peaches' eyebrows and Pearl is doing her hair in little bunches at either side, the radio blasting out as usual. I am tired from last night and from gym this morning, lie on my bed and actually manage to nap for ten minutes or so. Perhaps I am learning to sleep amid this racket.

I am woken by a noise from down the corridor. Janine is being moved to a different house along with someone else, and Billie and Marie are being moved downstairs, to one of the rooms on Skid Row. All on Nancy's say-so, and Pearl's too. Though I respect my roommate and accept her actions, I am learning that it is possible to cause a lot of grief in here if you are prepared to go running to the screws. The women are upset at being moved; they have friends on this wing, and

I remember the way the move at Holloway disturbed me. However much they annoyed me, these women were part of my spur. But I do wonder if life will now be quieter.

When we are unlocked we see a note on the whiteboard: 'Will all the silly girlies doing the ouija board stop, otherwise they will get moved.' Abominably patronizing, but the point is made. Some people feel all this is over the top; a quietly spoken Indian woman starts up a petition to get her friends back. I am happy to sign it, but one of the inmates says we could get into trouble, that a petition can be seen as an incitement to riot. It gets torn up. No free speech in here. Later on I discover that the ouija board is a common prison diversion from the day-to-day boredom of jail.

At 2.30 p.m. the screws open the gate so we can go out to the grassy area at the front of the unit. Determined to take advantage of the chance to get outside, I wrap up as best I can, take a book and sit on a wooden bench there, reading and smoking the odd dog-end. It is freezing, but at least I am outside, and I hang on until I start to shiver. When I get back in it takes me a good half-hour to thaw out, still in my coat and curled under my blankets. Pearl solicitously makes me a cup of tea.

□ □ □

The next morning is bright and cold. There is a blanket of white frost on the ground outside. No wonder I got chilled yesterday. I have had my first decent night's sleep since my incarceration almost two weeks ago and feel heavy from it, my head muzzy. At 7.30 a.m. we get the usual roll-check from the screws, looking through the small windows in the doors of our rooms, accounting for everyone. For once I am not up. Pearl comes to and complains that I have not woken her as I usually do. We get unlocked at 8 and have to get our milk for the breakfast cereal then, otherwise we miss it. I get dressed and lie on the bed, losing myself in the photos of my family.

Grace comes to borrow my bowl, as she has lost hers and wants some cereal. Accused of threatening a male screw and calling him a racist, she is due to go down to the block this morning for an adjudication.

'Maybe I did say he was racist, because I reckon he is, but no way did I threaten him.'

'The male screws are the worst,' I say. 'Doing this job, subjugating us women, seems to give them a kick.' Grace and Pearl agree.

'I could get days for this,' Grace says, meaning days added on to her sentence. She explains the procedure for the block.

'You have to walk yourself there at 8.30 a.m., I mean walk yourself, where are they at? Most prisons take you there. Then you wait on cardboard furniture till 10 a.m., or later, till the governors arrive. It's like a kangaroo court. You explain your case with screws standing each side of you, but they can say what they want and who they gonna believe? Not me, that's for sure.'

When she has gone, Pearl explains to me that Grace has already had days added to her sentence.

'She should be out by now. She should've spent Christmas at home. But she lets them wind her up. This place gets to her real bad.'

I go for a shower, and in the washroom a young woman approaches me, having heard that I've worked in homelessness. She tells me that she is due out in March but has nowhere to live. It turns out that she is from Huntingdon, not far from Cambridge, but has lost her flat through rent arrears and anyway does not want to go back. Everyone she knows in the town is on heroin.

'I want to stay off the brown,' she says, meaning the heroin. 'Would Cambridge be better?'

'There's a lot of heroin in Cambridge as well. The place is awash.'

'Yeah, the same story everywhere. Anyway, you know us addicts, if we want to find it, we will.' I talk about her options: the winter shelter in Cambridge closes in March, so all the projects will probably be full. I tell her about the other agencies, including our day centre, which would be the best first stop. She looks like an ordinary young woman, but I can see her all too easily getting sucked into the Cambridge heroin scene.

'You should get yourself some counselling from the local drugs agency, to help you keep off.' She brightens.

'I was getting counselling in Holloway and it helped a lot.' I wonder why she is not still getting it. She seems so young and I know she will have a hard time when she gets out: nowhere to stay, no job, no money, no family or support. Who is to blame if – when – she gets back on to the needle?

Pearl tells me that we are to be locked up all morning because the prison's most famous inmate, Myra Hindley,* has been taken to hospital with angina and they need a lot of the staff to guard her.

'I hope she doesn't snuff it, she needs to suffer and suffer,' says Pearl.

'Yeah,' says Grace, 'I don't believe in the electric chair for the likes of her.'

'She'll never get out,' I pitch in. 'Wouldn't ever be safe.'

'Just let me at her,' says Pearl, coming from a somewhat different perspective than mine.

'I'd cut her up good,' says Grace, 'for what she done to those kids. Let me take her to the forest, I'd do her in.' And she goes off to the block to face her own tormentors.

□ □ □

Pearl is reading her Bible out loud, to the accompaniment of the jaunty beat from her radio. Maybe it is through having a good sleep the night before that I can feel the anger rising in me now. What am I doing here, locked up? I see myself as a useful member of society, have a contribution to make, have been contributing for years, working in projects, running them, using my creativity to set up new developments. What on earth is the point of sticking me in this jail? Look at the financial cost of it, let alone the cost to me and my family. But there is nowhere for my anger to go. I have to hold on to it myself.

I worry constantly about my daughter, feel pure hatred for what the police, and the judge, have done: they have stolen her mother. I feel desperate at the thought that she will have to spend more time on her own while her father is at work, that I cannot care for her as I should. It is her right to have me. I wonder how I can make her situation easier. Gordon works for another homelessness agency in

*Child murderer Myra Hindley was jailed for life in 1966. She died on 14 November 2002, aged sixty, having spent thirty-six years in prison.

Cambridge. His boss was a colleague of mine. I write him a letter, asking if there is any way Gordon can be taken off shifts for a while, can be given a nine-to-five job, maybe doing resettlement, so that he would be around more when Rachel gets home from school.

As the morning wears on I become aware of temperature changes in my body. Perhaps it is to do with the contrast between the icy cold outside and the central heating inside, which seems to be permanently on day and night. I reach through the bars to open and close the windows. I have to leave the heater on because that is how Pearl wants it. The control knob is at the head of my bed. Secretly, I turn it off when I go to sleep and back on again at 4 or 5 a.m. when I awake, frozen with the cold. Pearl sleeps through it all.

I hope I do not have the flu; I dread being ill in prison. I have seen two people with flu in here, their faces brimming with the misery and trauma of being unwell in such a comfortless place. The other morning I heard Peaches spewing up while I had my morning shower. Later she tells me that she spewed up blood and that she has a bad pain in her belly, but she could only get paracetamol from the nurse.

There is a woman in here who had a hysterectomy a couple of weeks ago and is supposed to be on bed rest for twelve weeks. But she has to walk to medication to get her tablets three times a day. One day I walk with her. She has to go very slowly, tells me that at first the nurses would only give her paracetamol for the pain. Then she got an infection and was put on a child's dose of antibiotics.

'When the doctor heard, he went mad,' she says. 'He got me on to the proper tablets. Though the nurses complained that they were too expensive.'

'They don't have to pay for it,' I say, as I accompany her on her slow and painful walk back to the wing. 'They just don't want to give us prisoners anything.'

□ □ □

It's 5 p.m. – another early lock-up. Pearl has had her bath and is in bed in her nightie, listening to the usual inane stuff on the radio and thumbing through an ancient magazine. She seems quite relaxed; she watches TV a lot here and at home, does not have my urge for activity. Perhaps that makes prison life a little easier for her than me.

I really do have the flu now. My head burns and hurts, my throat is on fire and I can feel the infection spreading down to my chest. I am starting to cough up phlegm. I have managed not to smoke all day; I know it is damaging me. Now that I am ill perhaps I can completely stop again. Because we are locked up early, the nurses come on to the wing to give out the medication and I manage to get a dose of paracetamol out of them. I try to get more, to last me through the twenty-four hours until I am due medication again.

'Can't do that,' says the nurse. 'They were storing them up.' They? I am not 'they'. I am me, and I want to storm: 'Me, me, me. You bastards.' Grace butts in and starts to hustle the nurse for herself, but they are short with her too, will give her nothing more than the same old dose of paracetamol. It takes me all my strength to get my aching body back to my room and into bed.

By 8.30 p.m. Pearl is asleep, lying on her back and snoring. I feel bad, physically and mentally; I cannot get comfortable and sleep will not come. Prison really is a terrible place to be ill. The whole day has been incredibly boring and tedious, as well as increasingly uncomfortable as the illness took hold. I cannot bear to be restricted in such a rough and unstimulating environment, whatever my physical state. The feelings seem to get worse, not better, as time goes by. Being ill accentuates my deprivation. Why have people done this to me? It is a cruel and senseless injustice.

Pearl has left a precious roll-up out for the morning. I just cannot resist a puff and haul myself to Janine's room to hustle a light. There is much merriment from the bathroom. One of the women is leaving the next day and is getting the customary prison farewell: a thorough soaking. Buckets of water are launched at her, some filled with bits of soggy cereal. She takes it in good spirit. In the morning she will have left all this behind. Though I know from speaking to her earlier she is worried about what she will face when she gets out. Her two young kids have been badly upset by the loss of their mum, and her relationship with her boyfriend, their father, is at breaking point.

The fag smoke is hurting my chest. I leave most of the roll-up in the ashtray and hope that Pearl does not berate me. All night I toss and turn on my hard bed, but manage an hour or so of good, deep sleep. In the morning I refresh myself with a shower and go to Grace's room to retrieve my bowl that she borrowed. She is not there but I am faced with a dreadful sight of blood and phlegm in her washing-up bowl, in my bowl, and dripping off her table and on to the floor. I remember how dismissive the nurses were of her last night and wonder what on earth has happened.

As far as I am aware, I am not allowed another bowl and could get in trouble for lending mine out. So I pick it up and give it a good wash in the bathroom, hoping that I will not catch anything from it. Then I find Pearl to tell her what I have seen. She already knows.

'Grace has sickle cell disease. They took her into hospital last night.'

'Those bloody nurses,' I exclaim.

I wash and rinse the bowl with boiling water from the urn, over and over again. Hygiene is a problem in here and I have already had the shits; I am sure it is because of the difficulty of keeping your plastic plates and cutlery clean between meals. You get to wash them in a sink in the dining room after you have eaten, but only with a communal scourer and just a bit of very watered-down washing-up liquid. Then you have to keep everything in your room with all the general dust and dirt. As well as affecting our health, it is degrading, as if we are not worth properly hygienic conditions.

'It's like camping out,' I tell Pearl, remembering the good times I had tenting it with Gordon and the kids.

It is a Saturday and we have to go to medication in the morning instead of the evening, as the staff want to get away. My temperature is building up again: I am alternately hot and then shivery with cold. The pains in my head, throat and chest fight for ascendance. We troop off with the screw, through four gates unlocked and then locked back up by the screw when we have all gone through. At one point she laughs.

'What are you laughing at, miss?' someone asks. She will not say. I find nothing to laugh at, except for the ludicrous nature of locking and unlocking, and I concentrate on keeping my shaky upright.

The medication room is crowded out as usual. We form queues at each of the two barred hatches, one for A–L and one for M–Z; surnames, of course. The nurses have their records and studiously dispense what is allowed, stoutly refusing any requests for more. The crush of the bodies in this small space is stifling. I try to get three doses of paracetamol to last till tomorrow but as usual am allowed only one. That has to keep me going for the next twenty-four hours. When I am done I wait outside.

Annette is there and fixes me with wide brown eyes.

'Do you realize that we are all convicts?' I look back wearily. Annette has been inside for four months.

'Has that only just struck you?'

'Yes. It's a bit shocking, don't you think?' Annette is an ordinary Yorkshire lass, I am an ordinary middle-aged woman. She's right. To be placed here, like this, is shocking. I look up at some trees in the distance, their black shapes silhouetted against the blue of the clear sky. Then I realize that, just 40 yards or so away, past two bits of fencing, there is a road. I can hear invisible traffic swishing past, so close. I work out that the first fence would be easy to get over: it is not very high and there is a good foothold halfway up, in one of the gates. The second fence would be more tricky, standing at 25 or 30 feet with a double roll of razor wire on top. You would need a stout rope with a grappling iron and a piece of carpeting to get yourself over.

It is pure fancy, but the urge is very strong. It could be done with the right equipment. For a few moments I happily dream, imagine the getaway car waiting to whisk me away – to where? If I went to Cambridge, I would be arrested on sight, but there is nowhere else for me to go. All I want to do is to go home. With the rest of the women finished, the screw walks us back to the unit.

□ □ □

Grace peeks in through the window in our door: 'I'm back.' Pearl and I jump up, delighted to see her. She has been in the West Suffolk Hospital and had to have an operation for a tear in her oesophagus. Sickle cell disease made you bleed like leukaemia, Grace explains, so she had been in quite a lot of danger.

'They said I nearly died.'

'I bet that nurse was shitting herself after the way she treated you,' I say, remembering how they had only given Grace paracetamol.

'She was having kittens. Ringing the hospital all the while to check.'

Her parents came up from London to see her. I am jealous: an extra visit.

'My mum asked if I'd seen you,' says Grace. 'She'd read about your case and was really chuffed that you're on my wing.'

She sits on my bed and shifts her weight, trying to get comfortable. I apologize for the hardness of my mattress. Grace and Pearl inspect it.

'Pure Holloway,' Pearl pronounces. Grace tells me there is a mattress in her room that is better than mine. No one is using it; the bed is empty. We haul it up the corridor.

'What are you doin'?' asks Billie, who has been moved back upstairs after just two days' punishment on Skid Row.

'Bed-hopping,' I reply.

'Naughty girls,' Billie laughs and slaps me on the bum.

The bed is a little better with the new mattress: still pretty hard but marginally thicker. At least I cannot feel the criss-cross of the metal slats underneath. I stretch out and we all share a fag.

'How's things been here, then?' Grace asks.

'A bit quieter with Janine and that gone,' Pearl replies.

Whatever quietness there was, beneath the usual radios, is shattered by a scream from next door. It is Bet, the skinny Londoner who shares the next-door room with Peaches, the big Jamaican. We take a look and see Bet outside her door furiously berating Peaches.

'I can't do anything in my own room. It's my bloody room as well as yours, you know. You're so selfish. I can't stand it. I just can't take any more!'

We usher Bet in with us and she is off again.

'That fat cow, all she ever does is sleep. I can't smoke in the room, OK, she doesn't smoke, so I've been smoking outside. I have to go in the corridor if I want a fag. She wants the heating on all the time, OK, so I leave it on, never mind that I'm dripping with sweat. Then she wants the window open, it's freezing outside, but fine, I open it. Now she's going mad at me if I make the slightest noise. As if prison wasn't bad enough without all of this.'

We advise Bet to complain to the screws, to try to get a room move. She sits with us a while, then ventures back to her room. All is quiet for now.

I spend the rest of the evening working on an article for the papers. The *Independent* has asked Gordon for something from me and I decide to send a piece about the festive season in prison. I have spent a fair bit of time laboriously writing it and rewriting it by hand, but it helps to put my mind to something and writing things down relieves some of the stress. In the morning I post it in the letterbox, with my other letters. You have to leave your envelopes unsealed so that the screws can check them: nothing is sacred in prison. I have also written to the family, separate letters for my husband, son and daughter in the one envelope, plus one to my mother, and another for everyone at Wintercomfort. I try to put up a good front, as if it will shore me up and stop me from falling apart.

I have got the milk for my cereal and I eat it in my room, trying to listen to the news on the radio while thinking about what Gordon, Joel and Rachel would be doing right now: feeding the cats and the dog; getting up and ready for the day. Normal things. I gaze through the bars and out of the window, at the trees and fields on the other side of the fence.

Pearl bursts in: 'We've got induction, 9 o'clock in the lounge.' I wonder where the lounge is and follow her. It is the room that is my room, the one I use to sit in quietly by myself because no one else ever seems to be there. A screw is sitting there now; tall and grey-haired, he is known as Mr C. Pearl and I sit down with Billie and a few other women, all of us new inmates over the Christmas period. We get various bits of paper, one headed 'Standard of Behaviour and Performance', and others we have to sign and hand back. I can hardly take them in. The initial shock of imprisonment robs you of your ability to focus, and for some reason I find writing easier than reading. Even so, we all catch one section about having to respect the officers in the same way as they will respect us. It makes us snigger: we know the reality.

Halfway through Mr C. goes to get himself a cuppa and returns with it. He has a cheroot on the go, a Christmas present perhaps. We all eye it enviously; none of us have any tobacco. Mr C. takes a slow puff and goes through the prison rules. Pearl has stretched herself out along three chairs and looks as though her mind is elsewhere.

'Are you listening?' Mr C. demands. She assures him that she is.

'I'm just tired. But I'm listenin' for sure.' We are required to pay special attention to the anti-bullying strategy. Mr C. urges us to talk to someone if we feel low, describing how people can sink very fast, especially under pressure from others.

'I reckon the anti-bullying strategy is 75 per cent successful,' he says. Only 75 per cent?

'I don't want to be cutting you down,' Mr C. continues. He is talking about people hanging themselves. 'Women's prisons are very different from men's,' he adds ominously.

'What, because women are more emotional than men?' we ask.

'Exactly that.'

Then Mr C. takes us off to the gym, locking and unlocking as usual as we go. We are given a chat by one of the PE officers there, who says that we must get fitted out by the doctor and put in applications if we want to use the place. I keep quiet about the sessions I've already had. We're allowed two weekday slots plus some evenings and weekends. The ubiquitous prison bureaucracy. Mr C. says that the evening gym session clashes with the evening medication run.

'That's a bit unfair,' I say. He agrees and suggests that I make a complaint.

On we go for a trip to the chapel. A woman cleric sits us down and asks: 'How are you all getting on?' Everyone looks uncomfortable, especially with Mr C. there.

'Well, this is prison, isn't it?' I say.

'Yeah,' says Billie. 'We're not exactly supposed to be enjoying this, you know.'

We go out past the punishment wing, known as 'the block', or 'seg', and by the hospital unit. On the way Mr C. shows us which areas of the prison are off-limits without permission. There seem to be a lot of these. Back on House 3, a nurse is waiting in 'my' lounge to give us an outline of the prison healthcare system. She refers to us as 'girls' throughout.

'Women, we are women,' I say. The nurse looks surprised. I explain that I know we are often referred to as girls in this place but that I find it an insult; it is infantilizing. We are all grown women, all over twenty-one. The nurse looks confused.

'I like being called a girl,' says Billie, who anyway behaves like a ten-year-old most of the time.

Someone mentions House 1, which is described as a kind of community with group work.

'I've done some group work outside,' I say.

'It'll suit you,' says Billie, 'with you being quiet and all.' Mr C. says they usually come for the inductions but that he is not sure what has happened this time. From what I can gather the community has a Christian basis. Then Mr C. says that we might get moved to House 2, which worries me. It sounds a bit rough there, what with the trouble over New Year.

The final part of the induction is in the education block: a two-storey building next to the gym. At the front there is a hairdressing salon where inmates can learn the trade. Opposite it is a small library room, staffed by a librarian with a prisoner as an assistant. A screw is permanently stationed at a desk. The building has six or seven class-rooms and an art room.

We are taken upstairs and a member of staff outlines what's on offer: basic English, basic maths, basic computing, basic office administration, English for foreigners and the art class. I ask about Open University and am told that the staff would love to be able to provide it but their bosses will not comply. One or two people rather listlessly sign up for classes, but the staff do not know what to do with me and I am asked to wait until the end.

'Look,' I say, 'I'm a trained journalist and have been running a charity with a turnover of half-a-million pounds.' I feel embarrassed, as if I am boasting. Perhaps I am trying to remind myself as well as them of who I am. Though it hardly matters in here. There is nothing for me in this place, nothing to look forward to, just boredom and emptiness in the weeks, months and years ahead. I need to find a way of passing the time.

Everyone has to do either education or work, and the work options are pretty dire: cleaning various parts of the establishment; cooking; learning painting and decorating; sewing clothes for the third world; light assembly work; and gardening. I offer to help with the English class, to sit with people while they read.

'Oh, you can't do that,' they say. It seems that as well as being unable to help myself, I am not allowed to help anyone else.

'I guess you're disadvantaged in here if you have a bit of education,' I complain, knowing that I am not the only prisoner with this problem. It is good that there are the basic classes, but there are other needs to be met as well.

'I'm sorry, I don't know what we can offer you,' says one of the staff. 'You could try the art class.' I hate art, could not stand to do it all day, but agree to try it in the mornings. It will get me off the unit, if nothing else.

'I could do gardens in the afternoon,' I suggest, attracted by the prospect of getting out in the open air. They agree and seem relieved to have sorted out this difficult customer. I will be able to start the following week. Though one of the staff does look rather anxious about the gardening.

'If you're sure,' she says. I like gardening at home. What is her problem?

□ □ □

In the evening I feel very low. Evenings seem to be the worst in prison. They were very much a family time for me: preparing and eating a meal together; getting the kids to do their homework; reading or watching a bit of TV. There is nothing to interest me on the TV here – they are watching the usual rubbish. I feel my exclusion acutely, cut off from the outside world by the bars of the jail and inside by my complete lack of relatedness to this place. Though I have experienced constant kindness from other inmates, as a middle-aged and middle-class woman I fear becoming a target.

'You help us out there,' one inmate told me, 'so we'll help you in here.'

For a diversion, I go to the office to get a request/complaint form. Everything you want has to be applied for, in writing. I decide to do the one suggested by Mr C., to complain about the clash between gym and medication. I have also been told you can get black boot polish from the office, so, as my boots are filthy, I ask for some. Pearl is watching TV, which means I can do the two chores alone in my room listening to Radio 4 on her radio. I fill in the request/complaint form and the boots come up a treat. When I have finished I return the form and the polish to the office. A screw who is new to me fixes me with a malevolent stare and barks: 'Give the form to Mr C. and the polish to me.' I do so and pointedly say: 'Thank you,' as if I am trying to teach her some manners.

My mood is still fragile and the screw's impatience cuts through my façade. I seek out my only private space, in the small lounge, and weep with the light off so that no one can see. It is dark outside and my tears are mirrored by the rain that is sliding down the window panes. I peer out, look through the bars and the fences to more barred windows set in the building of House 2 opposite. Wherever I look I see the landscape of my containment. I know I need to speak to someone, to get things off my chest, but cannot bring myself to ask for help, dare not show any chinks in my armour.

Feeling that I have cried it out, I head for the office on a pretext. Miss Hardy is there, the screw with the rolling walk. She is generally liked, seems open-hearted, and is with Miss No-please-and-no-thank-you. I say I am worried about the possibility of being moved to House 2. My excuse is that Jo is there and she was a prosecution witness against me. Miss Hardy says I might be moved, but there are others in front of me; it all depends how many they get shipped over from Holloway. The other woman, who seems to know more about House 2, says she remembers Jo going to court.

'She was a client of mine at the day centre,' I say. Hardy changes the subject.

'Do you think you could stop calling us screws?'

'Do you know where the term comes from?' the other woman asks.

'Because prison screws you up,' I say, pleased to be quick off the mark.

'No,' she says, not prepared to take that one any further, and she tells me a story about how in the old days convicts at work used to spend their time turning a machine to make screws. When the finished product appeared, they'd call out 'Screw!' to get an officer to come and take it.

Now it is my turn to get on my hobbyhorse.

'Do you think you could stop calling us girls? We're all grown women and I find it quite insulting. It's infantilizing.'

'That's part of the system,' says Hardy.

'Ladies is what I prefer,' says the other screw. Women, I am a woman – but now I am close to tears again and I wonder if they notice. Probably they do.

It is time for evening roll-check and lock-up. Hardy says she will talk to the SO, Miss West, about the House 2 problem. I return to my room for another weep and then go in search of a fag paper to make a roll-up from my stored dog-ends. No one has any. Though I know Peaches has. She looks to be asleep on her bed so I nip in and nick one from her packet. When I am back in my room I hear her shouting at me. Her fury burns some of the upset out of me. With the food that I have given to Peaches over the last few days, I feel anything but guilty.

'Take no notice,' advises Pearl, and Peaches soon calms down again.

Annette comes in for a chat, with a quietly spoken Chinese woman, and we discuss the origin of the word screw.

'They called them "boss" at my last nick,' says Annette. I ask them whether they mind being called girls.

' "Ladies", "women", that is OK,' says the Chinese woman. 'But "girls"! I have a daughter of twenty-two. Even she is a woman. Girls, girls, girls. I hate it.'

That night I am assailed by the usual disturbing dreams: I enroll for a course, but there are no places left. I try to put my case. The others take a vote and vote me out. I wake up feeling hurt by the unfairness of it and cannot sleep, though it is only 4.30 a.m. This time I have woken with an ache that seems lodged deep inside me, a constant and steady feeling to remind me of my loss. Here I do not have my own life. I am living for someone else. My activities are dictated to me. The I that is me belongs elsewhere, resides elsewhere, and in this prison that life is snuffed out by the screws, at the behest of the trial judge, Cambridgeshire police and those who helped with the prosecution against me. They wanted to destroy me. I will fight them all the way.

At 7 o'clock I pad off to the bathroom in my prison nightdress to have my usual morning shower, drying myself as best I can with one of the small towels we get issued with. The only person about is the Chinese woman. She is washing. There is no privacy. Back in the room I dress and make sure I am decent for the 7.30 a.m. roll-check, when the screws look into all the rooms. Not long after unlock I am summoned to the office and taken into a side room where Miss West, the large black SO, is sitting at a table, waiting. She has hold of the article I put into the letterbox yesterday. I am told to sit down too. Miss Hardy comes in and stands over me. West looks really angry.

'Haven't you always been treated with respect by the officers here?' she demands. I hardly know where to begin – feel I have never been treated with respect, that it is endemic to the system – but I am afraid to say so. I can feel myself getting upset. West tells me to stop calling the officers screws, which I have done in the article.

'All right,' I say, not wanting any trouble. 'I can change that.'

Then she berates me for giving details about prison layout. I say I did not know that was against the rules and that I can take those sections out. She has already drawn a line through them, as well as circling the word 'screw' every time I have written it.

West saves her worst fury for the bit I did on the New Year's Eve riot in House 2. I had tried to write about the feelings involved, the pain of some of the women who had caused damage, that their behaviour could have been an expression of it.

'Those women are all bullies,' she states. 'They're in jail because they want to be.' Now I feel angry. None of the prisoners I have met want to be here. We all hate it and are hurt by it. This is presumably how West copes with doing this shitty job: demeaning the inmates to justify the shitty things she does to us day after day. But I cannot express my thoughts, or my anger, dare not do so, which only serves to make me more upset.

Hardy is hovering over me.

'You're not coping well,' she declares, venomously it seems. 'You should speak to someone.' It may have been meant as helpful advice but it makes me think they want to see me break down. Stamping their authority on me, making sure that I know who is boss. If I speak to anyone, it will not be her.

West moves on to my request/complaint about the gym and medication clash.

'We are trying to make arrangements,' she says through gritted teeth. I tell her I put the request/complaint in because Mr C. suggested it, during our induction.

'Of course he didn't,' says West. 'Mr C. wouldn't do that.' She makes it clear that I am dismissed. Feeling abused and unheard, I grab hold of what is left of my article and escape to fume in private.

When I have calmed down, I am able to reflect. The screws (and I will call them screws) seem discomfited by any emotion other than anger. And yet they are surrounded by a sea of pain, pain that they are directly causing by incarcerating us like this. Perhaps to acknowledge that would be overwhelming: how could they get on with their work? So they josh and tease and view us as beneath them, and anyone who questions their authority gets clamped down upon hard. All to protect themselves from this excess of emotion, which threatens to engulf them unless kept under iron control.

The situation is insane, but one thing is for sure: I have got to toughen up.

□ □ □

I am gradually getting used to the sounds of prison, the way the blank walls and corridors carry echoes of people shouting, laughing and moving about as well as the endlessly blaring radios. There is no carpeting in here to muffle the noise, and joking and fooling around is a way for prisoners, as well as screws, to blank out feelings and let off steam. So the screws are noisy too, yelling up the stairways for people, shouting for gym, medication, or whatever. The approach of our jailers is always heralded by the rattle of keys at their sides. My ear is getting attuned to it. I do not like to be caught unawares.

Today I get called in to see a probation officer. We all have to do so on admission.

'WYYNNNERRR!' As usual, we are kept waiting; our time has no worth. I go in last and the probation officer says: 'Don't I know you?' I tell her that I used to run a charity in Cambridge.

'Oh, you're Ruth Wyner. We've been expecting you.' Then, tentatively: 'How are you coping?'

'Well, it's better than Holloway. I use the gym when I can. But it's a disappointment that there's no Open University.' As usual, I do not want to let on about how bad I have been feeling.

'They sometimes do some distance learning,' she says. But most of all she wants to discuss the case. I give her an outline of it.

'What about prison governors, then?' she responds. 'They know drugs come in but can't stop it. And what about me? We work with addicts all the time.' We discuss how users and dealers are often one and the same, how it is hard to distinguish between them. I tell her about the police liaison we had set up at Wintercomfort before I got arrested and how they wanted me to be a police informer. That I had refused.

'I think I'm an exemplary sentence,' I say.

'Well, you seem to be taking it quite philosophically.' If only she knew.

'I'm writing like fury,' I add, meaning the journal I am keeping, and my letters. 'It helps.'

'I expect I'd do that if I was in prison.'

'But I'm running out of pens and paper.'

'Here,' she says, giving me her pen and some blank sheets of paper from her file. 'Stick it up your jumper.' And I do.

□ □ □

Thursday morning. I am on the wing as usual. Other people get to go to work or education, but I do not start until next week. I have slept little the last few days and wish I could catch up, but it is hard to rest in here – everything is permanently on edge and disjointed, and always implacably noisy. I am listening to my Walkman when Katherine, a small, smart, bespectacled woman, knocks and walks in.

'Hello,' she says in a slightly hard-edged Irish accent. 'I'm Katherine from the Kainos Community on House 1. The officers said I'd find you here and that you might be interested in joining us. It's quieter there, you know, and cleaner too.'

'But I'm not a Christian,' I say. I have been told a little about Kainos: that it is a part of the prison run as a community with a Christian basis.

'You don't have to be a Christian,' Katherine tells me. 'You just have to believe that there is something else.' She has a wheedling way of speaking, is smiling at me now – a tight, rather anxious smile.

'I believe in the collective unconscious,' I say. It is a Jungian term and I am boxing clever here, while getting tempted by the thought of a little peace and quiet. Why shouldn't I go for what is best for me? I have heard you get toast there, and easier lock-ups. 'To me the human soul is precious,' I add, feeling that to mention the collective unconscious might have been unfair. I presume this woman is trying to help.

'Ah, see?' she says, triumphant. 'I didn't mention the soul, but you did.' I wonder if her idea of the soul is the same as mine. She promises that no one would make me pray.

'Give it a try,' Katherine persists. 'It's much more homely over there. I'm sure you'll like it.'

I waver, knowing that I feel desperate in this place, and presume I always will. Katherine goes on to say that there are more people my age at Kainos. Perhaps it would be easier – anything for an easier life in prison. And perhaps Kainos would engage me. I do have an interest in communities, therapeutic communities, and a little knowledge of how they work. I say, 'OK, I'll give it a try,' and Katherine speeds off before I can change my mind.

I go downstairs and the screws surprise me by saying that I can move immediately, which makes me wonder if I have been somewhat impulsive. What is the catch? Well, the decision is made. As I pack, I feel sad to be leaving Pearl and the others, and put an apologetic note underneath her Bible, which she has placed carefully on her pillow as usual. Downstairs, Grace asks what I am up to. When I tell her, she cheerily helps me carry my two bin-bags of things over to House 1.

I am moving again and, as always, find it unsettling.

four

An Irish screw lets me into House 1, where Katherine's Kainos community is based. I wonder if everyone is Irish here. This one is tall and ginger-haired, with buck teeth and a couldn't-care-less attitude. He tosses me into Room 1 on this unit's Skid Row – six rooms set in a short ground-floor corridor. The other bed is not occupied. Great: a room to myself. But I do not get a chance to unpack my few things. As soon as I hit the unit women are wanting to drag me off to their rooms to talk. They introduce themselves rather formally, with a shake of the hand. Very nice, but for some reason I do not trust it and already I am nostalgic for the rough and tumble of my old wing.

An inmate carts me off upstairs for a cup of tea. After the stark emptiness of House 3, the place feels claustrophobic. All the rooms are painted different colours and confuse my deprived senses. At last I am sitting down and my tea comes in a china cup – very admirable; I have drunk out of plastic since being in prison. They ask what I am in for, and one woman – my host, wild-looking, with straggly brown hair, no teeth and a face like a sun-dried raisin – laughs when I explain.

'I'm doin' twenty months for pourin' boiling water on a paedophile's bollocks,' she says with the greatest of pride. Her compatriots congratulate her: 'He won't be causing any trouble for a bit.'

A fair-haired and rather podgy older woman wearing clingy leggings and with heavily pockmarked skin gives me the details of her drugs bust. Then I get another story from Evelyn, who is in her sixties and got five years for conspiring to defraud, reduced on appeal to three and a half. She tells me that her husband, who is sixty-six and not well, is also banged up for the same offence. Evelyn complains of being set up by the police.

Someone else pops into the room and out again, cheery-looking; I am told she is doing four years for manslaughter. She killed someone and is doing less time than me. The thought is deeply depressing. There are more long-termers here than at House 3, and most of them seek my sympathy. I would willingly give it but right now can hardly cope with my own situation, let alone anyone else's. I drink the tea fast and excuse myself. In my confusion, I have difficulty finding the way back downstairs and to my room. The Irish screw catches me.

'Change of plan,' he says. 'Room 5.'

'It's a good thing I haven't unpacked.' But he does not care one way or the other. We prisoners have plenty of time to fill, and packing and unpacking your stuff is as good a way to fill it as any other.

I am given new room keys and find Room 5, still on Skid Row. I am disappointed: it is painted a rather dingy mauve colour, is not as light as Room 1, and I am sharing. A tall, well-built and striking-looking black woman comes in, appraises me in silence, and then disappears. She comes back a few minutes later to announce: 'My name is Diana,' in an accent that sounds Dutch, and then is off again. Some welcome. I miss my Pearl already.

Katherine is wandering about, being very friendly, it seems over-friendly, her concern unreal. 'How are you today?' she asks, and, 'Do you feel all right?'

Everyone quickly assures her that they are absolutely fine. It reminds me of Holloway: how the nurse's kindness upset me more than the doctor's bloody-mindedness. I return to my room for a bit of time to myself, but the two middle-aged women in the room opposite call me over for a fag. Glenda, the dark-haired one, lets me roll one for myself while she lounges on her bed and tells me how she too was set up, had crack cocaine in her house but apparently did not know about it. Now she is doing four years, while her sister is caring for her daughter.

Glenda's roommate June pats her greying hair and sniffs her disapproval. She tells me that she was set up as well. June is in for conspiracy and gives me a long, involved story that I can make little sense of. Both of them seem perfectly ordinary people. They complain vociferously about the state of the prison and make it clear that they have a much better life outside, that for them money is no object. They have large wedding rings and gold jewellery to prove it. I can feel a headache coming on. Their angst is understandable but it is adding to my own pressure. I excuse myself, say I have to unpack.

The view from this room is not as good as the one I had on House 3. It is on the ground floor, on Skid Row, and the fence is closer. I feel my trauma returning, must be panicked as usual by the move. The younger ones on House 3 lifted me and I miss the more spacious feel of the place. Even the ceilings seem lower here, though they cannot really be. It is only an illusion. There is a kind of clinging atmosphere on Kainos, it gives me a sickly feeling that I associate with religious people who are two-faced about their beliefs, who use their faith as a cover. Working in homelessness, I met, worked with and got to respect many committed Christians. I also learnt that there were others whose kindnesses came from something other than genuine feelings of compassion.

Later on, I come across a noticeboard in the hallway on the other side of our spur gate. The minutes of the last community meeting are pinned up there; they have these meetings weekly, and I see that the last one ended with the Lord's Prayer. Katherine told me that I would not have to pray. This is the last straw. I storm back to my room and slam the door. The two women from the room opposite knock and come in.

'What's the matter?'

How can I begin to explain?

'I just need a little space.' Thankfully, they leave me alone with my frustration.

I want to get the gym and need to ask in the office whether there is a session tonight. The spur gate is open but the ones through to the office are locked. Someone dejectedly tells me that we are locked up till 5.30 p.m. My spirits are very low. I feel I am stuck in with a bunch of derelicts. At least there was some life on House 3, a bit of free spirit. During twenty days of prison I have been in two jails and four different cells. I need to settle but somehow do not think this is the right place, if there is one in prison. Back in the room, I try to sort out my post. I have loads of letters to answer but am too depressed to start on any.

Now I am pacing the room, clenching my muscles, pulling faces, trying to shed the stress. The phone – I need the phone, and go out to find it too is beyond the locked gate.

'All right, Ruth love?' someone asks. It is the manslaughter woman.

'Can't get to the fucking phone,' I curse and storm off. 'Ruth love': it is not love I feel, but fury.

□ □ □

We get supper at 5.45 p.m., queuing at the hatch and eating it in a dining room on the unit rather than in the draughty canteen. I have no place or table allocated yet and end up sitting next to the woman who boiled the paedophile's bollocks. Everyone is complaining about the food. Katherine is wandering about, ministering to us as we attempt to eat our unappetizing meal. I have got a spoonful of rice with a few peas, carrots, the odd green bean and a bit of sweetcorn in it.

'Am I supposed to live on this?' I ask the screw dishing it up.

'If you've got a complaint about the food, make a food complaint to the office,' he tells me. Katherine gives me a little wave. I ignore her. After supper, we wait at the office for our post, queuing up – ever more queuing. I also get my *Guardian* newspaper; Gordon has got it sent in daily.

I hurry to the phone to make my nightly call home. I am getting more organized as time goes by. Rachel seems chirpy enough, tells me about her day, then Gordon tells me that he has just done an interview for Channel 4. Very exciting, though it accentuates my feelings of being cut off from everything. I take a puff on my fag and he twigs that I am smoking.

'Ssshhh, don't let on. Rachel would kill me,' I say, forgetting that it is the fags that really will.

At 6.30 p.m. I catch the gym session and we walk over, glad to get a little air. There is only me and one other. I get stuck into my usual fast workout: rowing, cycling and jogging machines, followed by a few weights. I am covered in sweat when I get back and head straight to the shower. On the way I bump into Janine, the tough-looking Irish woman from House 3 who got moved to the non-Kainos side of House 1.

'I think I've made a mistake coming here,' I say.

'Believe me,' she replies, 'you have.'

□ □ □

There is a feeling of more restriction here on Skid Row than there is upstairs. The corridor, bounded by the spur gate at the entrance and a fire door at the end, has six double rooms. These are the same as on House 3: about 13 feet long by 8 feet wide, with two beds, wardrobes and lockers in each, plus a table and two upright chairs: soft-bottomed chairs here. Ah, bliss: a little luxury. This is the real benefit of being on Kainos: a soft-bottomed chair. The windows are quite large, shielded by the usual heavy set of impenetrable white bars, but giving us a good view to the grass outside which runs up to the perimeter fence.

After 8.45 p.m. lock-up and the 9 p.m. roll-check, when the screws come on to the spur to make sure we are all present and correct, Skid Row has a spur meeting. These happen weekly here, one for each spur, usually with Katherine or her assistant Linda acting as facilitator. But it had not been possible to arrange one for our spur this week, and the women have decided to meet together by themselves. There are ten of us – Room 1 is still empty – and we squash into June and Glenda's room. June seems to be a chairperson of sorts and, giving her usual little sniff, she calls us to order. I am feeling exhausted, need to catch up with my sleep, but am required to attend. At first I am happy to, then feel an urgency to escape. Everyone is full of complaints, about Katherine and the community.

'Kainos is a prison within a prison,' says Glenda, drawing hard on her roll-up. 'Once you're on here, you have to stay, you know,' she adds darkly. I feel very unnerved. People say that the community gives them more rules, more restriction, rather than less. A long discussion follows about how there is no clarity on the rules or as to what happens if you fail to comply.

'Any community needs boundaries,' I chip in.

'Thank you,' says my roommate, Diana, and off they go again with their chorus of complaints. After an hour, two of them, a bit younger and in their twenties, leave the room.

'They'll lose points over that,' says June. Points? What points? But my tiredness is taking over; I can hardly keep my eyes open and this meeting is making me feel worse. All those welcomes and smiles were false as hell. It is plum crazy here. Katherine lied to me. She said it was cleaner and it is not – it is less clean if anything, and I have not noticed that it is any quieter than House 3.

At 11 p.m. I say that I just cannot stay awake any longer and get myself excused from the meeting. I walk to my room opposite and change into my prison nightdress, desperate for bed. Then it erupts. The two who walked out of the meeting have been told about their loss of points. Everyone seems to be shouting at each other at once. The radio is on loud next door. The bed is extra hard. I have just one pillow, was not allowed to bring my other one with me. However tired I might feel, it is quite impossible to get comfortable and go to sleep.

Cursing Katherine, I grab my roll-ups and my *Guardian* and go to sit on the floor by the white-barred spur gate, as far from these goons as I can get. I have a fag and read, trying to shut out their shit. They quieten down a bit, but the discussions continue. Every so often someone comes up to me: 'Are you all right, Ruth?' Well, it's obvious that I am not.

'I just need some space, that's all,' I reiterate. But they cannot leave me alone, so I accept an invitation from Lulu, a short and rather stout

Londoner of South American descent, who has long curly dark hair and a personality as expansive as her girth. In her room she has a duvet on the bed – a privilege of acquiring 'enhanced' prisoner status. It is wonderfully soft to sit on, but I am caught in the clutches of my anger. Silently, I continue to read my paper. My fury does not abate. I storm off again.

In the corridor there is still lots of noise. I bash the wall and shout: 'For crying out loud can't you be quiet? It's midnight. I need to sleep.' They look at me as if I'd threatened to dope the Pope. Back in the room, the light is off but Diana is awake. We chat in the darkness, lying in our comfortless beds. She tells me how bad she thinks Highpoint is, how much better the prisons are in her native Holland. I ask if she could not serve her sentence there. She tells me she is doing seven years for bringing 200 grams of cocaine into the country – a long time for the amount. Her co-defendant got less, though he had been carrying more. I wonder if Diana did not play the game, can imagine her looking fierce in court – her way of coping. Diana is waiting for her appeal against sentence to come through and hopes to get deported after that.

'In Dutch prisons you get TV in your room, your own fridge, and none of these petty rules,' she tells me. We discuss Holland's social security system as well. Diana says that in Holland no one need be poor.

'Here in England you are such snobs. Look at our two queens, Elizabeth and Beatrice. Our royal family mixes with the people. They know what is going on. They do not separate themselves.'

Eventually I sleep but awaken with bad pains in my legs and bum again. I have got a worn mattress, have left the better one behind. When we are unlocked, I go to the office.

'I want to go back to House 3,' I demand. 'Katherine's told me lies about this place, fucking lies.'

'Don't swear,' says the screw. 'You're here now, you can't keep moving backwards and forwards.' I can see I will get nowhere with him.

Diana gets ready for work at the prison hairdresser's.

'I'm out of the room a lot,' she says. 'With my friends upstairs. But don't worry about that. You're OK.' When she has gone, I sweep and mop the room as Pearl has shown me and do a little washing, by hand as usual. I have not tried to figure out the washing machines and dryers; it is as if by using the prison laundry room I would be making things permanent. I wonder if my irritable behaviour on the wing has got into the grapevine. I am getting no nicey-nicey smiles and 'Are you OK?'s now. Good. Suits me. As usual, I have had no induction, just a one-liner from the Irish screw, who I now know as Mr McCafferty, about what time you do this and that. Well, my defences are well up and I have no wish to associate with anyone. I have some space at last and use it to write letters in my room, shutting everything out as best I can.

□ □ □

Whatever problems there were with House 1, there was one privilege on Kainos which meant a great deal to people suffering the deprivations of prison: toast. You could make it at around 8 p.m., using an industrial toaster at the back of the kitchen. I can remember the first time I made some: four slices, each one heavily basted in melted margarine. I took my plastic plate of goodies to my room and wallowed in the indulgence. It was hot and crisp. I washed it down with a cuppa and closed off my appetite with a fag. Sitting on my soft-bottomed chair, for a few moments I felt like a most fortunate prisoner.

□ □ □

I wake from a dream about living in a really grotty night shelter, a bit like one I worked at in Norwich for many years. In the dream I have lost my bag and am sure I will not find it again. I look across to Diana. She is still sleeping. Not wanting to disturb her, I peek out through the curtains, trying to acquaint myself with my new view. It faces the back of House 1 and takes in a small semicircle of grass. The high metal fencing is not far away, only about 25 yards. This is the perimeter fence. Behind it stand bare wintered Suffolk trees; I imagine them laden with greenery. I can see no birds but will try to attract some by flinging out sneaked-out bits of bread, though it is strictly against the rules. The best thing about this room is that it faces west: I will be able to devour the sunsets.

It is Saturday. Weekends are generally disliked in prison. There is more lock-up and even less to do than usual. Everyone takes turns in cleaning the spur corridor and toilet and today it is the turn of Room 5: Diana and me. We both want to go to the gym session at 9 a.m. so we do our duties fast. Diana gets bleach and disinfectant, well watered down as usual, from the office store. She does the toilet and shower and I mop the corridor, clanking the metal bucket as I go.

'Will you shut up!' comes a shout from June and Glenda's room. A little welcome reality. I clank more quietly, give our room a quick go and finish off. Then a disappointment: no gym. It's been cancelled.

'They wouldn't dare to keep cancelling gym like this on the men's side,' complains Diana. She goes upstairs to see her friends. Suits me: gives me time and space to myself. I settle down to do some yoga, though I am a bit tense with it, worried as usual that someone will see me through the small window in the door, or just walk in. Afterwards I write some letters, conversing with people on the outside, trying to hold on to what feels like a dangerously thin thread of connection.

At 10.30 a.m., on my way back from the loo, I notice that the front gate is open. We can go outside to the compound for a while. Not one to miss such a chance, I grab my coat and a book. The compounds here are basically just grass, bounded by narrow concrete paths which run alongside the high metal fencing topped with the razor wire. Facing us and separated off by the fence is the flat, squat building of House 2, set in its own grassy compound. House 3 is the next one down. The day is sunny but cold. I sit on the wooden bench near the gate and start to read. A Danish woman is marching fast round the path. She takes a break to sit with me.

'I hear you're out in a month,' I say, proud to be on top of the prison gossip.

'Oh, I can't wait,' and she tells me she has done four years of an eight-year stretch for importation of drugs; all the long sentences here seem to be for importation. Now she has got her parole.

'I'm desperate to get back to my kids.' She talks about her life at home, where she was a teacher. With her drugs conviction, she does not know what sort of work she will be able to get, or whether she will be able to get anything at all.

'I'll be opening a bottle of wine to celebrate when I get home,' she says. 'Or two.' We discuss the benefits of having a drink after a day's work, and how wine is most enjoyable when enhanced by good company. Maybe this woman could be a friend for me, but she is going soon – her head is already out of the gate. Going home. I have two-and-a-half years until my parole. The days ahead seem interminable.

The Danish woman goes back inside; the cold is getting to her. The only other person out with me is Evelyn, the elderly woman in for fraud. She is trying to loosen up her severely arthritic legs with a little slow walking and takes the Danish woman's place on the bench beside me. Evelyn has been given special dispensation to carry a kind of fisherman's seat that doubles up as a walking stick. It opens up and she can sit on it during the continual waiting and queuing we are subjected to: for our meals, medication, post, and the weekly canteen; to be let out for work, education or gym; and every morning if we need to make an application to the office through the request/complaint procedure for items to be handed out or in, to change our work detail, to get to see the doctor or the dentist, or to complain about one or other of the endless indignities we have to put up with in here. Applications can be made between 8 a.m. and 8.30 a.m. I have applied to get a typewriter sent in.

Evelyn asks how I am getting on and I tell her I start my morning art class and afternoon gardening on Monday.

'I do art too,' she says, 'though I'm absolutely no good at it.' Then I get further details of her case – she is turning it over in her mind continually. Evelyn claims she and her husband were set up by the police, says they were kept waiting for four years to get to trial. Four years! She has done over a year inside now, has another few months to go but does not know what she will do on release. She and her husband have lost everything: house, car, all their assets. Nothing is left. How these things take up our lives, not just the sentence but everything that goes on, before and afterwards. Evelyn seems very ordinary, very sweet, a million miles away from my idea of a criminal.

I roll a fag and obligingly chat for a while, but my legs are restless, they want to go, and I take myself on a brisk walk, following in the

Danish woman's footsteps round the concrete path. It is the first time I have walked this route, but it is one I will follow many times in the weeks and months ahead. The view of the prison is grim, functional and unattractive, with banks of fences in every direction keeping us penned in. This compound has three young trees in it. Their branches are winter-bare and they stand stark black against the bright blue of the sky.

I try to pretend I am somewhere else: the Cornish cliffs, the Welsh hills, an Alpine pass, looking to escape in my mind from these oppressive surroundings. My visual memory is still strong in this barren place. I feel as if I can remember every other location I have been to in complete detail: the towns and cities I have lived in, the holidays I have taken, and most of all my home. Every part of it, every inch. Now I have my dog with me, we are out on the common. I struggle to retain the fantasy. This is my escape, marching round the compound, shaking off the tension. I like the feel of it, but it is a bit embarrassing to be on full view, my desperate need for exercise on show to all. I take myself back to Cornwall.

Lunch is the usual Saturday fry-up. I refuse the soggy chips and the baked beans, dining on barely warm fried eggs, which I make into a sandwich, with a vegetarian sausage on the side. During the lock-up afterwards I feel the depression; it swings in from nowhere and takes a hold, pulling me down. I am alone with it. Despite the surface goodness here at Kainos, I do not feel the same camaraderie of House 3, where we somehow supported each other in our common adversity. I feel that there is some suspicion of me here and wonder where it comes from. My normal way of speaking is coming back: I have lost the Cockney accent, the cussedness, the swearing. Perhaps that is why I am being viewed differently. Is my anger becoming more muted, leaving the depression to settle deep inside? I worry that I will lose my fighting spirit, and will sink without trace, destroyed.

□ □ □

We are unlocked from behind the spurs but still stuck on the unit, and the depression stays with me. I am desperate to get outside. The hustle of sixty-odd women in this small building continually annoys and unsettles me. My guard is up all the while, which is stressful and exhausting, and there is no quiet room I can get to as on House 3. I try to walk my mood off. Starting at the front gate I go up one set of stairs, along the spur, down another set, past the dining room – the TV's on in there – past the kitchen and the phones in the corridor, into the hallway in front of the staff office and back up the stairs. Round and round I go, trying to unwind. It feels dead in here, it all feels dead; there are people about but I feel separate. Bars are everywhere. They contain me physically but cannot contain my feelings. I stop to look out through the bars of the front gate, breathe in the fresh air, but it is by the staff office and I hate the feel of the screws near me.

I explore a ground-floor corridor that I have not been along yet and find a new room: a small games room with the usual pool table, its green baize ripped, and a table-football game propped up against a wall. I feel destructive and start to unscrew one of the legs of the table football but it will only go so far. I walk round and round the room. Chairs line the walls. I have a real desire to fiddle, to mess around with things. There are phone points here, left open. Very remiss. I could unplug them and cut the connections. I resist, do not want to end up in the block, and anyway those phones are for my fellow inmates.

A find: a small piece of wood, just 1 inch wide and 6 inches long. My piece of wood. I invent a game. Standing on one side of the room I have to toss the wood on to a chair on the opposite side without it bouncing on to the floor. I pace about doing it, getting the greatest satisfaction when I miss and have to retrieve the wood by pulling chairs out roughly so that they bang on to the ground. Bang bang bang. I feel murderous.

□ □ □

On Sunday morning I cannot sleep past 5.30 a.m. The pains around my hips and upper legs have mostly gone, but I still find the hardness of the bed difficult to cope with. It is annoying that I cannot switch the light on to read. I try to roll a fag in the dark and knock the ashtray over. Diana stirs. So I go to the loo for my smoke. Although the light is broken in there it is not quite as dark as in the room. Then I take my usual early shower.

At 7.30 a.m. a screw comes to do the regular roll-check. I am desperate for a cup of tea. A hot-water urn is boiling, barely 10 feet away on the other side of the locked spur gate. As the screw unlocks and comes in I hold out my cup and ask for some hot water. He ignores me. When he goes out I ask again.

'I'm doing roll-check,' he states importantly. I respond with as much dignity as I can muster, feeling small and insignificant locked up in here.

'It wouldn't hurt to give me some hot water while you're there.' It is futile. He ignores me. Here I am, Oliver Twist with my plastic mug, asking for 'more'.

Most of the women on the house have a Thermos flask. They fill them at the hot-water urn before lock-ups so that they can make hot drinks when they want them. Until recently you could get flasks sent in. Now this is disallowed for 'security reasons'. If I want one, I will have to buy it on my canteen, but they cost £7.99 – over half of my weekly spend. I simply do not have the money if I am to keep buying my phone cards; those calls home are too precious to lose. I will have to save up over time. Meanwhile, I cadge hot water when I can. But at this time in the morning no one else is up and about.

I get my tea at unlock and by 9 a.m. am ready for the gym. This time they do come for us and on the way there I see Pearl and others from House 3 being walked back from medication.

'You traitored me,' she accuses. I make some feeble excuses and ask who she is in with now.

'No one.'

'What about Grace?'

'She's in the block.'

I feel terribly anxious, the thought of lovely Grace in the block, in isolation and only half an hour out of the cell every day. Grace is headstrong and prison is making her increasingly desperate the longer she stays.

I get two hours at the gym. There are seven or eight of us, including three women from House 1: Lulu and a couple of her friends, gabbling away in Spanish.

'What part of Spain are you from?' I ask.

'We are South American.' Of course. How could I be so stupid? They are in for importing drugs. Two Colombians and one Bolivian. They chatter incessantly. I have seen Lulu annoy people with her non-stop gabble but watching her with the two others, I wonder if her voluble nature is a cultural thing.

A young butch Scot from House 3 is there, spending her time necking with her girlfriend. The PE officer lets them get on with it. The two women are kept on different houses and gym is their only real chance to be together. I find an appropriate moment to ask the Scot if she knows what happened to Grace.

'Oh, she shouted her mouth off at someone in the dining room – blood clots, dykes and all that stuff – and she wouldn't shut up when the screw told her.'

'What is this blood clot thing about?' I ask. I hear lots of the blacks in here use the term as a sort of swear word. 'I've never heard it before.'

'You hear it all the time in London,' says the Scot.

Back on the unit and drenched with sweat, I have another shower and queue up for the best meal of the week: Sunday lunch. It seems that everyone else has the same idea. I feel quite petite, surrounded by these large women. Many get very overweight through the inactivity of prison. I am pushed into someone's bum to the front of me and can feel a pair of huge breasts squeezing into my back. Though I am getting used to holding my own while queuing, this crush is extreme. Even so, I do not allow myself to be ousted from my place and am rewarded with a feast: a leg of chicken (this vegetarian allows a weekly chicken lapse in here, as well as the odd bacon lapse), roast potatoes, gravy and rather cold broccoli and cauliflower. Sometimes we get roast parsnips as well.

Then we go into the afternoon lock-up, which for me, three Sundays out of four, is punctuated by a visit, my highlight of the week. Joel is back in Birmingham studying, so today Gordon and

Rachel are coming with my mother, who has travelled up from London. I am desperate to see them and ready way before time. At 1.45 p.m. we get called out from behind our spurs, escorted off the unit and to the back door of the visits building. There are six of us; most of the women have made a real effort to look nice. Miss Turney, a dark-haired screw with a wicked grin, is doing the frisking today, under the eyes of a second female officer. We go in one by one.

More waiting. I get my usual feeling of rising anxiety as we sit patiently at our tables, straining to look through the windows to see if our visitors are there. They get frisked too and my special three arrive at last. I stand up to exchange huge hugs with them, which we are allowed to do at the start and the end of the visit. I make my only physical contact of the week last as long as I can.

Rachel is wearing a new top; she has brought it here to show me, wanting to share her pleasure with her mum. As always she sits next to me so that I can keep an arm round her shoulders and get as close to her as possible. Gordon is sitting opposite. We hold hands, unusual for us, but in here the need for contact is urgent. Unsurprisingly, my mother looks overwhelmed by the surroundings, and I try to reassure her that all is well with me. It is distressing for her to see me in this harsh place, with the screws all around us, continually watching. Everyone talks at once and the noise hits the roof, but we persevere; there is always so much to say. Rachel goes to get some drinks and chocolate from the machines. For just over an hour we are a family again.

At the end a screw shouts for us to finish. I get up again for the farewell hugs and kisses, we hold on to each other for as long as possible, and, hustled by the screws, our visitors reluctantly troop out. The room is suddenly quiet and empty, as empty as we prisoners feel inside. With the visitors gone it is as if they were never there. We all strain to look through the windows, to catch a last glimpse of our loved ones, to remind us that they were here, that it was not an illusion. Then someone makes a joke and we get on with being prisoners again, going through the frisking, searching and processing before being marched back to the units. A half-decent Sunday lunch and then an hour with the family. I guess this should be a good day, but I find it hard to feel at all grateful.

□ □ □

We get unlocked at 6 p.m. and I see my name on the whiteboard when I go down: Wyner. It means I have to pick something up from the office. But it is not good news: my application for a typewriter has been turned down.

'Oh, fucking hell,' I say.

'Now, now, you don't have to swear,' says the screw.

'Why not?' I demand. 'I am an adult, you know,' and I storm out, muttering 'Bastards' as I go. It is the sort of thing you can get nicked for if the staff have a mind for it, but I hear one of the screws saying that I have had bad news. Indeed I have. The form says the typewriter has been refused for 'security reasons'. What bullshit. How is it less secure for me to write with a typewriter than a pen? They will not let me have the one small thing that would make my life in prison more bearable. It is as if they want to make things as difficult for me as they can.

I go upstairs to find Diana with her two friends, Yvonne and Nita, in their room.

'It's nice in here,' I comment. All the noticeboards are covered with pictures and cards. There are ribbons around the edge of the boards and the curtains are tied back with more ribbons. Both beds have comfy duvets on them and eight of the 6-inch-square mirrors we get issued with have been attached to each other to make a long one, nearly full-length.

'This is the penthouse,' says Diana.

Yvonne, a bright young black woman, adds: 'Come up here any time that you want.' It feels cosy and I settle on one of the duvets, giving out the bad news about my refusal on the typewriter.

'You must appeal,' says Nita. 'And if they still turn it down, you can appeal right up to the governor. Don't give up.' She is just out of the shower, is sitting with me on the duvet, her skin deep black against the cream colour of the towelling dressing gown she is wearing, a handsome woman in her thirties with strong features and a quick smile that warms. Her body is strong, solid and muscular, and, starved of physical contact as I am, I feel an urge to sink into it, to allow myself to be enveloped, shielded, protected and comforted. I begin to understand why so many women form sexual relationships inside. 'Prison bent', it is called: people who are straight on the outside but make do in jail.

The penthouse feels like an island of sanity on the unit, but I am restless as usual and wander downstairs again. My temper is now contained and I go back to the office to pick up the *Observer*, which Gordon has got delivered for me on Sundays. I check the letters page to see if there is any response to Nick Cohen's article on us and see that there is: a whole bunch of letters, all supporting us. There is even one from America suggesting that, with the prosecution of the Cambridge Two, the 'war on drugs' has gone a stage further in Britain, even further than in the United States.

Then I glance across to Cohen's column and see he has done another Cambridge Two piece. This time it tells how our trial judge had reportedly blabbed at the lawyers' dinner party before my sentencing, informing those present that he intended to send us down, me for five years and John for four. As the article points out, judges are expected to maintain at least a semblance of having an open mind until the pleas of mitigation and the various reports have been presented in court. The article is delightfully wicked as well as outraged. Nick Cohen writes that scores of letters and phone calls have been received by the newspaper from people wanting to help us. He adds that the way local lawyers have stuck their necks out to speak to the press about a local judge's gaffe says a lot about their attitudes to the case. Perhaps I am less forgotten than I feel.

I spend the evening reading my own letters and writing replies. Many are from people who want to get involved with the campaign for our release, which started as soon as John and I were banged up. I write back to them with a contact phone number for the campaign or send their details on to the campaign chair. Another correspondent, a fellow day-centre manager, bemoans the fact that national homelessness agencies have not dared to stick their head above the parapet to help Wintercomfort. Too eager to curry favour with the government, he reckons. Too concerned about protecting their own skins.

People working on our campaign have sent me a copy of the campaign petition calling for John and me to be released. My Rachel and John's son Dylan have been lined up to deliver it to the Home Office. But first we have to get the signatures. Prisoners are not allowed to sign.

'No petitions in here,' the senior officer barks at me when I show it to him.

'But it's nothing to do with prison. People will be signing it as members of the public.'

'People in here aren't members of the public. They're in custody.'

Along with shock/horror letters, I get chatty ones from people who cheerfully tell me about their day, or their week, presumably trying to relieve my prison boredom and keep me in touch with real life. I quite like it, cherish them all and respond as best I can. By the end of the evening, I have thirty replies ready to send out. The weekend's work. All written in longhand. My fingers are hardening up.

Diana is asleep. As usual in the evenings my thoughts are with the family. Taking myself through my night-time routines, I think how there is more time in here than at home: getting everything in order, changing, washing, brushing, tidying up my papers and sorting the letters for the morning post. My reward is a nightmare, in which I have something like chewing gum in my mouth, or perhaps it is glue. It stops me from speaking, or even opening my mouth properly, and it is all happening in a weird kind of secure hospital. I cannot get the gluey stuff out. I have been shut up, cannot express how I feel, cannot even speak at all.

I wake shaking from head to foot with the terror of the dream and once again take myself to the loo for a fag, so that I do not wake Diana. The shakes continue for half an hour. This dream has taken me by surprise. I thought my defences were getting up well. Maybe my subconscious is reminding me that however much I try to bury my feelings, they are still lodged within.

□ □ □

Nothing happens quickly in prison. All you can do is wait for the bureaucracy to churn through. Today, Monday, my time has come: I am starting the new regime of art in the morning and gardens in the afternoon. I look forward to having something to do and being able to get off the unit, but am furious that I cannot do what I want. I have to do art when I just ache to get on to one of the idle computers in the education block and do some writing. But that is not allowed. I worry that gardening will be demeaning. I am used to using my mind rather than my muscle.

'This isn't rehabilitation,' I write in one of my letters. 'It's de-habilitation.'

At 8.45 a.m. the unit's front gate is opened and we are allowed out to work or education. A screw marks us off on a clipboard as we go. It is a chilly day and I have my coat on, to walk the path 150 yards down to the education building, a route which is now crowded with other inmates. This is known as 'movement'. Women greet their friends from the other units, the black women being particularly demonstrative. Diana walks to hairdressing with Yvonne, who is doing a basic office-administration course – somewhat lackadaisically, which is not surprising as she is already educated to degree level. Nita stays on the unit to work in the laundry. I walk down the path as slowly as I can to make the most of the brief time outside. At the education block, a screw with another clipboard checks us in. Once movement is over, they will be working to get the roll correct. No one can go anywhere until it is.

The art room is on the ground floor. The tutor greets me and I am as polite as I can manage in return. I really do not want to be here, bitterly resent it, but it is better than doing wing-cleaning or working in the kitchens. She gets me to draw some daffodils. It is restful and centres my mind a little, but I cannot concentrate for more than fifteen minutes at a time. This is a continual problem for me in prison. My head flits here and there, just will not settle. I am still having difficulty with reading. Writing comes more easily: it feels good to get things out on paper, and with the letters there is a change of focus whenever you start a new one.

Everyone in the art room is engrossed. Two women are doing huge oil paintings on large canvases. Three others are lined up doing drawings like me, or watercolours. Old Evelyn sits fiddling with an abstract design she is working on. I am impressed by the quietness in the room but still do not want to be here. So I sneak off to the library up the corridor. Ten minutes later the tutor comes to see where I am.

'I'll be back in a minute,' I say, which I am, in time for the 10 a.m. fag break: excellent timing. We take ourselves off to the loos, as smoking is not allowed elsewhere.

Puffing on our roll-ups, we are entertained by two women complaining about life on House 2.

'I hardly dare leave my room. You never know when someone's gonna chuck a bucket of water at you.'

'Yeah, the bathroom is always awash. It's not as if we've got unlimited supplies of clothing either.'

Everyone complains about the restrictions on the clothes we can have in. Unlike most men's prisons, women can wear their own clothes and many take great care about their appearance. But we are allowed only six tops and six bottoms, and four pairs of shoes. I am happy to be casual. My friend Jenny in Norfolk has sent me three T-shirts and I have Rachel's stripey jacket, which I wear constantly. Plus two pairs of jeans, some jogging bottoms and a pair of loose trousers, also from friend Jenny. For shoes I have a pair of boots, some slip-ons, and Rachel's old tennis shoes, which I wear at the gym. I want to get some slippers and a proper pair of trainers. Rachel knows what to buy. But it will take a lot of organizing with applications for hand-ins and hand-outs. They will not let me go over my allocation.

Listening to these women, it does sound as though I am better off on House 1 than on House 2. I begin to think that I have made the right choice. When we get back to the art room, I doodle away at my daffodils for a while but am relieved to finish at 11.30 p.m. Time for movement again, back to our units for lunch, then lock-up for an hour and a half. I take my slow walk to the unit as if closed off inside myself, while being constantly alert to what is going on. There is a strange paradox in prison: we are in a supposedly secure environment, yet feel personally insecure. This makes it hard to relax at all, and the constant tension is debilitating. My new way of walking is not so new. I see other people doing it.

□ □ □

At 1.45 p.m. there is movement again. We crowd around the unit's front gate waiting to be let out. This time I make my way to gardens. Our work base is a large shed by the education building. Next door we have 'paints', where people do painting and decorating, and next to that 'works', where they assemble and pack things for commercial firms, though they are not paid commercial rates. My weekly wage will start at £6.

In the shed half-a-dozen other women are sitting on old chairs set in a line against the back. I sit on a chair too, maintaining my protective air of insularity and unconcern. All this hanging around. I am used to working hard and fast from the moment I set foot in the office. Bet arrives and breaks into my mood.

'Hiya, Ruth. You coming on gardens, then?' She gives me some gossip from House 3 and tells me that gardens is the best place to work.

'It's hard, but at least you get outside, and I like that,' she says. Everyone is kitted out in bright-green overalls, steel-toe-capped boots and donkey jackets or dark-green bodywarmers. Pete, the boss, is in a small office reading a book. After a bit he rings through his twice-daily liturgy of numbers. This time it is: 'Two from House 3, three from House 2 and two from House 1.' Then he casually wanders out to allocate the work. Bet and one other are told to move a pile of old turf, shovelling the stuff into wheelbarrows. Two others tend the greenhouse plants and another pair are sent off to do some digging.

Pete takes me into the office for my induction: a run-down on the rules, health and safety and so forth. He makes it clear that he has total power over his workforce and that the payment of the wages is entirely at his discretion, going up to a princely £9 a week for his best workers, though he will pay as little as 10 pence if someone messes him around.

'Do you really want to do gardening, or are you just doing it to get off the unit?' he asks.

'I like gardening at home,' I tell him innocently, and quite truthfully. He sorts out my allocation of gear and I change in the loo. Then I am sent off to do some wombling: picking up rubbish from around the houses.

'I'll get you on something else tomorrow,' Pete says, a little apologetically. It does not bother me. I enjoy the chance to be outside. We finish at 4 p.m. and there is another wait while the roll is checked. It is a very short day, less than two hours' work in the afternoons. We are then due to go back to the unit at 4.30 p.m. but people from House 1, who pick up their medication at 4.15 p.m., get to leave early. I am glad to be off. The continual waiting around is interminably boring. The two women who tend the greenhouse seem well prepared for it and have their noses stuck in books to kill the time.

Back on Skid Row, everyone roars with laughter to see me in my gardening gear.

'All I need now is the peaked cap,' I say ruefully, and quickly change back into my usual clothes.

Bernice, a lively black Londoner that I hardly know, comes into the room. She is feeling chatty. First she tells me to trust no one on the community, and she goes through a list of those who in her view are most likely to grass you up.

'Did you see Marianne in art?' she asks. I can place her, a thin, sad-faced woman who keeps herself to herself.

'Watch her, and tell her nothing,' says Bernice. 'She goes to Katherine with whatever she hears. Katherine will try that on you too. She'll see that you've got brains and will try to use you.' I wonder how much of this is fact and how much is paranoia, which would be understandable given the power differentials.

Bernice goes on to spill something about what happens on the Kainos Journey, which is billed as 'A Short Course on Christianity'. Everyone has to do it and Bernice already has.

'It's not Christianity, it's a cult.'

'Evangelistic?' I ask.

'Very. For the Journey you go to the chapel for four days, all day. They get all these people, widows and that, and they tell you their sad stories from thirty years ago, and cry and stuff. Then they try to get you to tell them your sad stories. That's all they want to hear. They don't want to hear that you're happy with a nice life outside. They want you to be sad.'

It sounds pretty ghastly. 'Why should we be burdened with their problems when we've got enough of our own?'

'Exactly,' says Bernice. 'And that's not the end of it. They hug you all the time – I don't want to be hugged by people I don't know – and they pray. At the end they put this cross around your neck.'

'Oh, well, I can't do that. I'm Jewish for a start.' Hiding behind my neglected Jewishness seems a good ploy right now.

'Well, you have to do it. They say that Kainos is not Christian, that it's for all beliefs, but believe me, it's Christian all right – hard-hitting Christianity.'

'I think faith and belief are private matters,' I say.

'Yeah, me too, you're like me.' Bernice gives me a Bible reference: Matthew 6:5. 'Quote that at them when they hustle you. It says there that you are a hypocrite if you parade your belief and prayers, that prayer is private. But this lot is different, really pushy.'

'If they try that stuff on me, they won't get anywhere.'

'Believe me, they will try it. When Katherine gets you in for the one-to-one, just don't let her make you angry because that's what she wants, and then she'll say you have an attitude. That's what she did with me.'

'But of course I'm angry, for being here.'

'Take your press cuttings to the one-to-one, then she'll see who you are. That you are someone, not a nobody.'

I reckon everyone is someone. Though in here it is as if we are all nobodies. It does not matter. I never get the one-to-one.

Bernice continues to advise me: 'On the Journey you have to forgive, they'll ask you for the names of people you need to forgive.' I wonder who I am expected to forgive. The judge? The police? The prosecution? Well, they can stuff that. I wonder if there is any way I can avoid this Journey. Bernice has alarmed me. Am I really trapped in a religious cult?

□ □ □

Now Bernice is complaining about the loss of our toaster. We have been without it for weeks. Someone cut the mains cord and it had to be sent away for repair, but when it came back it ended up in the screws' office. No one has actually said anything to that effect, but we know, and can often smell toast from the smaller office at the back of the main one. At times like that I linger. Smelling toast is the next best thing to eating it. But Bernice is furious.

'That's our toaster,' she complains. 'What right have they to take it?'

'They do what they like,' June sniffs.

'They can eat as much toast as they want when they go home,' I chip in.

'Thank you,' Bernice says. 'And we all know who cut the cord, the bitch. I'll fucking have her.'

We do indeed know who it was: Lois, a grim-looking black woman who works in the servery, where the toaster was kept. She strikes me as being very depressed.

'Lois always complained about the mess that was left,' Bernice continues. 'She didn't like people going in there at all, like the servery was her territory. I tell you, just watch: she's for it.'

Every Friday we have the community meeting at Kainos. Most of the time people say little at the meetings, enveloped by the negativity of prison. I use the meeting to follow up on Bernice's complaint.

'When are we going to get our toaster back?' This sparks an animated response.

'It was supposed to be fixed.'

'We shouldn't lose it because one person vandalizes it.'

'Yeah, that doesn't make us all vandals.' Stevenson, the prison officer who is sitting in on the meeting, says he will look into it.

'He only has to look into his back office,' Bernice whispers into my ear.

During the evening there is lots of activity and giggling coming from Bernice's room. I keep out of it but learn what it was about the next day. Someone has slipped an anonymous note under Lois's door, made up of letters cut out and pasted from newspapers.

'We'll burn your boats,' it says. 'Own up or you are toast.'

Stevenson produces it at lunch the next day.

'I want to know who did this,' he demands. 'It's stupid and childish and you ought to know better. You're all grown women, aren't you?'

'Treat us like it, then,' someone mutters.

'Maybe Lois has something to say,' says another voice. But she does not.

After lunch there is a kerfuffle. Bernice is fronting Lois, backed by several others, and is yelling at her about the toaster. Lois stands her ground, laughing in Bernice's face. This toaster thing is getting far too heated and I am worried that I have fanned the flames. My shelter instincts come to the fore and I stand between Lois and Bernice, trying to stave off a real fight for Bernice's sake. At last the screws appear. The toaster is not returned to us.

□ □ □

I am still writing all my letters painfully by hand. Following Nita's suggestion, I apply to the governor for the typewriter but am turned down again. I try once more, making my points carefully. A message comes back that I should speak to the education department about my needs. They have computers, but I am not allowed to use them because they are only for prisoners doing courses. And I am not allowed on the courses because I already know what is being taught. I speak to a woman I know at education.

'We can't do anything,' she says. 'I don't know why they referred it to us.' So I apply once more to the governor and try to get the letter forwarded to 'Governor Number One'. It is like a game of ping-pong, but at least it helps to keep me amused.

This evening the Quakers have booked a session in the chapel. I decide to go, always keen to get off the unit. It might give me a little peace and quiet. Indeed it does: an oasis of calm amid the continual frantic hustle of prison. We sit in a circle, mostly black women, just a few whites. Even the most boisterous sit peacefully for a full half-hour. No one speaks, except for a Methodist minister who is there. She reads out something from a book. I find it patronizing and out of place, and say as much. Not very Quaker of me, but I cannot help it. Afterwards, when we all get a cup of tea, the minister tries to explain herself to me, but she seems hopelessly out of touch with how I feel.

Somehow, it is doubly annoying when people trying to do good in this prison get it so painfully wrong.

□ □ □

The downside for most of us on Kainos is that we have to attend the various meetings. I was originally interested in them, thinking that opportunities for communication are always worth developing. It is not long before I get infected by the general atmosphere of resentment. Every week there is the large community meeting and also small group meetings for each spur. Skid Row's spur meetings are usually badly attended and most of the discussions centre around hygiene: the toilet not being properly cleaned; leaking water in the washroom; the difficulties of having one washbasin between the twelve of us. It is a metaphor for our situation: all of us stuck in this squalid environment and made to feel like shit.

One or other of the co-ordinators facilitates the spur meetings. They take these hygiene issues at face value, are not able to read between the lines. Sometimes we get confrontations between individuals, which make the co-ordinators anxious. I hear that in the past there have been fights at the large community meetings, which explains the co-ordinators' eagerness to keep feelings under wraps. So people are routinely shut up with lectures on needing to show respect, but the co-ordinators' fearfulness makes things feel even more unsafe. They do not have the skills for the job.

'I was like you when I first came to Kainos,' says Kath, a middle-aged heroin addict who knows the prison system inside out. She is a deeply religious woman but is not fooled by Kainos.

'I questioned everything too,' she continues. 'We know what

Kainos really is, it's not what it's cracked up to be, but it's better than nothing, believe me.'

I do believe her, but Kath has not completely given up the fight. At one of the community meetings she stands up looking very serious, holding some papers in her hand. Kath has prepared a speech about the needs of women in prison and how these are not being met.

'We women have different needs than the men,' she says. 'Yet we're always compared to the male prisoners, usually unfavourably, which is not surprising because we're in a system set up for men.'

Kath has some relevant statistics: 70 per cent of women prisoners are on prescribed medication and half self-harm. Eighty-six per cent of male prisoners have their partners to look after their kids, but only 17 per cent of women get that support.

'Two months ago we were promised meetings with the one and only woman governor here,' Kath continues. 'Nothing has happened. We want to know why, and when the meetings will be set up.'

Once again, Stevenson is the screw sitting in with the community. I am disappointed to hear him let himself down.

'I can't understand why you say women have different needs to men,' he says. 'You're all prisoners. Family things are the same for men and women. Why do you have to see the female governor? She's not married, doesn't have kids. Why not see a governor who's a family man? It doesn't matter if they're male or female.'

Everyone looks stunned. Doesn't he understand at all?

'I suggest that the officers have some training in gender issues,' I say. Stevenson visibly reddens.

'Perhaps Miss Wyner would like to see all the certificates we have from courses we've done on women in prison.'

'Perhaps I'd question the quality of those courses, then,' I respond. Stevenson suggests that a few people take their issues up with the unit's senior officer. Bernice is sitting next to me.

'They don't want us to go direct to the governor,' she hisses into my ear. 'This lot have got plenty to answer for.'

□ □ □

'Godparents tonight, and you've got to go,' June sings across to me from her room opposite, allowing herself a rare smile. I am sitting at my table, on my soft-bottomed chair, looking through the window at a pretty wagtail examining some old bread outside. I have been feeding the birds regularly and am beginning to attract them now. The wagtails are quite aggressive and compete for territory, while the huge crows are much more nervous, despite their size. A blackbird and a few starlings sometimes come by as well, and most mornings two large pigeons drop in for breakfast. Reluctantly, I go across to find out what June is on about.

'You know: godparents.' It is lunchtime lock-up and she is sitting on her own soft-bottomed chair, smoking. 'They come every Wednesday evening. You've got to go or you'll lose points.'

'Who are these godparents, anyway?' I ask.

'Good Christian people,' says Glenda, lounging on her bed. Both of them are enjoying my discomfort and keen to make the most of it.

'Come along, Sister Ruth, they'd love to meet you.'

'And what's all this points stuff?' I demand, making the most of my annoyance as I know it cheers them up. June explains that we lose five points for every meeting missed: spur meetings, community meetings, godparents and any other sessions we are supposed to go to.

'If you lose thirty points you can get chucked off Kainos.'

'Well, that's one way of getting moved off the house,' I say.

'Ah, it's not that easy, Sister Ruth,' says Glenda. 'Come on, we've got charades tonight. And you've gotta join in.'

June rolls another fag for herself and offers me one.

'I hate this place,' she sniffs, now melancholy, looking out of the window. As ordinary as any fifty-year-old you could expect to meet, she gives me her tale of woe once again: talking about evidence being hidden to protect a police grass; police harassment of her and her family; diverted mail; and false charges laid on her when she tried to bring all this into the open. She is a local woman and I recognize the name of one of the policemen she mentions. He was involved in my case, went to see some of the eight people convicted of dealing at my day centre, offering them inducements to give evidence against me.

'The justice system in this country is rotten to the core,' says June. I wish I had the conviction to contradict her.

At 7 p.m. eight well-meaning middle-aged to elderly people file into our dining room. They sit at the six round tables there with the Kainos inmates, offering effusive greetings to those they've met before. Diana motions me to a table that she is sitting at with Yvonne, Nita, one or two others, and a godparent, who looks decidedly uncomfortable. I am alarmed to see that they are about to start a game of bingo and feel relieved when the charades takes over. This is a welcome diversion from the daily prison grind. I get the first one right by mistake, with what I thought was a foolhardy guess, so have to take my turn, getting it over and done with as quickly as I can.

I continue to join in the game as best I can, but after half an hour the noise and the bustle dig under my fragile defences and I suddenly feel extraordinarily tired. Unable to stop yawning, I sink into my chair, the tiredness moving to upset and an anxiety about losing control. I have been holding myself so tight in this place, in order to cope with it, internally fearing an onslaught of anger, grief and uncontrollable emotion should I let go, even a little.

As soon as the game is over I absent myself and sit at a spot outside the dining room to enjoy a fag and a cup of tea with a few others. There are a table and a few chairs there. Puffing and sipping, we watch the world go by. The inmates have named the place the Bus Stop.

'Mind you,' says Glenda, 'you'll wait here forever to pick up a bus.'

The godparents file past, smiling to be on their way home. Our relief is mixed with anger at their good fortune, that they can walk through those gates that pen us in.

At 8.45 p.m. lock-up the screws herd us like cattle, walking around the unit, keys jangling, and bellowing at the tops of their voices: 'ROLL-CHECK! BEHIND YOUR SPURS!' They lock the spur gates behind us and return at 9 p.m. to do the roll-check: 'ROLL-CHECK! IN YOUR ROOMS!' I ignore their presence as best I can and read my paper while they march up and down the corridors. They check each room and mark us off on their clipboard lists. Then they retreat, leaving us to it, noisily clanking the spur gates as they go. Lock-up lasts till 8 a.m. I am enormously weary of it all but can do nothing apart from endure.

Tonight Diana wants to talk about her five-year-old son. She regales me with stories of his habits, his food preferences and the toys he likes. Photographs of him adorn her side of the room. Then Diana tells me her good news. She has a date for her appeal against sentence to be heard, in ten days' time. She hopes the sentence will be reduced; if it is, she will then apply for deportation. Finally, she turns over to sleep and I take the opportunity to pen a couple more letters. But the writing is getting increasingly difficult. I am developing very bad sores on my thumb and on the inside of my second finger from overuse of the Biro. I know that if I keep at it they will eventually develop into hard calluses, but at the moment my letter-writing is pretty painful. At 11.30 p.m. I hit the sack, feeling the usual deep loneliness until I drift off to sleep.

□ □ □

I am about to start my Kainos Journey, three-and-a-half days of what is described in the Kainos leaflet as 'A Short Course on Christianity'. Already unnerved by Bernice's descriptions, down on Skid Row I am teased by those who have already done it.

'Now, now, Sister Ruth, get ready to pray.'

They tell me about the goodies that come in: cakes, biscuits, crisps and chocolate. Looking to share this largesse, some of them have volunteered to help out on the Journey. They have been designated as Angels, which amuses everyone, knowing each other as we do.

'Fallen angels, more like,' sniffs June.

On the Wednesday afternoon we all go to the chapel for a talk with the chaplain. He tells us that he hopes most of all that we enjoy our Journey.

'It's like a box of chocolates. You may not like them all but you can select what you want.' He goes on to say that Jesus came to show the Jews how to live. I make an uncomfortable protest. As the only Jew here, and indeed the only professed non-Christian, it makes me feel uneasy about what is to come.

The next afternoon the Journey begins. We are ushered into the dining room where the Journey helpers are waiting, seventeen of them for twenty-four inmates, mostly middling to oldish women. I am paired up with Jeanette, who tries to give me a hug, which I automatically sidestep.

'Don't hug me, please,' I say. Unexpected intimacy from a stranger who seems predatory is not welcome at all. Jeanette sits me down at a table. I eye up the munchies and proceed to devour a bowl of dried fruit: figs, dates, apricots and papaya. I have not tasted anything like this since my imprisonment and apologetically explain that the prison food is terrible. Someone else is going at some crisps and sweets.

During this session we are supposed get to know each other. Trying to make conversation, Jeanette asks me if I am looking forward to my Journey. I say I do not know, that with the content of it a secret I have no idea what to expect. Poor Jeanette – she had been expecting a grateful prisoner. For me the Journey is a means to an end. I have to do it to stay on Kainos; I know that the rest of the prison is worse. Other people have the same predicament but wisely hide it better. I try to be a little more friendly.

The session ends with a few words from our leader, Irene, a tall woman with long grey hair. She has a great facility for patronizing us. Afterwards I tell her that as a Jew, I cannot take the cross at the end of the Journey.

'Don't worry,' says Irene. 'We've had non-Christians before. The co-ordinators have told me about you.' I wonder what she has heard.

In the evening we are ushered into the chapel and sat in a large circle. Everyone has to say a little bit about themselves. People's embarrassment cuts through their prison bravado. After a much-needed fag break we are sat at separate tables again. We have three helpers on ours, including Jeanette, and are told where to sit. As for the inmates, Hester is with us and so is Mary, a middle-aged woman with fresh cuts on her arms. We have two black women: Lola from Nigeria and a Jamaican called Georgette. They are both deeply and openly religious and I do not want to upset them. Sitting as close to me as possible is

Allie, a pretty but rather overweight twenty-three-year-old whose spell in prison is providing a break from a chaotic life outside. She spills over with bubbly energy and has a great sense of fun, which serves to hide a deep sense of insecurity. Allie sticks to me like glue throughout the Journey. Like me, she feels threatened by these earnest women. Maybe she thinks I will protect her, but I do not know that I can.

Irene reads from a large Journey book, telling us what a wonderful experience our Journey will be. Then we have short talks, described as meditations, from three of the helpers. They exhort us to let God into our hearts, tell us how Christ died for us. Their conviction is total and I am sure the religious ones among us find that a comfort, but to me it feels like an attack. We finish with a few hymns, taking the chance to exercise our lungs. The helpers pass round tambourines and enthusiastically get us on to our feet. I notice some people looking very uncomfortable. Between verses Allie whispers to me: 'We've got three full days of this.'

The next morning we are ushered into the chapel first thing. I dodge the oncoming hugs.

'Jesus is reaching out to you in Kainos,' Irene reads from her book. Believe, believe, believe and you will be saved. Then more singing, during which some of the helpers dance enthusiastically, bang their tambourines and wave their arms aloft. More meditations follow.

'Jesus came to show the Jews the true religion,' pronounces one of the speakers. During the break I tell her that as a Jew, I find that an affront.

We get the first of several personal talks from the helpers. One of the women comes to the front to tell us how she used to drink too much, how that became a prop for her, but then she found Jesus and everything became all right.

'A new prop,' I think, but she is welcome to it if it helps her – if only she was not trying to put it on me. In the middle of her talk she starts to weep and one of the other helpers comforts her. I wonder if she has any concept of what we prisoners are suffering through our incarceration and what dreadful difficulties some of my fellow inmates face outside. It seems an insult for these free people to parade their past hurts when our anguish is immediate, right here, right now. I discover that many of my compatriots find it as annoying as I do. We make the most of the goodies: sweets, crisps, biscuits, cakes, and Jeanette thoughtfully makes sure our table always has a dish of the dried fruit.

More singing, more dancing, talks, readings and prayers; it gets harder to bear as the time wears on. We are a captive audience and a generally reluctant bunch, ferried back and forth between the prison unit and the chapel. I soon give up joining in, sit in silence most of the time and manage to sneak out the back during most of the singing and dancing, my main excuses being a headache or needing the loo. Seeing me struggling, one of the Angels passes me a thoughtful and reassuring note: 'Don't worry, you are loved even more by people on the outside.'

At the end of the first evening Allie and I make a dash for the unit gate.

'Let us in,' we beg the screws. 'Lock us up, please.'

The next day it is my fiftieth birthday. My cellmate celebrates by throwing a bucket of cold water over me when I am not expecting it. Allie makes a card and gets everyone to sign it. That I do like, and I stick it up on my noticeboard with a drawing pin I have filched from the unit's noticeboard. Reluctantly, I follow the others to the chapel. We are asked to say how we are finding the Journey.

'God is in my heart,' says Lola fervently to applause, but most of us decide not to comment. Keen to change the subject, people shout that it is my birthday. They sing a hearty 'Happy Birthday to You' and force me to my feet.

'I never expected to be spending my fiftieth birthday with a bunch of evangelicals,' I say to laughter. Some of the helpers look annoyed at my turn of phrase, so, trying to be more diplomatic, I add: 'I'm glad some people are enjoying the Journey. It's helping me to define some of my views.' I get hearty applause too and am relieved to sit back down.

In the afternoon we have the weird forgiveness ritual that Bernice warned me about. People have to write the names of those they want to forgive on pieces of paper, which they take turns to place in a large bowl of water ceremoniously set between two burning candles. Irene stirs the brew and tells us it will be emptied at the foot of the Kainos tree – a young maple that grows at the side of our unit. A saying from that infamous prisoner Oscar Wilde comes into my head: 'Forgive your enemies. Nothing annoys them so much.'

We are stuck in the chapel till lock-up. During prayers, Irene tells us that unless we believe, we will not have eternal life. For me, that is a step too far: to load this fear on to women already made vulnerable by their imprisonment. Afterwards someone anxiously asks me if Irene is right. I say I do not think so, that we are all equal in the eyes of God.

The following morning we have a session in the dining room. The chaplain is there.

'How are you finding it?' he asks me.

'A bit much, really.'

'I know, it's American evangelism. We have to take the whole package or we don't get anything at all.'

I realize that this is all paid for by Kainos: the Journey, the community and the co-ordinators. They have bought their way into the prison.

Back in the chapel, after the usual singing and dancing and preaching, we get what Irene calls 'an experience of agape'. She tells us how Kainos people have been praying for us on our Journey and the chapel is adorned with pictures and messages from some of them. Bags full of letters and cards are distributed to each of us. I must have forty messages in my bag; everyone does. The ones that touch me most are from prisoners in America.

'Dearest Sister at Highpoint,' writes Vince from Hancock State Prison. 'I have been praying for you to be richly blessed over your weekend walk. May you find the peace and joy of Our Lord Jesus Christ. Sit down every morning and often in the day to say, "Lord Jesus, I know nothing, I will be silent, let the spirit lead me." The full blessing of the spirit is promised to the obedient.' Poor Vince; I bet the prison he is in is worse than mine. It is hard not to feel a little moved, and I know these letters and cards are particularly welcomed by people who do not get much post, do not have the support from the outside that I do.

At the end everyone is ceremoniously given their Kainos cross. I sit and watch while they go up one by one to receive it, and then they have to run a gauntlet of hugs and kisses from the helpers and the Angels. Thank goodness I got out of that one. The only hitch is when an Angel refuses to kiss one of those on the Journey, presumably for reasons of her own.

On Sunday, the last evening, we are penned in behind our spurs while the chapel is made ready. When we are unlocked, we have to walk over while our laughing Angels clap and sing at the tops of their voices 'When the Saints Go Marching In'. The chapel is packed full of Kainos people from the outside. With great embarrassment, we sit as directed at the front by the altar and face the crowd.

A couple of prisoners come forward to thank everyone for the Journey and say how much it has meant to them.

'Out for their parole,' someone hisses. Then one representative from each table has to talk about the experience of their 'family'. I do it for mine – no one else had the nerve. The throng erupts with a final burst of singing and dancing, and at last it is over. As we leave I accept a few hugs from insistent helpers, too worn down to resist to the last.

'Jesus loves you,' laughs Glenda when I get back to the spur.

'Praise the Lord,' I reply.

five

At Highpoint all but half a dozen of the rooms on House 1 are shared, so one of the most important people in the prison is your cellmate. I have three different cellmates in succession while living on the Kainos Skid Row. Diana, the first, is a confident and reassuring figure who enjoys giving me the benefit of her experience.

'I don't like being upstairs,' she says. 'Too many arguments, too many drugs; I just end up getting wound up. I got thrown off for fighting before, but they let me back after I made a whole lot of fuss and the others spoke up for me. I don't like the other houses.' I certainly would not like to get into a fight with Diana: she is big and powerful and would make mincemeat of me. But Diana did say she thought I was cool – a great relief.

Diana knows in detail what everyone on Kainos is in for and how long they have all got to serve. Most of those doing the longer sentences, seven to twelve years, have been convicted for importing hard drugs. As for the small-time dealers, four years seems to be a standard. I remember Annette from House 3: she got four years for selling one hit. Yvonne got her four years for merely being found with a small amount of heroin on her, but she was arrested outside a prison and, though not listed to make a visit, was convicted of intent to supply.

Few of the women are in for violence. Diana tots up three doing time for manslaughter; they each got four years as well – less time than me. Then there is Janis, who stabbed a guy, plus the woman who boiled the paedophile's bollocks. But a high percentage of the Highpoint women are doing short sentences for thieving, almost invariably drug-related: getting money to fund their habit. Previously, Kainos was reserved for long-term prisoners. Now they are bringing in short-termers as well, to fill up the beds: people who are vulnerable or not coping with prison well, or those who the officers feel need more help to stop them reoffending. Kainos is more or less all that the prison has to offer.

I lose Diana when she has to go to Holloway, to be in London for her appeal against sentence. She wants to be deported, and, having a misguided view of Home Office efficiency, she does not expect to be returned to us after the hearing. Diana is getting worried about the special prison farewell.

'On my birthday I was covered with cereals, creams, talcum powder – anything anyone could get their hands on. I tell you, I had cornflakes up my arse.'

On Diana's last evening nothing happens until the 8.45 p.m. lock-up. Then, as Diana walks downstairs, Yvonne pours a bucket of cold water over her from the landing above. Diana is furious. That does not stop Connie and Jade, the two black women from the room next door, from sprinkling lashings of talcum powder over her as she walks past. They are screaming and yelling with delight. Diana manages to scramble into our room and shuts the door fast.

'Diana, you've gone white,' I say, laughing.

'Shut up, you traitor,' she fumes.

Diana starts to pack, stuffing everything into black bin-bags. There is a knock on the door. It is Glenda, peering in through the small square window. Impatiently I open up and Glenda bursts in, flinging more talcum powder around indiscriminately. The others are outside shrieking with glee: June, Karen, Bernice, and Connie and Jade. The room is awash; we are shrouded in a mist of fine white snow.

'I'm not going to touch that door again,' I promise after we get rid of Glenda. We open the window and sweep up what we can. Diana eventually trundles off for a shower, muttering revenge.

A few days later, she unexpectedly returns. Coming back from a stint on gardens, I see her disappearing up the stairs, hauling a plastic HMP bag full of her belongings. Was it really Diana? Why is she back? I find out that she has had her sentence reduced, but that is all people know. Diana will not talk to anyone and has shut herself away in a room upstairs. I go up to knock on the door but she waves me off, will not even talk to Nita or Yvonne. No one has seen her so upset before.

In the morning Diana is given a room on her own, back down on Skid Row. She lies on the bed all day, in darkness, the curtains drawn. After supper I hear voices in there and, armed with a little chocolate, I go and peek through the small window in the door. Yvonne is talking to Diana, still in the dark. I knock and go in.

'I've a present for you,' I say, and give her the chocolate, which she eats straight off. Then she gives us her story.

'Holloway was terrible,' she says. 'Evening association only twice a week, nothing but bang-up, bang-up, bang-up.' She did get a result with her appeal: her sentence was reduced from seven years to five and a half.

'I'll miss two more of my son's birthdays.' That is her real sadness; her son's too. But what also upset her was that her male co-defendant had his sentence reduced even further, down to three-and-a-half years.

'He was carrying more drugs than me,' Diana complains. 'He doesn't have a child at home.'

'Typical,' says Yvonne. 'They always sentence the women to more.'

This is a common and much-debated perception. There is a credible view that it is seen as less acceptable for women to offend than men, and consequently women are more severely punished. I certainly got a longer sentence than John, even though John was working closer to the client group and was therefore closer to what was going on. Throughout our court case I felt I was being portrayed as an evil witch who had led this poor misguided man astray. It is a fact that the prison population is rising much faster among women than among men, despite far fewer women being convicted for violent crime.

The child-care responsibilities of women do not seem to be taken properly into account by judges when sentencing. As a result, every year an estimated 8000 children lose their main carers due to imprisonment, a terrible punishment for these young innocents. Surely there must be a better way.

□ □ □

We had not expected Diana to come back to Highpoint at all. On the day she left for court, Janis hustled the screws to let her move into Diana's bed and share with me. In her thirties, Janis is a childlike figure who does not seem ever to have grown up. Despite a twinkle in her slanted green eyes, her mouth is thin and sad and her expression lank, like her jet-black hair. She has already cornered me in the washroom to tell me about her adventures.

'I used to take a lot of amphetamines,' she says, adding apologetically: 'All the time.'

Sometimes during the lock-ups Janis would pop her head into my room, asking to talk. Diana did not like Janis and always beetled off to see Janis's cellmate, Karen, down the corridor, or, if the spur gate was open, her friends Yvonne and Nita upstairs. Janis would sit herself down to tell me how she got into using amphetamines, saying she graduated on to heroin afterwards but that speed was always her favourite hit. Though she lived in the country, she often came to Cambridge to score.

'Lots of drugs there,' I say.

'Lots,' she confirms.

Janis explains that what she really wants is to get into a drug rehab. She has heard of a good one at HMP Send in Kent and is waiting for a transfer.

'It'll be good for my parole.'

'And good for your head,' I remind her.

'Oh, yes, my body is detoxed, but I know I need help. I'm still an addict.' She looks at me woefully, her overweight body slumped in the chair. She tells me she was skinny as a rake when she came in. Typical. The addicts come into prison half-starved and then fatten up fast.

The top of a large tattoo curls around Janis's breasts. She has several others on her arms and legs.

'It was all like one bad trip, really,' she says. This is not her first offence and her future looks bleak. She worries about ever finding a job.

'Perhaps you could work with drug users.'

'Yes, my probation officer suggested that.'

'With all your experience,' I say, 'you'd be very valuable indeed.'

But she has a long and difficult road ahead. Both of us know that there are no quick fixes when it comes to hard drugs, and services inside and outside prison are desperately overstretched.

'There are drugs on this house,' Janis tells me. Although I have occasionally smelt cannabis being smoked along the corridor, I have not yet seen any heroin on Skid Row, but have been told by various people that there is a fair bit going around. Heroin is usually the drug of choice in prison because it is easy to get in, being much more compact than cannabis, and it stays in the blood stream for just three days – handy in case you are called up for a piss test. Cannabis lingers in the system for a month.

We can all tell if someone has taken heroin – or at least we have our suspicions. I presume the screws can figure it out too. Or do they turn a blind eye? Like I was supposed to have done.

□ □ □

Janis does not like sharing with Karen down the corridor because Karen plays her radio loudly. At least, that is what she says before organizing her move in with me. She hauls her stuff through and changes the lockers and noticeboards over, mentioning in passing that she has hepatitis C. I am a bit alarmed, though I know I should behave as though everyone in the prison has the hep. C virus.

I tell Janis I am trying to get a typewriter in. She says that it would not bother her and produces a ring binder plus several cardboard folders for my letters and my writing. In return, I let her pick out some pictures that she likes from the cards I have received. I have too many to fit on to my noticeboard and Janis still has lots of space to

fill. We spend the first evening writing letters, Janis asking me for the
spelling of words now and again. She has her radio on but not too
loud and turns it off at 11 p.m., which is a relief.

June and Glenda have been watching from over the way.

'You'll regret it,' they say when I pop my head round their door in
the morning. 'Janis is always nice as pie at the start, but she'll turn
against you; she always does.'

□ □ □

Janis wants to talk again, needs someone to listen, to hear her, and I
know I cannot give her everything she wants. No one can. Inevitably,
that will make her angry at some point – a righteous anger, as she has
clearly been deprived in some way in the past, but it does not belong
with me. I can, however, chat, which helps both of us to pass the time.

Sometimes, like naughty schoolgirls, we find ourselves in fits of
giggles over the least humorous thing as the tension we are holding
is released. One evening Janis prepares to shock the screws during
the 11 p.m. roll-check. She covers her face with white moisturizing
lotion, sticks two pieces of cucumber left over from lunch in her eye
sockets and waits, her head right up to the window in the door. I
turn off the light. When the screws come and look through the window, seeing it is dark they turn the light on from the outside and are
immediately confronted with Janis's apparition. One of them gives
out an involuntary yell and we fall into uncontrollable giggling fits
again.

'Next time I'll take my top and bra off,' Janis splutters. 'That'll
make 'em yell twice as loud.'

□ □ □

Janis has prison pen-pals. Lots of the women write to other
prisoners, usually men, and some of the letters get quite salacious.
It is generally little more than harmless flirting, and I can understand
the desire to write to other prisoners. They really do know what
prison is like. Right now there is something in Janis's manner that
makes me uneasy and I ask: 'What's up?'

She tells me that her pen-pal had arranged an inter-prison phone call for them, but Highpoint had disallowed it because they had put a stop to inter-prison phone calls two days previously.

'Why didn't they tell me? I've been looking forward to that call, really looking forward to it, for ages.' She stomps off to the office to complain, saying: 'You just watch me now,' as she goes.

I know Janis will not make a scene. She is an unsettled young woman and the screws are her security. Whenever we have a roll-check, Janis is at the door of the room wanting to be noticed by them. As soon as we are unlocked in the morning she is up by the office, hanging around. June reckons she is a grass, but I think it is all about her insecurity, her feeling of not being safe.

□ □ □

After three or four weeks Janis's manner towards me begins to cool. One lunchtime she gets the broom, mop and bucket from the bath-room and sweeps and mops her side of the room only. I am sitting on my bed reading and leave her to get on with it, hoping that her mood will pass. But it does not. Janis begins to spend most of the lock-up time in the room opposite, with June and Glenda. When the spur gate is open she goes upstairs. It seems that her greatest mate is the woman who boiled the paedophile's bollocks. She talks about paint-ing her half of the room. That would certainly be original. But getting the cold shoulder from your cellmate is hard to cope with, on top of all the other stresses of prison life. I think Janis partly enjoys my dis-comfort, and partly cannot control her behaviour. Making me feel bad makes her feel better. In here we all need some relief.

I escape down the corridor to see Bernice, who gives me instructive talks about how to import hard drugs. More usefully, Bernice works in the stores and gets me things I need: spare prison T-shirts, some prison jogging bottoms, extra drawers for my locker, a plastic basin for doing my hand-washing, and an extra coverlet which becomes my yoga mat.

I still nip across to see June and Glenda and occasionally catch Diana and Karen in there with them. They have a good chuckle at my expense.

'See: we told you Janis would turn. She always does.'

'I wish she'd stop coming in here,' June complains. 'She listens to everything, you know, and she can't be trusted.' Glenda puffs knowingly on her fag.

'You wait. She'll be asking for a room-move next.' I remember the laughs Janis and I had together and try not to feel sore.

□ □ □

Glenda was right. Janis has asked for a room-move. She is going upstairs to share with the bollock-boiler. I look forward to having the room to myself for a day or two, but no such luck. When I come back from working at gardens, I find what appears to be a child lying on Janis's bed. She sits up and, with a mischievous look, introduces herself as Viv. She looks about fifteen.

'I'm twenty-one,' she says, anxious to make the point, 'but I've been in prison most of the time for the last six years.' I express sympathy.

'I was at Bullwood Hall,' she continues, 'but I got into bother and they sent me here. I'm fucking pissed about it, you know. All my friends live near Bullwood. I won't get no visits, nothing.'

Off she darts, a pretty little thing, but dead skinny. I must seem like an old lady to her.

A few other new people have come on to the unit. Viv says they have come to Kainos for a laugh and, like most of us, for an easier life. But she is annoyed that she is being kept on Skid Row, away from her friends upstairs.

'They think I'll get into bother,' she says, with a shrug and a wicked grin. She shows me a photo of her baby daughter.

'She's with my mum. Not my real mum. I was fostered. Mum wants to adopt her, but I'm gonna do my best to stop it.'

Viv is like a yo-yo, always up or down: up the stairs to be with her friends, then back down to Skid Row to escape from them, flinging herself petulantly on the bed.

'They're all winding me up,' she complains, before sweeping herself off again; she is a real wild child until she takes her night-time medication. Then, like Pearl, she quickly falls into a deep and impenetrable slumber.

Viv's mates pop into the room from time to time. Franny is a young mixed-race Londoner in for shoplifting, no doubt to fund a drug habit, very pretty but desperately thin. She is a bundle of nervous anxiety, with long Afro hair that bursts from her head in all directions as if in response to her pent-up energy. Leah is a little older, a confirmed heroin addict who has a large, toothless grin. She describes herself as 'a gypsy girl' and has an endearing habit of looking after everyone. Looking after herself is much harder. Shula is a young Jamaican in her early twenties, and she desperately wants to fit in. She is another one in for importation – off the plane and straight into a police cell. Working through a lengthy prison sentence is a terrible start to her adult life. Shula fancies Viv and makes desperate plays for her. Viv, who sees it as sport, flirts back.

The activity of these young women is frantic: a desperate attempt to escape the emotions brought on by prison. Viv plays her music loudly and continually fools around, but I see another side of her when she retreats, seeking sanctuary in our room. She takes to eating continuously: crisps, chocolate, packets of biscuits got from her canteen, or more often scrounged from anywhere and anyone.

'I'm eating for England,' she announces. We watch her little stomach grow. Viv puts the weight on fast.

'You've got a right handful there,' June sniffs.

'Viv's all right,' I say, somewhat defensively. 'A bit mixed up but basically a good-natured kid.'

□ □ □

Prison is frustrating in its monotony, but there is the occasional surprise along the way. One afternoon I am stopped in my tracks at the sight of Nancy from House 3. She has been in the hospital wing all this time and has now been deposited on Kainos, on Skid Row. Blinking owl-like through her specs, Nancy greets me like an old friend. Remembering the problems she caused, and her engulfing neediness, I respond gruffly and walk quickly past. Am I becoming a tough con?

Nancy is put in with Diana.

'Why do I always end up with these fat women?' Diana asks. It is a difficult issue, the number of overweight women in prison. The food is stodgy, we are inactive and it is hard to work up the motivation to go to the gym, not that we get much time there anyway. June, Diana and Bernice discuss some of their other former cellmates.

'What about Mary?' says June. Mary is a tank-like woman in her fifties, kindly but very depressed and known to cut up. I sat with her on the Journey. Bernice screws up her nose.

'She stinks,' she says. An accusation from the playground.

June sniffs: 'Not as bad as Hester.'

'Who's Hester?' I ask. 'Do you mean the one I did the Journey with?' Hester was on my table as well.

'Yes, she's the one who shaves.'

'What? On her face? Is she butch?'

'Well, she is and she isn't,' says June, laughing. 'She's just lost a baby, so she must like men.'

□ □ □

It is not long before Nancy is up to her old tricks. She submits a written complaint about June and Glenda. We think she has been put up to it by a couple of the women upstairs, one of them being the bollock-boiler. Some other people have joined in, saying June and Glenda have made racist comments. In Nancy's case, she alleges she was got at for being fat.

June and Glenda vehemently deny everything, but are put on 'bully watch' for a week. I am not quite sure what this means, but the two of them can hardly contain their fury. It will go on their prison records, known as P16s, which are looked over when you come up for your parole. A day or so later, Mr Jones, a tall officer who walks duck-like, his big-booted feet splayed out, comes to say that the complaints are disproved. Even so, the incident will remain on their P16s. June and Glenda crave revenge.

There is uproar at the next community meeting. June and Glenda say their bit, then Nancy defends herself in the worst way possible, saying she has made complaints about other people too. She even

CHAPTER FIVE / 119

accuses the bollock-boiler of using drugs. The bollock-boiler leaps up to protest her innocence and threaten violence to Nancy, but she allows herself to be held back by two other inmates. Amid the general mayhem I shout out: 'This is just what happened on House 3.' Instantly I regret it. I have been roused by the mob.

Viv creates a diversion by broadcasting a headlice scare.

'They're full of it on House 3,' she says. 'We all mix in education and the like. I bet some people have got it here too.' So everyone gets their head checked and Viv reckons she finds lice on Nancy, who has hair down to her waist. Viv gets the electric razor from the office and Nancy submits, ending up with a drastic skinhead and her lovely locks strewn around her feet. We all watch the spectacle, June and Glenda with more satisfaction than most.

□ □ □

Glenda has received some news that she has been waiting for. She is being transferred the next day to HMP Send. For 'security reasons', prisoners only get a day's notice of their transfers. Glenda and June have been waiting for months to go to Send and they had wanted to go together. June is very jealous. Meanwhile, we prepare the usual prison farewell.

At lock-up we go for it, shrieking with laughter as we hurl buckets of water over Glenda, one of them laced with a variety of cereals. She gets completely drenched but takes it in good spirit, splodging off to the shower clutching some dry clothes. One of the screws is watching from behind the spur gate.

'Ruth,' she says, 'I wouldn't have expected it from you.' But I am well into prison culture, can be as childish as the rest, and do not feel the least bit ashamed. It is what prison does to you.

Glenda packs her stuff during the evening. She has a few small tins of food from her canteen and offers them around. Diana takes the hotdog sausages and I am up for the tins of pineapple and peaches. Diana makes for the spur gate and shouts to Yvonne upstairs.

'You got the tin-opener?'

'Yeah, wait.' Yvonne gets one from somewhere and throws it. We use a broom handle to pull it towards us and open up our tins. I eat the pineapple straight off and savour every morsel.

'Exquisite,' I pronounce.

'They aren't that marvellous,' says Glenda.

'Oh yes they are,' I say. They do taste absolutely delicious after our prison fare. Diana has got hold of some bread for a hotdog sandwich. I move on to the peaches. They are like nectar, and I resolve to get myself some on my canteen when I can afford it.

□ □ □

With Glenda gone, Diana is planning to move in with June, away from Nancy. Meanwhile, my cellmate Viv is becoming very friendly with Jan from up the way. Jan is sharing with Lola, the deeply religious African woman. She is in for smuggling quantities of cigarettes and views these muddle-headed drug addicts as an incomprehensible puzzle. For Viv, Jan is a reassuring presence, self-assured and easy-going. A big-built woman in her thirties, she is doing a few months for shoplifting and has half-a-dozen kids by a variety of fathers. They are all in care now and Jan desperately wishes she could get her life back on track. Right now she is composing a letter for Viv to send to her prison pen-pal. She is on the third page and it is utterly explicit.

'The screws'll blow a blood vessel when they read this one,' Viv says with a contented grin. I tell her that a friend of mine suggested, in all seriousness, that female prisoners should be allowed to bring in vibrators. Viv is shocked by such a matter-of-fact approach. She is still young and not as experienced as she makes out, not so confident when faced with reality.

Later on, the inevitable happens: Diana gets transferred to another prison. June has taken to coming into my room most evenings, to tell me her troubles. Viv wants to share with Jan from next door. So I move in with June in an attempt to keep everyone happy.

This turns out badly for me.

□ □ □

Most of the other inmates know that outside I have worked in housing and homelessness, and occasionally they ask me for advice. Statistics show that over 40 per cent of women are homeless when they leave prison, and I am shocked that Highpoint, like many other prisons, does not do more to help. There is not even a list of local housing agencies for each area, which would be relatively simple to provide. It is vital for people to have somewhere to live on release if they are going to stand a chance of staying out of trouble. Some months later I discover that attempts are being made to provide more housing advice in prisons, but it is a slow response to an urgent problem.

When I first moved to Kainos I got a typical request. A young woman from up north asked me to help with her resettlement. She was due out in a couple of months, and had a daughter who was living with her mother, but said she had custody of her child. I told her she ought to have a statutory right to housing and set about writing some letters with her. I do not know how it went for her. Many female ex-prisoners find it hard to get reunited with their children, whether or not they previously had custody of them. Their situation is pure heartbreak, for the child as well as for the mother.

□ □ □

I only once become incensed with another inmate. It happens before Glenda's transfer. I am in June and Glenda's room one evening, listening as usual to their complaints against the prison and the police, when Gabrielle puts her head round the door and rudely demands to see their copy of the *Sun* newspaper. June and Glenda are not willing to comply with such a brusque request and tell Gabrielle that they have not finished reading it. Gabrielle storms off after shouting liberally at the two women – that they are a couple of arseholes and so forth. They try to ignore it.

As it is late, I go back to my room to get some rest. Janis is sitting there.

'I wish I could be like that,' she says of Gabrielle: 'able to say what I think.' We can hear Gabrielle talking and laughing loudly in her room. I do not respond to Janis's comment and try to get on with a letter or two.

Then at 12.30 a.m. I hear Gabrielle shouting into June and Glenda's room again.

'Have you finished with the paper?' She launches into a diatribe about how June and Glenda slag everyone off, how Glenda's daughter is the ugliest girl she has ever seen, that June's son is evil, anything she can think of that might hurt, and away she goes to her room laughing uproariously. Fifteen minutes later she is at Jade and Connie's door, yelling at them about how June calls them rats and cats. I am full of fatigue; it is nearly 1 a.m., I need to get some sleep, and I burst out through my own door to give Gabrielle a piece of my mind.

'Will you fucking shut up! It's 1 o'clock in the morning and people are trying to sleep. Keep the fucking noise down and stop keeping everyone awake.'

Gabrielle looks completely shocked that my usual mild manner has given way to such fury, and then she starts to give me some back. But I am already in my room again, having slammed the door behind me, and, getting no response, Gabrielle slopes off. I am relieved. I do not usually shout at people and thankfully there seem to be no repercussions. It reminds me of my night-shelter days, when I occasionally did yell to bring about some order.

'Do you still want to be like that?' I ask Janis, referring to her earlier comment about Gabrielle.

'No,' she says, with feeling.

The next day, when the officers hear about what happened, Gabrielle is moved upstairs.

□ □ □

A major prison diversion is the making of hooch, a crude alcoholic drink for which there are various recipes, mostly based on what you can get hold of at the time. The main thing is to make something that works. I get my first taste of it on the Kainos Skid Row, in the middle of an extra-long lock-up: twenty hours non-stop, which makes me feel as though the stress of it is literally dripping off me. We are shut behind the spur gate, confined to our six cramped double rooms along the narrow corridor with the one toilet, shower and washbasin at the end for us twelve women. Deprivation and despair. I tell myself that some prisoners have an even worse life: twenty-three-hour lock-ups as routine and shut behind the cell door. Enough to drive you completely barmy. Perhaps that is the point.

During the evening I mutter: 'I could do with a glass of wine.' Diana laughs, and I think she passes my comment on. She has been in and out of the room for the past hour, helping Karen set up her huge stereo at the end of the corridor. Karen has got some new batteries. They turn the machine on and blast us out. Then Bernice comes in holding a lemonade bottle.

'Get yourself a glass,' she says. 'This 'ere is hooch.' I do not have a glass; where am I supposed to find a glass in prison? Bernice disappears and returns with two plastic tumblers. She pours the hooch and goes out again. I drink mine down fast and almost instantly feel it hit my stomach, the warmth spreading like tentacles through my body. Ah, relaxation. The racket in the corridor is getting worse, but it does not bother me anymore. I am grinning hugely, and glowing from the inside. Bernice pops her head round the door.

'Come on an' dance!' she yells. I look out: she is grooving away with Karen, Diana and the voluble Lulu. I leave them to it and flop on the bed. Contentment at last.

I sleep soundly and, unusually for me, do not wake until the 7.30 a.m. roll-check, with the screws turning the light on in the room, doing their usual chore of making sure we have not escaped in the night. Bugger off – I have a headache. And my stomach is churning. The morning after the night before. But it was worth it. Then, half an hour later and out of the blue, there are three officers on the spur, ones I recognize from House 3. They are looking for Bernice. When they find her, they bark out that under Section 67 of some Act or other they are taking her for a drug test. Bernice is very cool as she goes off with them.

'Does alcohol show up?' I ask Bernice when she returns. She tells me not to worry.

'It'll come back negative and be good for my parole.' Parole: two-and-a-half years to go before mine comes up. What can I say to them?

You are supposed to show remorse. I could say: 'I'm sorry I didn't know about the dealing at the day centre.' But that would sound as though I didn't accept responsibility for my crime. Maybe: 'I'm sorry I didn't do more about the dealing that I didn't know about.' No, no; definitely not right. It would have to be: 'I'm sorry I didn't do more about the dealing,' full stop. And I suppose they would question me on it, dig deeper.

'What you say at your parole hearing can be used against you for an appeal,' says Bernice. That could be difficult. If we lose the appeal at the High Court, Liberty might help us to take it to Europe, as they are worried about the confidentiality issue in particular, and it was that which really got us convicted. It takes years; the hearing would happen after my parole. So I would have to be very careful about what I said. Quite a quandary.

A few days later, a parole officer is on the wing and some of us get chatting to him. I ask him straight: 'What would you suggest to someone who doesn't think they're guilty but wants to get their parole?'

'Lie,' he says. I am shocked, but suppose that he is right. Telling the truth has not worked up to now.

□ □ □

It did not take me long to decide that gardening was the best job in the prison. I am continually desperate to get outside, and, while not being outside of the prison, the grounds are at least under the open sky. The afternoon session, the one I do, only lasts a couple of hours. But it is better than nothing. Along with two or three of the other women on the gardening team, I develop a reputation for hard work. I enjoy using up my energy, and I am in any case well imbued with the work ethic, know the satisfaction of achievement.

Some of the others do not have that experience and expend more energy avoiding the work than doing it. Gypsy-girl Leah uses the opportunity of being out and about to call up her mates in the different houses, hustling them to pass her cups of tea and fags through the bars of their windows. Pete is an easy-going boss most of the time but he comes down hard on people who mess around. One day he decides that he has caught Leah and Viv skiving once too often and finds them a particularly heavy, dirty job, digging out the compost from the compost heap and then putting it all back.

'It needs airing,' Pete says.

'I'll fucking kill him,' Leah curses, ankle-deep in filth. 'I've had enough of Pete and his fucking gardens.' Pete comes by to inspect the work.

'Good job,' he comments. 'Well done.'

□ □ □

On my first afternoon of real gardening, Pete takes me out on my own to weed three beds close to the main gate. Armed with my spade, hoe and wheelbarrow, I get on with it, looking out of the corner of my eye at the activity around the gate. Vans come and go, people come and go. I feel envious and angry, take it out on the weeds and pretend not to be peeking. After an hour I take a break, lean on my shovel and roll a fag, unnerved that I slip so easily into character. A little later on, Pete comes to check up on me and is pleased at the progress.

'I can see you've done this before,' he says. 'You can finish it off tomorrow.' After weeks of continual denigration, his praise is a pleasant surprise.

Afterwards I am shattered. A full gardening session: pure delight. It has given me longer in the open than I have ever had since being locked away – nearly two hours – and the fresh air has exhausted me. My body is a dead weight. I can hardly move to get changed out of my gardening gear. Half dressed, I stretch out on the bed and, though it is not yet 5 p.m., fall asleep straightaway.

□ □ □

Feelings seem to come up from out of nowhere in prison. One afternoon I am working away, weeding another bed on my own and quite enjoying the activity. Then, unexpectedly, I am flooded with emotion and an urge to weep. It is as if my body is dissolving, the deep sadness forcing its way up to my throat. I am besieged with images of being at

Wintercomfort: the bustle and chatter on the Bus; people working hard and getting things done; the friendliness; the commitment to the job and to our homeless clientele. I chip at the earth with my hoe, chipping away at the pictures I am getting, trying to cut them out of my head. There are the staff, cheery and good-hearted, and I have been wrenched away into this bleak place. I wonder if the images, and the emotion, have surfaced because I have let my guard down just a little, for just a moment. I am in mourning for the life that was once mine.

A screw walks by and comments in the jolly manner they use that somehow still asserts their authority over you.

'Doin' a good job there,' he says. I suppose he enjoys seeing me engaged in menial work and pointedly ignore him.

□ □ □

Quite often the work in gardens is decidedly unpleasant. One day three of us have to haul sacks of a heavy peat mixture from where they are piled near the greenhouse to the shed, 50 yards away. We have a large handcart and feel like pack animals, one of us pulling the cart from the front and the other two pushing from behind. Dragging the heavily laden cart over the uneven grass to the shed takes every ounce of our strength. We end up covered in sweat and exhausted, and desperate for a shower. Such demeaning work reinforces our lowly status.

Another time I am laying 3-foot-square concrete slabs. We have to dig the path out, spread sand on top and then position the slabs, making sure they are flat and solid. Again it takes me all my strength, hauling along the muddy, stony soil and piles of sand in a rickety wheelbarrow, and then lifting the heavy concrete slabs. I work with Gerrit, a German woman in her thirties, and when we have finished we use a trowel to scrape our initials on the path. Pete is pleased with our efforts but not with the signatures. Then Gerrit picks two daisies and puts one in her hair and one in mine.

Gerrit becomes my greatest friend, and we are close companions during my next couple of months in prison. She is tall and slim with a mass of black curly hair, has intelligence, maturity and a tremendous sense of humour. We laugh at everything. It is a tragedy that she is doing an eight-year sentence for drug importation so many miles from home, but I admire her for bearing her burden with the greatest dignity, though she suffers from crushing depression like the rest of us. 'I did wrong and now I'm paying for it,' she says philosophically.

We work together on gardens, play badminton in the gym, share reading material and do our best to lighten each other's load.

After the afternoon gardening sessions, Gerrit and I walk together to healthcare to get our night-time medication. Today, as usual, the small, grimy room that we have to wait in is absolutely packed. I am squeezed in the queue by yet another pair of massive boobs pushing into me from behind. Suddenly Pearl surprises me, jumping through the door to ask me how I am. She has been moved on to House 2.

'It's OK there, except the woman I'm in with is giving me the silent treatment.'

She proudly shows me her nails, which are painted black. I do not ask where she got the nail polish from.

Then Grace turns up. She has just had another session in the block, with its twenty-three-and-a-half-hour bang-up, and cannot stop talking or keep still, wide-eyed at the sight of all these people after seventeen days of intense isolation.

'Boy, it's so good to see you guys,' she sings out. 'Fucking marvellous.'

□ □ □

Gardens is a good place to catch up on the prison gossip. Bet is the one who tells me that Pearl is out. She has got her days back. Her solicitor must have got it together at last. I am over the moon, knowing how Pearl will be feeling. It is as if she is out there for me.

'I've got another eighteen days to go,' Bet says. I count my time in years, not days.

I am sent off with Gerrit to dig over a flower bed. We work on a bed beside the main pathway and everyone who passes by greets us, except for the screws, who mostly ignore us, or taunt us with sarcastic remarks such as: 'Call that work?'

A huge Jamaican who does the bins yells at Gerrit and throws a clod of earth at her when she looks up. Gerrit responds in kind. Stupid fooling around helps to cheer us all up. Then a tutor I met in education says a cheery 'Hello' as she goes by. I am polite in return but am more interested in hearing from my fellow inmates. Working in the grounds, you can catch up on the news.

That morning the whole prison had been on lock-down and each spur was searched in turn. It was an unnerving experience, being invaded by gangs of screws. They shut us in the dining room while they searched our rooms, leaving some of them in a terrible mess. While Gerrit and I have a fag break, we hear the reason for it. A knife had gone missing from the kitchen. Our informant, who has been visiting the prison library, tells us that the screws on House 2 were not too happy about things.

'They were so pissed off they didn't even touch the rooms downstairs.' Apparently, we had got let out when the cook found the knife safe in his kitchen after all.

The door to education bursts open and McCafferty comes out for a fag.

'Get back to your unit,' he bawls at our informant. She wanders off, very slowly, no doubt wanting to make the most of those precious few moments outside.

□ □ □

One afternoon I am sent out to cut the grass in the compound outside House 2. It is my favourite location for mowing, as it has a group of tall poplar trees to one side. The trees whisper secrets to the wind, oblivious to the miseries being enacted beneath them. I am set to work away from the poplars but am nevertheless happy to be there wheeling my little petrol-powered mower; I had as usual been urgently impatient while waiting on the unit to be let out into the fresh air.

I have only just begun to mow when the rain starts, slowly at first but quickly building up to a torrential crescendo. I take shelter under one of the fire escapes outside the unit, reluctant to go back indoors.

The rain comes down in sheets and the prison grounds are deserted. They are being washed clean. I am alone, crouched in my hideaway. For those fifteen minutes I belong to myself in the world, in my world, feel like an independent person. I feel almost free.

□ □ □

After a couple of weeks in my job, Pete puts my weekly wage up to £7.50, for which I am supposed to be grateful. Along with the £10 weekly spend that I am allowed from my private cash, I have got to the point where I can buy phone cards to call home every evening. It is great to speak, is normalizing and helps keep us together as a family. Even so, there is always sadness when the calls are over and their voices are gone. I also ring my mum once a week and occasionally call my sister or a friend. I spend £4 on tobacco and buy a few other bits and pieces: a small jar of Nescafé every fortnight so that I can have one half-decent cup of coffee every morning, batteries for my Walkman, shampoo, honey sometimes, some fruit and the odd snack. Like all my fellow inmates, I work it out to the last penny.

I can get paper and envelopes sent in, provided they are sealed and wrapped. Even then, if the screws open the parcel too roughly and break the wrapping, it does not get through. I am still getting lots of stamps from various people. My companions have found out and they come to see me when they are in need. Nobody abuses the situation, which means there is enough for everyone. Though, according to prison rules, we are not supposed to give anything away and can get nicked if we do.

□ □ □

Gerrit and I get dreadfully frustrated when gardening is cancelled, which happens often, sometimes for days in a row. It is always a relief to get off the unit. One day I am sitting with the others in the shed, waiting to get started, when they come for me: two screws who confuse me with pronouncements on Section this and Section that.

'They're taking you for a piss test,' one of my colleagues helpfully explains.

'What do they want to take her for?' another person says. 'It's obvious she doesn't take drugs.'

'To get a good result,' comes the reply. 'It doesn't look good for the prison if they get too many positives.' The official explanation would be that the piss tests are random, but official explanations are routinely treated with suspicion in here.

Along with three other women I am marched off to the block. We are locked in a room that resembles a cupboard, having been searched and had everything taken off us, and are allowed to drink only a specified amount of water to help us pee. A dark-haired woman is really panicking and drinks as much as she can, aiming to dilute whatever is in her system. We are not allowed to smoke while we are waiting, presumably to encourage us to get on with it. I am taken out third and am watched over while I pee into a jar. The pee jar is sealed and packed away for analysis. I sign various forms and then am sent back to the unit. I have nothing to worry about but the process itself is unsettling. I will get the results in a week or so. Perhaps, like Bernice, it will be good for my parole as well.

The next afternoon I am extra anxious to get outside. I don my greens early and as usual roll a couple of fags to take with me. I would be endlessly hounded for a smoke if I took all my tobacco. But we are not unlocked as we should be at 1.45 p.m. No one knows what is going on. Ten minutes later we find out. Peering through a little window and past a locked gate, we can see there is activity by the office: lots of screws are coming on to the unit, the place is crawling with them, ten, maybe fifteen. Then they come on to the spurs, two at a time, to pick people off. Bernice is first, followed by two of her friends.

'They're not suitable material for the house,' says one of the screws.

We all wait, furious but impassive, and terrified it will be our turn next. I say goodbye to Bernice but she cannot respond, has been told to say nothing. We wonder if those chosen are going to be shipped out.

They do not take me, just Bernice and the two others. I am relieved for myself but sad to have lost a good friend. Bernice had an independence of mind that I valued and appreciated. We all wonder why the overkill, with so many screws to do the job. Do they really think we would riot? We are supposed to be a community at Kainos, but it is pretty clear where the power resides. The raid has an effect on the community meetings. We all shut down.

'They've finally got the idea,' says a screw. 'If no one says anything, the meetings are over with quicker.'

□ □ □

Everyone is supposed to have a sentence plan. So here I am, in a room with a young female probation officer and my personal prison officer, Mr Jones, who sits impassive, his duck feet splayed. I have no quarrel with Jones; he is reasonably decent to me most of the time. As ever, there is a form to fill in. I am asked about my acceptance of guilt. I explain that I am appealing against my conviction.

'We'll leave that bit blank, then,' says the probation officer, adding that if my appeal fails I will have to do the prison's drug importers' course, which presumably is not about teaching people how to import drugs but to encourage them to stop doing it.

'I'm not in for that,' I protest.

'It's all we have to offer,' the probation officer replies, meaning in terms of rehabilitation. Is this a joke, an insult, or both?

She then goes on to look at what my goals in prison are. I need to have at least three.

'It's pretty limited in here,' I begin, but the probation officer has done this before.

'How about completing Kainos as one,' she suggests, 'and carrying on in gardens could be another.' That is two. We struggle for a third. I tell her about my efforts to get a typewriter, and that a publisher has asked me to write something for him. I have got him to write back saying that everything has to be typed and I get his letter from my room to show them.

'I want to write about homelessness,' I explain, worried that they might think I would write about prison, which feels far too dangerous to do in here.

So it goes into my sentence plan, the third goal being to start a book on homelessness (which is not quite how it has turned out), and under the 'Actions' section the probation officer puts the need to get a typewriter in. I leave feeling pleased that I have manipulated things to my possible advantage and get outside for the last half-hour of gardens.

□ □ □

A couple of weeks later I have part two of my sentence planning. It entails a meeting with one of the governors, as well as a probation officer and a prison officer. I wait in a queue, feeling as though I am about to face an examination or an interview. When I get in, the panel treats me quite respectfully, which is a welcome surprise.

'Do you like working in gardens?' the governor asks.

'Yes, I like to get out, and Pete is a good boss.' It might sound like arse-licking, but I mean it.

'This bit about a book . . .' the governor begins.

'I need a typewriter to do it,' I say.

'Yes, it's been agreed.' I am ecstatic, but try to look nonchalant.

'Does that mean I can arrange for one to be brought in?'

'Yes.'

I pride myself that my manipulations have been effective, but one of the screws tells me later: 'You could have asked for one to work on your appeal.'

'Why didn't you tell me that from the start?' I ask.

The screw just smiles.

□ □ □

While in prison I was initially only dimly aware of the massive efforts being made to get John and me out. The first meeting to try to address the situation was held at Wintercomfort, on the floor of the day centre, a few days after we were sentenced. Although it was just before Christmas 1999, fifty or sixty people turned up. They were a real mixture: Wintercomfort trustees, staff, volunteers and general supporters; local councillors; homeless people; academics and townsfolk; homelessness staff from other agencies; all of them united in their outrage. They became the Cambridge Two Campaign Committee, with Alexander Masters, who had worked with me on fundraising at Wintercomfort, as the chairman. Fighting and Support Funds were set up to cover the campaign's costs. John and I remain indebted to everyone on the committee, to those who ran the campaign, the contributors to the Fighting and Support Funds and to the countless others who stood by us and gave up their time to help prise us out of jail.

Only now, as I look through the files of press cuttings, do I realize how much publicity the Cambridge Two got around the country: sympathetic and thoughtful articles in the national press; in magazines for the housing, charitable and legal sectors; in the *Big Issue*; even *Private Eye* took up the story. Radio 4 sent me a tape of their *Face the Facts* programme about us, which was well researched and presented, and certainly on our side. Trade union members produced resolutions supporting us. People connected to churches around the country expressed their deep concern, with the Quaker movement being especially supportive. We were even reported in the media abroad.

The Cambridge evening paper was more ambivalent, presumably having to cope with letters from irate antagonists as well as supporters, and needing to keep their police contacts happy, though supportive 'Letters to the Editor' easily outweighed the 'hang 'em and shoot 'em brigade'. And they also used letters from John and myself, thanking people for their support and generally bemoaning our plight.

The *Independent* and the *Guardian* were particularly helpful, as was the *Observer*, which ran the two articles by Nick Cohen, the first headed 'Jailed for doing her job' and the second being the one relating how Judge Haworth was reportedly heard boasting at a lawyers' dinner party that he was going to send us to prison, before he had seen the court reports or heard the mitigation.

Cohen came up with a heart-warming rant:

When the suspects did not have criminal records, when they had abandoned comfortable lives to provide what help they could for the destitute, when no one was suggesting that they had taken heroin, or sold heroin, or laundered drug money – when, indeed, the police had approved their policies of banning drug users from their day centre and rehabilitating drug addicts – most people would consider it to be no more than common courtesy that they should be the first to know they were going to be banged up for years in our stinking prison system.'

The only unhelpful journalist was Melanie Phillips, who slammed into us in the *Sunday Times*. 'Why are the Cambridge Two being championed?' she asked in the article, and suggested three reasons. The first was that 'most people know little about the case other than what a well-organised campaign is putting out'. This brought a chuckle from Alexander. ' "Well-organised?" ' he said. 'If only she knew.'

Phillips' second reason was that 'the outrage of the privileged class is always greatest when their own are jailed'. That one made *me* chuckle, at being considered a member of the privileged class. I saw myself as an ordinary middle-class woman, even though I had taken on a somewhat unusual job and had attacked it with an unusual amount of gusto. Her third reason was that 'in our most influential circles, drugs are increasingly tolerated; drug law enforcement is not', which is not something that I was aware of, but then I did not mingle in influential circles. Perhaps she did.

I wondered if Phillips' annoyance had been fuelled by an exchange we had had shortly before my arrest. I had heard her speak as part of a panel at a National Homeless Alliance conference, and had written to her afterwards because I felt she was out of touch with the realities of homelessness. For a start, she believed that if any homeless person was mentally unwell, they would get all the treatment they needed from our overstretched NHS. If only that was true. In my letter I had invited her to visit our day centre in Cambridge, to see things for herself. She had declined the invitation, which was a shame. If she had come, she could have written a much more interesting article.

At one point a freelance journalist got in to see me, and this led to yet another story appearing in the *Observer*. I was not long over my New Year dose of flu, and when the article came out I was annoyed to see myself described as 'a frail woman with huge dark circles under her eyes . . . she looks gaunt and sickly and punctuates her

conversation with a hacking cough'. I knew the journalist was look-
ing to generate sympathy but was so incensed that I wrote to the
Observer insisting: 'I am not frail,' which probably amused them.
Perhaps I did not dare acknowledge what prison had done to me.

□ □ □

I continued to get innumerable letters from sympathizers: people
saying how shocked they were at what had happened; that they had
written to their MP for the first time in their lives; or that they had
written to Jack Straw, or even the prime minister. Peter Bottomley
championed our cause in the House of Commons, getting backing
from various MPs. I wrote to him and he passed a copy of my letter to
the prime minister. I also heard that the Home Secretary was being
briefed about the case, along with Keith Hellawell, the government's
drugs tsar. I felt it must surely all help, though I knew that Parliament
was not supposed to interfere with the judiciary. They could, however, apply pressure. If we could be patient, that pressure would
hopefully pay off.

Overall, I was amazed by the support and wondered if the case was
acting as a touchstone for people's concerns about homelessness and
drug addiction, about the shortfall in services. There were not
enough beds to give shelter to people, let alone rehab and detox for
those ready to take them up. People had real concerns about heroin
addiction, concerns about the fate of addicts which seemed at odds
with what was almost a demonization of these hapless souls by government and in much of the media.

Traditionally, charities filled in the gaps of community welfare
services. They acted as a form of public conscience. It was as if, by
prosecuting John and me and sending us to prison, that role had been
brutally violated.

□ □ □

A month after my imprisonment, the campaign organized a protest
in Cambridge. Hundreds of people turned out on a cold winter's day
to march through the city and hold a rally in the market square. My

husband and John's wife spoke from the steps of the Guildhall. I was sent photographs of the rally and I scanned the crowd for familiar faces. I knew it was happening, had been told about it in advance, but was stuck in a lock-up throughout. I tried to be with them in my mind, to imagine what was going on, and when they were due to start I heard a familiar tune on one of the radios down the corridor. It was the theme from the film *Local Hero*. I had to chuckle.

Then a benefit gig was organized at the Junction, a good venue in Cambridge. There was a pretty impressive line-up, including Martin and Eliza Carthy, Norma Waterson, Eddi Reader and Boo Hewardine, and Dr Robert. One thing you could do in prison was send and receive cassette tapes, so I made a recording for the concert – a message for the audience. Janis agreed to let me use her tape machine, provided I got my own batteries and a blank tape from my canteen. First of all, I had a special introduction in mind. When we were due for unlock, I nonchalantly hung around at the spur gate clutching Janis's machine. As soon as the screw came up with his keys I surreptitiously switched on and recorded the rattle and clang of us all being let out, the bustle and chatter as we women pushed through.

Then I added my message for the benefit. Janis sat on the bed listening, and every so often we collapsed into our schoolgirl giggling fits. But she had some good advice.

'It's for a gig, innit? Don't be so fucking formal.' At last I got it down and was back at the spur gate with the machine when it was time for us to get locked up again. Mr Stevenson was there, a rotund and jolly man with a boom of a voice. He looked at the tape recorder suspiciously.

'Come on,' I said encouragingly. 'Give us your usual "Roll-check! Behind your spurs!" yell.'

Stevenson would not oblige. Instead, I got a beatific grin as he urged us, polite as never before, with a: 'Come along, ladies, time to get to your rooms, if you would be so kind.'

'Bastard,' I railed, but I did get a good recording of the spur gate being locked for the end of the recording.

Later, I heard that the benefit was a sell-out.

□ □ □

Not long afterwards, I was busy making a second tape recording. The campaign crew had organized a march in London this time, ending up with a rally at Trafalgar Square, and they wanted another message. I gather I ended up sounding excessively posh, probably the result of overcompensating for my flattened prison accent. People said my voice sounded slightly shrill as well. I reckoned the batteries for the tape recorder were a bit low, making the tape play slow during the recording. It was always difficult, getting things done in prison.

Despite my own minor technical difficulties, I was told the march went off well. I was with it throughout in my mind, imagining people waiting at Hyde Park and then walking through the streets with their banners, arriving at Trafalgar Square, the speeches, the camaraderie. I was sent the press cuttings and lots of photographs. They were a goodly crowd and as usual I enjoyed picking out familiar faces. At the end my daughter got up on the podium to thank everyone for coming. It must have raised her spirits; it certainly raised mine, and I treasured a photo of her dancing up there with some of her friends.

The campaign ran the 'Free the Cambridge Two' petition for several months. It was supported by the unions UNISON, MSF and the TGWU, Release, the Big Issue, and several cross-party MPs. People worked extraordinarily hard and got a formidable 20,000 signatures from all over the country, an indication of strong public feeling. John's eleven-year-old son Dylan and my Rachel delivered the petition to the Home Office, after Alexander and some of the other supporters had valiantly slept outside the building for several nights. My mother brought them sandwiches. Things got harder and harder for our kids, the longer our imprisonment went on, and I am sure Dylan and Rachel were glad to do their bit for the campaign.

□ □ □

The campaign crew may not have been as organized as Melanie Phillips suspected, but they were certainly ingenious. When the singer Joan Baez visited London to receive the BBC Radio 2 Folk

Awards Lifetime Achievement Award, they managed to get her on board.

'On my concert tour of the US in March and April, I will dedicate a song nightly to Ruth and John, tell their story and continue to demand their swift and imminent release,' she was quoted as saying in the local press. 'The arrests of and imprisonment of Ruth Wyner and John Brock are the result of drastically misguided police vigilance.'

Then there were the comedians. Mark Thomas was the first to come on board, but others followed later, including Jo Brand, Robert Newman, Alexei Sayle, Arthur Smith and Victoria Wood. Mark ran a hilarious stunt on his TV show, *The Mark Thomas Product*, during which four people turned up at a Cambridge cop shop and asked to be arrested because they had committed the same offence as John and me.

'I am a felon,' said Professor David Brandon, a colleague who ran his own homelessness project in Cambridge.

'This is a farcical position,' he told the press afterwards. 'Ruth Wyner and John Brock, two sensible and intelligent people, are getting convicted and getting longer sentences than the drug sellers. What message is that? The only people who are laughing are the drug barons.'

□ □ □

The case of the Cambridge Two became a major issue in the city. Most local councillors were disturbed by our imprisonment. Two of the city representatives wanted to table a resolution supporting us unreservedly. But they had to temper the wording to concentrate on the sentences rather than on the convictions themselves, in order to maintain support.

The local paper reported that

Cambridge City Council was undivided in calling for the early release of the pair who were jailed for allowing the supply of heroin at Overstream House centre for the homeless in Cambridge. Two councillors – John Hipkin and John Durrant – put forward a resolution expressing sympathy for the families of Brock and Wyner, and condemning the sentences as 'inappropriately severe' … . City councillors also urged the council to seek clarification of the law regarding drug misuse in hostels.

Coun Hipkin ... spoke of the dilemma facing workers dealing with the homeless across the country in the wake of the Wintercomfort court case, adding that some felt they were now expected to act as 'casual informers' to police ... . He warned the repercussions of the case could force hostels to exclude all drug users, creating 'a pariah class of outcasts, utterly rejected by everybody in the rest of so-called respectable society'.

Coun Durrant said: 'The treatment of the Cambridge Two has shocked our community and reverberated into the wider world.'

Alexander, our campaign Chairman, managed to get a quote into the paper too, telling them: 'People are extremely worried about the implications of what's happened to Ruth and John. I had a call from an agency in Edinburgh where the workers are literally terrified. They couldn't understand how homeless workers could end up in that situation. The council's response was fantastic, it would have taken a person with a heart of stone to vote against it.'

A couple of stony-hearted individuals did decide to abstain, including Gaynor Griffiths, a councillor who seemed to have a vindictive dislike of Wintercomfort. She had given evidence against me in court, charming the judge with her apparently perfect memory of meetings we had had up to two years previously. Presumably she was happy to see me behind bars. Some local people also did not support the council's resolution.

The *Cambridge Evening News* quoted both sides:

Sonny Mayner, former landlord of the Jolly Waterman pub in Victoria Avenue – where police camped out during the surveillance operation leading to the convictions – said: 'I'm absolutely furious the council is backing criminals. It's scandalous.'

James Mount, deputy manager at Wine Rack, on Chesterton Road, said: 'The issue is about the judgement of the court, not about the individual traders and their problems here. It's a case of misinformation. People don't really know what happened at Wintercomfort and they're making judgements based on the fact they don't like travellers in Cambridge.'

□ □ □

The Welsh National Assembly agreed a motion expressing its grave concern about the prosecution and imprisonment of the Cambridge Two. The House of Commons was not so easily persuaded, though my own MP, Anne Campbell, did her best to lobby her fellow Members on our behalf and got a fair amount of support. She also urged ministers to clarify the position of people running homelessness centres which seek to help those addicted to drugs and managed to get some recognition of the understandable concern within the sector, with the Home Office saying it would consider the need for further guidance.

'People need some guidance otherwise nobody will want to work in this field,' Anne was quoted as saying in the local paper. 'I have been pressing the government to look at the implications, particularly for people in Ruth and John's position. A lot of people are extremely worried that they are also going to be charged.'

□ □ □

Anne Campbell came to visit me in prison. Gordon had told me about it the evening before, when I made my usual call home. I felt very nervous. Anne was usually really well turned out. In here I could hardly compete. My hair was a terrible mess. I scrounged some decent hair conditioner from down the corridor and sloshed loads of it on.

In the morning I reluctantly endured the art session and then walked back to the unit with Evelyn, slowly because of Evelyn's arthritis. I heard from her that the prison would not let her have the herbal remedies she used on the outside and that, as a result, her joints were stiffening up badly and her legs were getting seriously ulcerated. Evelyn repeatedly told me how she had lost everything because of her prosecution: her house, her savings, her health – the lot. She was due out soon but said that the police were now rummaging up some new charges in an effort to keep her under lock and key.

'I know too much,' she muttered darkly as she struggled up the path, leaning heavily on her stick. Those police officers did manage to lay new charges on Evelyn, which meant she painfully spent yet more weeks and months in prison waiting for her case to come up in court. Thankfully, the judge threw it out at the very first hearing and Evelyn regained her precious freedom at last.

After lunchtime lock-up I made my way to the door of the visits hall and, as usual, knocked and waited along with a few other inmates who had turned up. Eventually, Miss Stratford opened the door and let us in one by one.

'Oh no, not Stratford,' said one of my fellow inmates. 'Being frisked by her is like being frisked by a man.' I was surprised. Stratford came across as a bit more posh than the other screws, and was often teased by them about her middle-class accent.

'I've never seen her as a lesbian,' I said.

'Come on, it's blindingly obvious,' came the response. 'Why else would a woman like that work in a place like this?'

Quite a few of the female screws were lesbians, at least half of them. Many of the inmates were as well, though often they were prison bent. People's sexual orientation had never bothered me before. But in prison it could feel overpowering, even threatening, particularly if you were not used to it.

At last I got into the visits hall, and, after a fifteen-minute wait sitting on my red plastic chair, I saw my MP at the door. We greeted each other warmly and I was relieved that my normal social persona was still operational. Anne asked me how I was and I made light of my difficulties, said the separation from the family was the worst thing and did not mention anything about the daily deprivations. Afterwards, I wondered why I protected her from it.

'Ruth is in quite good spirits and keeping well,' she duly reported to the local media.

Sitting together, we discussed the case. She told me that the Home Office was considering issuing fresh guidelines on Section 8.

'That's all very well,' I said. 'But it's being done on my back.'

'I know,' she said, looking smooth and in control, living the good life while I was stuck in here. Even so, I was grateful for her efforts.

When visits were over and we were steered out one by one, I had my first and only post-visit strip-search – pretty chilly, standing on a mat by the door. I coped by being amused: did they think my MP had passed me something? The screws kept saying that it was just routine, that I just happened to be the one who came out when the strip-search was planned. But it was their decision who came out and when. I reckoned they were making too many excuses, that they wanted to punish me for getting my MP in and to ensure that I still knew my place.

It turned out that Anne was annoyed about it too. I was sent a press cutting about a question she put in the Commons to Jack Straw, the Home Secretary, asking him why I was strip-searched after her visit.

'I feel rather insulted by it,' Anne was quoted as saying. 'I just want to know what the prison authorities feel is the purpose of such an intrusive search after an MP's visit. I don't know if the prison authorities thought I was passing her drugs. That is the obvious implication.' Peter Bottomley joined in. He tabled a highly unusual parliamentary question asking how many times prisoners had been strip-searched after an MP's visit.

Perhaps it was a shock to them: that prison can be so insulting and intrusive. But me, I was an old lag, and had come to expect it. After I got out, Anne told me that the prisons minister, Paul Boateng, offered her an apology and said he made sure that the prison authorities were aware of his disapproval. A quite satisfactory response, but it did not do much to address the real issues. It would certainly happen again.

As for my apology, I am still waiting.

□ □ □

There was a vigil in Cambridge to mark five months of our imprisonment. It lasted from 12 noon to 6 p.m. and I sat quiet at the start and the end. In between, I was furiously cutting grass on the compound outside our unit, mowing as fast as I could. It was a hot day. The Kainos co-ordinators came and went, but completely ignored me. Stevenson walked past and jokingly, in true officer fashion, told me to go faster. Then I saw Alicia the Colombian and she gave me a cheery wave. Gerrit was picking dead heads off a flower bed nearby and came over to share a fag break. I was dripping with sweat and hassled the people inside the unit for a cold drink. Someone passed me a mug of squash through the bars of the locked front gate and I drank it straight down. Frantic hard work in gardens kept my mind off things for a while, but it was an exhausting way of doing it.

□ □ □

On 12 June 2000, Anne Campbell got a debate in Parliament on the plight of the Cambridge Two. She had already raised the issue in the Commons three months earlier, asking the local government minister, Hilary Armstrong, whether my jail sentence might deter other charity workers from helping the homeless. At that time Ms Armstrong had said she believed the case would have no impact on other charity teams helping the homeless. Judging from the responses I had been getting from around the country, she was misinformed.

Anne had just a little more luck in June, with a clause she wanted inserted in the Misuse of Drugs Act, adding the word 'wilfully' to prevent other unwitting people being prosecuted as we had been. Speaking at length, she expressed her admiration for people working in the homelessness sector: 'I feel in awe of the dedication that, day after day, takes charity workers into situations where people are often hostile and unfriendly, and desperately in need of help.'

Then she came to her main point:

> We know from surveys that many people who are homeless are addicted to drugs ... . I would never condone homelessness shelters becoming havens for drug abusers or places for dealers of hard drugs to make a quick buck. That is not shelters' intentions ... . If, however, there is drug taking and drug dealing on a shelter's premises, despite the best measures being taken, it should be a defence for a person charged under Section 8 of the Misuse of Drugs Act that it was not wilfully permitted. That provision is needed to safeguard the livelihood of the many dedicated men and women who do a very difficult job to the best of their ability and to protect them from possible criminal prosecution.

Anne went through the issues: that, as was shown on the police surveillance tapes, the dealers did not pass drugs openly; that 'difficulties arise if people are banned and the police then require the names of those who have been banned'; and that essentially 'charity workers are worried that their shelters will not be used if users perceive that any information handed over in good faith will be passed to the police. There is a conflict of interest.'

Peter Bottomley weighed in, pointing out that the rate of detection of drug use at HMP Highpoint was lower than at Wintercomfort and roundly demanding that our appeal date be set for the very next week. He suggested that people running schools were in the same position as John and I had been, when they knew drugs were being bought and sold on the premises, wanted to stop it but just could not do so. 'We have seen in the newspapers this week how many glamorous writers in this country appear to have had a heavy drugs habit, but should we convict editors and proprietors for knowingly employing those who misuse drugs?'

Simon Hughes and Paul Flynn were among the other MPs who added their support. 'Unless people with important management responsibility in social work in the wider sense are able to risk being with potential criminals, a lot of work will not be done,' said Simon Hughes. And Paul Flynn could not resist mentioning that cannabis had been found at Buckingham Palace the previous weekend. Who was going to take responsibility for that?

One MP talked about an evening he had spent at his local night shelter. 'Those workers and volunteers were extremely worried about their positions, in the light of the case in Cambridge. Even the first whiff of concern about drug dealing led to the police being called immediately, with sniffer dogs, and to the whole place being searched .... The search, which in fact revealed nothing . . . was profoundly disruptive to what had been a pleasant evening at Christmas.'

It was down to Paul Boateng to defend the government's stance, stating initially that because there had only been one prosecution of charity workers, there was no need to worry. As far as he was concerned, it was simple: you took all reasonable means to stop drug use and dealing, and that was it. Peter Bottomley's mention of drugs in prisons was irrelevant: 'Prison governors are given a range of powers and facilities, which they exercise.'

Paul Flynn picked him up on that: 'Are not prison governors much better placed to be responsible for drug misuse than those who run such places as Wintercomfort?' Of course they were, but Paul Boateng would not be drawn on this. By that time, I was on an upstairs spur on House 1 and had seen first-hand the extent of drug use in HMP Highpoint. The prison staff knew it went on but were in the same position as we had been in at Wintercomfort: they just could not put a stop to it. It all seemed heartily unfair.

Anne's amendment was not going to be accepted by the government, and she had to withdraw it, but she made her disappointment clear:

> I believe that reasonable steps were taken in the case of Wintercomfort when people who were suspected of drug taking were excluded from the premises. That does not appear to be a sufficient way of demonstrating that reasonable steps have been taken … . There is a concern held by many in the sector, that having once brought a successful case and gained a conviction, the police might be encouraged to bring others.

Somehow, I think and hope that the publicity and the support of people like Anne stopped that from happening. But Cambridgeshire Police was, in my view, acting like a rogue police force. Later, I heard there were direct government moves to bring them into line. I was told that they were criticized for not drawing up the required policies for dealing with homeless drug users and people on the streets. Of course, they were far too busy prosecuting the Cambridge Two to bother with any of that.

six

Cigarettes are my only comfort in prison. As soon as I wake I get my first one on and the effect of it envelops me, like getting drunk, or getting a hit: nicotine. It does not last long, but it is the first measure of the day. After that, I have to space my smokes out, because there is a limit to how much tobacco I can afford and because my chest is getting tight and sore. I know that smoking is damaging me but that gives me a certain peculiar satisfaction, as if I deserve the damage. Or perhaps it is a way of showing how damaged I feel inside.

The next fag is after my breakfast cereal, before I go to art. Then one in the mid-morning loo break, one before lunch, one after lunch, one while waiting at gardens to get started, one halfway through the afternoon, sitting on the ground or leaning on my spade, and so it goes on, ten or twelve a day. Except when I run out. I can afford to buy two half-ounce packets a week and would manage fine on that if people were not on the scrounge all the while. When I go to art or gardens I take just a small amount with me, but even so I still get begged for a puff, for twosies, for a fag paper, or a light. It is constant. But I oblige when I can, knowing how desperate things feel. In here, we have so little.

Nothing else comforts like the fags. The rest is routine, what has to be done in order to survive: eating, drinking, showering, laundry;

keeping fit in the gym and with the walking; doing the art and gardening to get time off the unit and to keep the prison staff off my back. My real work is writing: the letters and the articles. Art and gardening are leisure activities.

'It's what I would do at the weekends, after a fifty-hour week,' I tell the screws. Anything to embarrass them about this pathetic regime that they are running.

My evening phone calls home and the family visits also feel like a necessity, though many prisoners have to manage without them. The contact is a comfort, but it burns my heart too. When the feelings get too much, I turn to my Walkman, play angry loud music to sear at the emotion or something plaintive to connect with the other side of it. But it is the fags that give me constant comfort, taking in the smoke to get instant relief. Tobacco is currency in prison. People pay for drugs with it. I use it to measure out the time, to get through the day.

Suck, smoke and choke. It feels like all I deserve.

□ □ □

When I first hit prison, I could not concentrate on anything: reading, writing, watching TV. My head would not settle. I knew it was the trauma. As time went by, writing became easier, particularly writing letters. It felt good to get things out on paper. Reading was a continually frustrating problem, as for once in my life I had all the time I wanted to sink my head into books. Things improved after three or four months, and I began to devour any decent novels I could get my hands on. I could not manage anything too heavy.

The TV was mostly rubbish. Sometimes the women would watch horrendously violent movies, and for some reason that was what I began to like best. But if the unit gate was open, I would spend the evening TV time walking the compound, round and round as fast as I could go, the manic walker, using up my surplus energy, trying to block out the stress.

At Highpoint I also developed that slow prison walk, to maximize my time outside the unit when walking to art or healthcare. It was linked to a demeanour of being closed off inside myself, while being constantly, if surreptitiously, alert to what was going on around me. I saw other women using the slow walk too. It was protective, if not particularly comfortable. I never felt properly relaxed in prison; the constant tension undoubtedly caused the searing headaches I got every two or three weeks. But this air of insularity, disinterest and unconcern was the way I found to maintain myself and feel safe. In prison you had to be on your guard all the time.

Alongside this, we all had to cope with the waves of sadness that came upon us, often when we least expected it. I imagined that there was a spirit of despair inhabiting the prison and that it moved indiscriminately from inmate to inmate, so you never knew where it was going to descend next. When it was my turn I could feel it knitting my brows, churning my stomach, pulling every part of my body into itself. All I could do was endure, and await its departure. I fought it in the gym and worked furiously in the gardens, but this demon spirit made its own choices about when to move on.

□ □ □

We were always locked up for the night by 8.45 p.m., sometimes much earlier. Not long after I came to Highpoint, the staff stopped doing their 11 p.m. roll-checks, which meant that we were chucked behind our spurs and left till the morning. Though I exhibited the prisoners' common 'don't care' demeanour, I never felt 100 per cent safe. Each spur had a call button and every couple of evenings an inmate would press one of them. More often than not it was a false alarm, someone fooling around or wanting a bit of attention. You could get nicked if you were caught doing this and sent to face an adjudication the following day, but all of us felt neglected in this dreadful place. Occasionally there were fights, which was hardly surprising in these conditions. Thankfully, I never got caught up in one, but I heard about them, and sometimes heard or saw something from a distance.

One evening, just before I settled down to try to sleep, I allowed myself to remember my daughter in a way that I usually suppressed: remembering and feeling all the love that I had for her, every bit. A huge chasm grew inside me, dark and raw, and my throat constricted as I felt enveloped by the sadness. This was what was inside of me when I permitted myself to touch it. This was what I was holding on to as I went through the days, chatting and joking alongside the other women as best I could. This was why I had to hold myself tight, in order to avoid being overwhelmed by feelings that we all had in here. I could see it in the hard set of the women's faces when you caught them unawares, the hint of anguish seeping through each mask of indifference. I saw it with Pearl: the way she would sometimes drift away from me when we were talking. Then I knew not to disturb, not to speak, to wait for it to pass.

Diana had her moods too.

'Just don't say anything when I go quiet,' she insisted. We all ached for our kids in here. The loss of the life you once believed was your own was hugely painful, but the loss of your children was the worst pain of all. I could hardly bear to watch them on visits, racing up to mum as soon as they saw her and then becoming desperate when it was time to leave. Some of the women chose not to see their children at all, because of the heartbreak it caused. Others didn't have that choice, banged up so many miles from home that their kids could not ever make it over.

As ever, Bernice had plenty of advice for me. 'If you think about it, about your life outside, about the time you have to do, it'll do your head in,' she said. 'Forget about the outside. Don't think, don't think at all. That's what it's about.' She found her own advice hard to follow. Her little boy, aged just two, lived with Bernice's mother and she was having problems with her 'baby father' – a common expression among the black women in the prison. The baby father was being difficult about handing over the child-benefit book, was cashing it in for himself, and Bernice was consumed with worry. I offered her my sympathy, unable to imagine the agony I would have felt if I had been imprisoned when my kids were young. Those attachments are as crucial to life as breathing, and such separation can do deep and irreparable damage to a child, quite apart from the effect on the woman herself. The barbarism of imprisoning young mothers was such a thoughtless, primitive vengeance that I felt ashamed to have been blind to it for so long. As a society, we ought to know better.

□ □ □

During my first few weeks in prison the days passed excruciatingly slowly, but then time seemed to find a pace of its own: the individual hours were long but the weeks went by fast. I wondered whether this was because prison was such an empty, routine existence: there was so little stimulation, so little going on; just drudgery, boredom and restriction; nothing of note to fill the days.

In the mornings, I always woke early, my head full of dreams about trying to speak and no one hearing me, about being excluded while everyone else was preoccupied with having their own good time. Usually my very first thought on waking was: 'Shit, another day in this place.'

One morning I woke with a new thought: 'I would rather have been publicly flogged than endure this.' The hurt inside me was tangible, and it was going on for so long. I feared the psychological damage it was doing.

'Prison: a very British form of slow torture.' That was my second thought. And my third was about the prison service's 'Statement of Purpose': 'looking after people with humanity'. Pure Orwellian double-speak as far as we inmates were concerned. Humanity? They had to be kidding. The system itself was inhumane.

I was in with Viv, who was still sleeping like a child, but I heard sounds from the room opposite and went to tell June and Glenda about my preference for a flogging.

'Anything but this,' June sniffed. 'It's not just the prison, it's what goes on before as well: the months of waiting, then the trial, and then getting banged up. It's all pure torture.'

The night before she had tuned into BBC Radio Cambridgeshire and had called me over. The presenter was discussing my case on a phone-in. One guy rang in to say, in all seriousness, that he reckoned John and I should be thrown into a pit, our arms and legs tied up, and left to rot. Perhaps that had brought up the thoughts about torture.

Slowly, inexorably, the days were piling up, adding to the agony, infiltrating my bones. Even if I got out on parole I would be on licence, still in the grip of the punishment system. And when that grip loosened, how would I know what to do, and what to be? A part of my life, of my person, would have been destroyed forever. I rolled an extra fag and waited to get unlocked.

□ □ □

As time went by, I gradually acclimatized to prison life. I became institutionalized. After about three months, I hit a relatively good patch, felt quite steady and reckoned I could manage things, though I still permanently yearned to be at home, and little things would unexpectedly cut through my defences. In prison your mood can change abruptly and you never knew when it was going to hit you. Nevertheless, I discovered I could enjoy gardens for what it was, I endured art, had learnt how to get through the lock-ups, and kept up the gym and the letter writing.

It was a good feeling: of being more in control and able to cope with prison privations. I kept pretty much to myself. I still chatted to people but was no longer anxious to be part of the crowd, to fit in. My accent was more or less back to normal and I felt I could be me. I did not have to hide who I was. This gave me a reassuring sense of internal freedom, strangely paradoxical when I was locked away.

While on my plateau, couched in relative equilibrium, my general moods inevitably remained low. I woke with the sadness and went to sleep with the sadness. In between was the tedium of virtually identical days without stimulation, without any real pleasure or enjoyment. My life had been caged. It felt like an endurance test, but I got to know that when the deep depressions came, as they inevitably did, they also passed. The prison's spirit of despair always moved on.

Not everyone could hold on to that certainty. When I was on a different spur, Viv, my mischievous young friend, cut her wrists. Even she found prison life too much to bear. When she got back from healthcare, I managed to corner her.

'I meant it, Ruth,' she said.

'Why didn't you talk to someone if you felt so bad?' I asked. Viv knew all about cutting up. When she was in Holloway her cellmate had done it late one night, and by the time the screws arrived young Viv had watched the woman bleed to death.

The self-harmers seemed unpopular with most of the officers at Highpoint, who just did not know how to cope with them. At lunch one day a screw came up to someone sitting at my table, a large, over-weight woman who had scars all over her arms from cutting herself. One of her arms was bandaged; she must have been at it again.

'Don't you ever do that again when I'm on duty,' shouted the screw, thrusting his face right up to hers. The woman carried on eating her meal, apparently unperturbed. I was pretty shocked. When the screw had gone she looked up and gave me a jolly smile, the smile she always had for the outside world.

'All right?' she asked.

'Yeah, are you?'

'Oh, yes, you know . . .' Later in the day she was taken off the unit and admitted to the prison hospital.

□ □ □

So there I was: locked away, a menace to society. I needed to be taught a lesson, this woman who dared to care for the feckless homeless. What a disgrace! Walking the compound, I watched a screw come out and stand by the gate, giving off an air of arrogant importance in his black-and-white uniform. Stuffed penguins, the lot of them. But by now I had regained some of my power, could stay pretty balanced amid this abuse, this unholy repression. It was getting to feel increasingly ludicrous, being banged up in here. Completely mad. I supposed these thoughts were coming up because I was not afraid of prison anymore. They had done their worst and I had survived. So had my family. It had been hard, still was hard, but we knew that we could get through it. That was my triumph. That was the triumph for all of us. We became strong. And thus prison defeated its purpose.

□ □ □

Rumours were circulating about my writing. While I was out on gardens, someone I did not know, but who had recently moved on to Skid Row, passed me and hissed: 'Written any more books, then?' Later, back on the unit, I began to see what had been going on. One of the governors wanted to see me. Red in the face and his belly hugely distended from too many rich dinners, he was exaggeratedly friendly.

'Take a seat,' he said, after he had got me into the screws' back office. 'Do you mind if I smoke?' The man lit an ostentatious cigar. His politeness was unexpected, a rare commodity in prison, and it caught me off guard. He told me there had been nine complaints from the unit about my writing, that people were afraid I was writing about them and that my safety was a concern for the prison. I explained that I was writing about homelessness and, at his request, brought the material to show him. He asked to borrow it to read over the weekend, promising to return it to me on the Monday. I knew I could not refuse him and, because I supposed he probably knew, admitted that I also kept a personal journal. That was a mistake.

'Well,' said the governor, 'I'll take this stuff now, but it also may be necessary to see the journal. As it's personal, we'll get a female officer to look at it, with you there with her all the while.'

He did not keep to his word. He tricked me. I should have known he would. My writing was not returned after the weekend, and a few days later, during one of the lock-ups, a senior female officer came bustling on to the spur and dramatically seized my journal. That was kept too. I wrote to Lord Avebury about it, as he had had some interest in my situation, and he spoke to a governor who pompously told him that prison was not a private place and that 'we need to satisfy ourselves that what she is doing is appropriate'.

I racked my brains for anything in the journal that could incriminate other inmates but reckoned I had been careful enough. In true prisoner style, I put in complaint after complaint but was fobbed off each time. They said they were seeking advice from the Prisoners Administration Group to see if any of the writing violated Prison Service Standing Orders. I had no idea what they were referring to. One week, two weeks, three weeks; would I ever get it back? Someone on the unit must have stirred this up for me. On gardens I heard that the prison was awash with rumours about what was coming off my typewriter.

Without the writing I felt utterly bereft. My anger turned inwards, creating an empty depression. It was a torment to think of prison officers going over the pages that contained my innermost thoughts. I took to going to gardens in the mornings as well as the afternoons, could not do art or write anything anymore, could not think, just let the days slide, feeling constantly tired and worn down. My self-containment deepened into a kind of dissociation. I inhabited a world apart, a world that felt safe but disconnected and vaguely unreal. This was what they wanted: to break me down; and I did not much care if that was what they got.

One lock-up, sitting in the room on my own, I got a mental picture of my father and my brother, Rickie. Though in reality they were dead, there they both were: I could feel their presence; they were standing in the doorway and smiling. Dad put a cheery arm around Rickie's shoulders. I thought to myself: 'They're OK, together now and out of all this.'

They seemed to want to give me support, as they would have done had they been alive. My father said the words he always said to me on parting: 'Look after yourself.' I promised him that I would – my father, who gave me his strength, conferred it on me through his warmth and through the generosity of his being. And my brother, who I had missed so much of, who never connected with this world. Rickie was my reason for working in homelessness. Suffering from similar problems to many of my homeless clients, he had eventually taken his own life. His loss was my loss. Now he gave me his unused masculine power, to protect me in this masculine environment, imbued with its masculine hierarchies.

With them inside of me, I felt that I could not be destroyed, however hard the prison tried. I had my place, as the lowest of the low, but knew I was not that. I remained myself and would express my being thus, and thus; always so. I would refuse to submit. I would survive.

Having done its work, my vision disappeared.

□ □ □

Looking back, many months later, I could see that I went through the three well-documented phases of separation and loss: protest; despair; and detachment. The protest was exhibited by my tears; the despair by my deepest depressions; and then the detachment was the equilibrium I found, that made me feel that I had beaten prison, that I had won. These were all common feelings among inmates.

'I can do it standing on my head,' was a phrase used frequently by the other women. I got to know what they meant and why they said it. I liked to say it too.

All of which made me wonder what the point was. Prison was punishment, that was for sure, but the main thing we inmates learnt from it was how to cope with the incarceration, how to work the system, and how to stop it hurting too much. The best way of doing that was to cut yourself off from your feelings, to become hard and brutalized – surely the opposite of what would have been helpful in terms of socializing and rehabilitating inmates. Prison, as I experienced it, was making people feel even more alienated than they had before.

□ □ □

Maintaining your physical health in prison is always difficult. The headaches are my biggest problem and it takes two 400mg doses of Ibuprofen over four hours to make the slightest impact on them. One afternoon I feel one coming on and join the crush at medication, amid the usual hassle of people trying to get extra doses. It is strange at healthcare, always crowded out with the drug addicts, who are prescribed various medicines but not the stuff they so desperately desire. Lots of us, drug addicts or otherwise, are on anti-depressants, tranquillizers, sleeping pills. Prison messes you up and then doles out drugs to reduce the symptoms it has caused.

My turn comes and I ask at the hatch for the Ibuprofen.

'Did you put your name down for special sick this morning?' demands the nurse.

'No, I didn't have the headache this morning.'

'You can't get anything unless you're down for special sick.'

'What can I do, then?'

'Remember to put down for special sick next time.'

'But I don't know when a headache is coming on. I can't predict it.'

'You can't have anything without being down for special sick. That's the rules; I don't make them, but that's how it is.'

'Bloody stupid rules,' I snap, and storm off.

Before we walk back Bernice sidles up to me. She has witnessed my fury.

'I have painkillers,' she says. 'I'll bring them to you.' True to her word, Bernice comes to my room as soon as we are back on the unit and thrusts a bag of pink tablets into my fist. There they are: Ibuprofen, thirteen 400mg tablets – that is double strength. What a haul. I take one straight away, and one later on in the evening, and by the time I get ready for bed the headache is much eased. Cursing healthcare, I put all the other tablets away in my locker; I could get nicked for having them but will take the risk. If those nurses were more helpful, I would not have to, and I resolve to find ways to keep my supply going for the future.

Healthcare is a constant battle for everyone. One of the nurses gets called Nurse No-No because she seems to take particular delight in turning down our requests. I am there another day and see the gardening crew on the other side of the fence. Franny races up to me, her wild curly hair framing the desperation on her face.

'They wouldn't give me anything for my toothache,' she tells me. Her hands press against the fence, and I touch them; she is starting to cry.

'The nurse held out two Ibuprofen in her hand and said I wasn't going to get any because I'd made a fuss,' she weeps. 'But I didn't make a fuss, I just hustled them 'cos I needed something bad.'

'That's cruel,' I say. 'She shouldn't have done that. I'll give you some painkillers when we get back to the unit.' Pete calls Franny away from the fence and she goes back to work.

Waiting inside healthcare, I am hassled by an Irish woman, who talks so fast I can hardly understand her. She is telling me about some fight she got into, graphically swinging her arms to demonstrate. I agree with her, whatever she is going on about, alarmed at the way she throws herself about, getting worked up. Later on, I find out that she is constantly in and out of the block for fighting. She has bad, painful teeth too, and I commiserate. Getting to see the dentist is a real problem in this prison. I have a couple of fairly drastic holes that need filling and put in my application months ago. Thankfully, the holes don't hurt me too much, but they are getting larger the longer I wait. An appointment eventually comes through for me after six months. I am examined and told I need £2000 worth of treatment. When I get out, and back to the real world, I have the work done for £500.

□ □ □

One of my greatest fears in prison is of contracting hepatitis C. Many of the addicts have it. The condition is ultimately terminal and there is no cure. There is some useful treatment that will slow down the progression of the virus, but you cannot get it while you are in prison, which is scandalous. I try to protect myself against getting infected but sometimes catch myself slipping up, like with the nailbrush at gardens. At the end of each session, we clean the muck off our hands in the washroom. After I have used the communal nailbrush a few times, I realize that I am putting myself at risk. A small risk, but a risk nonetheless. Then there is hepatitis B, also incurable once you contract it, and HIV, and countless other infections.

Some of the women get enormously anxious about what they could pick up from their fellow inmates, about the rough-and-ready hygiene of the prison. Here at Highpoint we share the toilets and the showers, and the wing-cleaners are not particularly motivated to do a good job. Every so often I get disinfectant from the office and use it to give the toilet seats an extra wipe over, but it is little more than a gesture. Many of the toilets do not have seats at all, or they are half hanging off. The locks on the doors are often broken and the sanitary disposal units regularly overflow with their stinking contents. As for the showers, you cannot help wondering who has been in there before you.

As time goes by, I see a lot of new faces. Highpoint starts to take remand prisoners, which means a higher turnover of inmates. They are always very wound up, these remands, consumed with uncertainty, not knowing when they will get to court or whether they will get a custodial sentence if found guilty. Some of them stew for months on end, and if they get acquitted there is no recompense, no compensation for being wrongfully imprisoned.

'Sorry, ladies.' A screw has poked her head round the door at healthcare. 'I'm gonna have to lock you in.'

Everyone groans. It is claustrophobic, being shut in a small, windowless room with twenty-odd other people. This usually happens when they're moving Myra Hindley, our infamous 'Moors Murderer' prisoner. They are worried that another prisoner might attack her. Child killers are constantly at risk in jail, though I have met inmates who are sympathetic to Myra's cause. Today she is coming back from hospital. Myra is unwell, which is not surprising. At Highpoint she has her own room in the healthcare block and is allowed no contact with the rest of us. The effect of living like that, over such a long period of time, is unimaginable.

□ □ □

Hester has arrived on Skid Row. I catch her unashamedly shaving her face in the washroom.

'Morning, Ruth,' she says cheerfully, scraping the razor around her jowls. I remember June telling me about Hester: how she was butch but not butch at the same time. Hester has been in healthcare since losing her baby and now she tells me a bit about it, about her upset. Despite being in labour, she was chained when she left the prison to go to the hospital outside, and the chains stayed on throughout her giving birth.

The way this works is that you have one end of the chain attached to your wrist and the other end attached to a screw. It is quite long, so that you can be treated while the screw is not in the same room, but the experience is nevertheless acutely shaming. It is ridiculous that Hester was chained while giving birth to her dead baby. Did they really think she could do a runner? I thought this practice of shackling had been outlawed for women prisoners, but clearly I was wrong. Various people have told me how terribly embarrassed they feel, walking through the hospital and hanging around in the waiting areas chained to a screw, with ordinary members of the public staring at you.

Tanya has been brought over to Kainos because she was being bullied in the main prison. Skinny as a rake, she is in for a minor fraud. She comes to talk and I hear how she had to go to the hospital to have pre-cancerous cells removed with laser treatment.

'I had the chains on all the while,' she says. 'It was so embarrassing. The screws were standing next to me during my consultation with the doctor, and throughout the laser treatment they were right outside the curtain. Me lying there with my feet in the stirrups. I don't know how in heaven's name they expected me to escape.'

That day I have my own problems, having pulled a muscle badly in the gym. To get off gardens I need to go to healthcare in the morning. I hobble over there and the nurse responds as if I am a total shitbag, just out for a skive; as if by being in prison I have lost the right to decent treatment.

'I'll give you one day's rest in cell, no more,' she says tartly. I hobble back and spend the morning catching up on my post. After lunchtime lock-up I ask my cellmate to get my paper from the office. The screws refuse to give it to her.

'Mr Jones told me that just because you're on rest in cell, it doesn't mean you can stay in bed all day,' she says. I painfully limp to the office to get the paper and wonder why these screws feel they have to take every opportunity to demean us.

'I haven't actually been in bed all day, if you want to know,' I tartly inform Jones.

Those bastards. The screws are always 'those bastards'; that way, I do not sink into being what they want: compliant, accepting of this abuse, depressed and downtrodden. I will fight them all the way.

□ □ □

Bernice tells me which officers to be wary of.

'Watch the female ones,' she says. 'They are the worst.' I wonder whether it is not the other way round: that the men enjoy dominating us, having such power over women. Bernice persists.

'The women are sneaky,' she says. 'And they have their favourites.' It is pretty obvious that I am not Miss Turney's favourite. One afternoon, when we get unlocked, I discover that gardening has been cancelled yet again, and so has gym. I have been shut inside for days with all these cancellations, and it is so bright and clear outside. Turney is on duty and I complain vociferously.

'Regulations state that I should get one hour of exercise daily,' I say, but I get the usual answer.

'Fill out a request/complaint form in the morning.'

I storm off to my room to get the Walkman. Time for some loud music. With it blasting in my ears I wander through the unit, ostensibly seeking inspiration for another prison drawing for the art class. I have taken to drawing prison views. Turney stops me and says that they need some help with the bins today – one of the women is sick. If I want to go outside, I can do it. She is laughing her wicked laugh at me, but I do not care.

'I'll go,' I say. At least I will get a bit of the sun.

I work with a large Jamaican woman and we go around with wheelie bins, collecting the rubbish sacks from the three units and the education block. We also do some 'wombling' – picking up litter from the ground with our special hand-held litter-pickers. I find an orange in some long grass. It looks OK and goes into my pocket. I eat it when I get back to the unit.

'Did you enjoy doing the rubbish?' Turney asks when she sees me, not bothering to conceal an evil grin. She seems to get a lot of satisfaction from seeing a middle-class professional woman doing a low-grade job. Well, it's her hang-up. I tell her that indeed I did enjoy it. I could not care less that she is amused.

□ □ □

My inept drawings of the prison raise some anxieties, especially for the screws working in security. I reckon Turney set them off. While nosing around the art room, she showed particular interest in a drawing that she saw me working on of the inside of House 1. A day or so later, two screws from security pay me a visit. They sit me down in an interview room. It feels threatening.

'We hear you've been drawing pictures of the prison in art,' says one.

'This could be a security risk,' says the other. 'Might be part of an escape plan.'

I reckon these two have been watching too many adventure movies, but, endeavouring to appear unmoved, I tell them about the pictures I have done and say they are in the art room.

'Well, we'd better go and see them,' says the first screw. At the art room they 'hum' and 'hah' for a while, and then agree that the drawings are inoffensive enough. I am instructed to keep them in the art room in case they get into the 'wrong hands'.

I cannot see what harm could come from my clumsy sketches, but I comply. The next day I tell the art tutor what has happened. He is equally unimpressed. 'All you're doing is using the drawing to try to come to terms with the environment here,' he says.

□ □ □

No doubt years of running appalling prison regimes have contributed to Turney's cynicism and general demeanour, but not all the female screws are as bad. Miss Croft, relatively new to the trade, is a tall, handsome and well-meaning woman, with a stated intention of doing some good. I see her in the compound, sitting on the bench and chatting to some of the prisoners: Hester, little Naomi, Allie and Mary; the most vulnerable women, all being hurt further by their incarceration. One day Croft comes to join us during the morning fag break in the art-room loo to regale us with tales of her life before she joined the prison service. I feel she genuinely wants to help, to be a friend, which some of the women appreciate, but none of us can trust it totally. The system sets her apart.

I cross her once, when she is sitting in on the community meeting and doing her best to maintain order during a particularly heated discussion. Throughout she refers to us women as 'girls', and I complain about it. She snaps back at me. After the meeting is over, I say to her: 'Can we have a word?' She follows me to my room, where I sit her down and explain how offensive I find it to be called girls.

'We're all grown women, you know,' I say.

'I don't mean to offend,' she says, and adds: 'I feel you're always out to have a pop at me.' Which is perhaps what a lot of the screws feel, as I am more articulate than most. Croft is the one who tells me that before I came to Kainos the meetings were often very rowdy, that they even had one or two fights. It helps me to understand the screws' anxieties about allowing open discussion. I try to make amends.

'I think you're a really good officer,' I tell her, somewhat embarrassed, though she seems to find it reassuring. It feels like talking to one of my own staff.

□ □ □

The inmates do not always side against the screws, as Nancy finds out when she puts in one of her famous complaints, this time accusing Miss Stratford and Miss Croft of touching her up. The response on the unit is complete outrage.

'We all know Stratford and Croft are lesbians,' says Glenda, 'but just look at Nancy. She's the last person they'd go for. This sort of thing can ruin people's careers.'

Nancy is taken to the block and the officers are sent off the unit. All three of them are back the next day. A senior officer speaks to us over lunch, saying that Nancy is returning and that he wants no 'funny business'. The only funny business comes from Nancy. She hides in her room, refusing food and her medication. We call an emergency spur meeting and people tell Nancy what they think of her. Then, having got their feelings out in the open, they put up with her again.

'A bit cracked, that one,' Bernice comments.

□ □ □

The worst male screws are the ones who are not regularly on the unit. I dislike Mr Cockburn on sight. He is a stout, ruddy-faced man who likes to appear tough. One evening, either out of boredom or devilment, he decides with a compatriot to check all the rooms on our unit. I have my two pillows on my bed. Cockburn takes one.

'Two aren't allowed,' he says.

Other women lose pillows too, and their extra mirrors. We have little ones, only 6 inches square, and people like to tie them together so they can get a better view of themselves. Yvonne loses hers.

I find Mr Jones and tell him about my pillow. Jones is clearly annoyed at the way his colleague has infiltrated himself and his way of doing things on to his unit, but Cockburn is operating entirely within prison regulations.

'Come and see me later,' Jones says. After Cockburn and his mate have gone is what he means. I do so and he gives me my extra pillow back. Viv is impressed and tries it too, but Jones tells her to fuck off. She must be out of favour. The screws can use their power indiscriminately.

Mr C. is next to visit, coming over from House 3. It is Sunday morning and, with the better weather, we are allowed outside in the compound for an hour. For some reason, Mr C. decides to get us in earlier than usual. I try to finish walking the lap I am on; it will only take twenty seconds.

'Get in, Wyner!' he shouts, as if he is calling a dog. As usual, I have to take it. I thank my stars that I managed to get off House 3 and away from him.

From time to time we get officers over from the male side of the prison. They tend to look uneasy and some of them are unbearably arrogant. Maybe they find working with women prisoners discomforting. Too bad; life in prison is a whole lot more uncomfortable for me. One day, when I nip up to the office to pick up my *Guardian* newspaper, I meet a young screw from the men's side who I have not seen before. I ask for the paper.

'What's your name?' he demands.

'Ruth Wyner.'

'Right then, inmate Wyner, what paper do you have?'

'I have the *Guardian*, and it's Ms Wyner. Ruth if you'd prefer.' I have never been called inmate Wyner before and I am aware of a memo that went out to prison staff months ago, telling them to address female prisoners by their first names, or to use 'Miss' or 'Ms'.

'You're inmate Wyner to me,' this one replies, adding: 'The *Guardian*, eh? Very posh.' I often get teased in the office about my paper. The young screw looks in the desk drawer.

'It's not in. Are you sure you don't want to read this instead, inmate Wyner?' He holds up a copy of yesterday's *Star*.

'When are the papers coming over?' I ask, trying to avoid telling this guy to fuck off. It could get me put on report and disciplined. Punishment can include days in the block, days on your sentence, or a fine, but it would surely just be a fine for a 'fuck off'. Mr Stevenson puts his head round the door of the back office.

'Ruth: I'll send someone over for the papers once roll's correct,' he says.

'Thanks,' I reply, and walk out on the idiot kid.

□ □ □

Stevenson is my favourite screw. He is an open-hearted man, expansive in personality as well as in girth, and most of the time he does not patronize me, which makes it easier to talk to him. I tell him of my worries about doing the Kainos Journey, my disappointment with the co-ordinators and my annoyance at the evangelism. He sympathizes but advises me to stick with it, reminding me that the rest of the prison is worse.

Sometimes we discuss prison policy. We both enjoy the sport. I point out the deficiencies of the place, and he puts on his hard-man act. One evening, I show him an article from the *Big Issue*, which is being sent to me every week. The article is about Britain's biggest independent survey of our jails in a decade. Two-thirds of the prisoners surveyed said jail did not work. One-third had no home to go to on release. Over half said being jailed had ruined their personal relationships. Three out of five were not getting any education or training while inside. One in ten claimed to have tried drugs for the first time in prison.

Stevenson is on shift with Miss Stratford, so I am aware he will be wanting to make a good impression. The screws are often different when you get them on their own.

'It's that crucial first two weeks in prison,' says Stevenson. 'If we could somehow bottle that experience and give it to people throughout their sentence, I bet prisons would work then.' Stratford laughs.

'That would be inhumane,' I say, remembering the trauma of my first fortnight. 'People would be completely destroyed.' Eventually, Stevenson backs off.

'I suppose what we really need is proper rehabilitation.'

'We get little more than four hours' work a day here,' I say. 'That is, when work isn't cancelled or we're not on extra lock-up.' Stevenson can only shrug and accept my frustration. What can either of us do?

□ □ □

For all his good-heartedness, Stevenson is still a screw and has to stick to the system like the others. This is made clear to me over the Sparks incident. Sparks is a cocky white woman with an addict's bad skin and close-cropped bleached hair. She sees herself as hard and is always attended by other young white women: her gang. One night the alarm rings from Sparks's spur and we can see a bit of what is going on from June's window.

'They're fighting,' says Diana. The screws step in and Sparks is escorted off the unit along with Hope, a young woman of Indian descent.

'Going to the block,' Diana informs us. The next morning they are marched back, except for Hope, who is taken on to House 2 instead.

'What they doing that for?' Bernice complains. 'That Sparks is coming back and she's the real troublemaker. If anyone should go off the unit it's her.'

Over the next few days, Sparks becomes increasingly annoying, strutting around the unit, surrounded by her lieutenants. She seems even more arrogant since the fight and everyone wants to knock her off her perch. I hear various mutterings. Bernice saw Hope at the gym and says that she has scratches on her neck and bruising where she was kicked in the back, and that Sparks had called her a black bastard. Things continue to brew. Perhaps it is my night-shelter training: you develop an instinct for this kind of thing. But the screws seem blissfully unaware. After tea I start to get panicky, know there is going to be a fight and do not want my friends to get involved, do not want them sent to the block. I can hardly contain my anxiety and hover around the office uncertainly, wondering what to do. Surely the screws will pick it up. You can almost touch the violence in the air.

Stevenson pops his head round the office door: 'All right, Ruth?'

'Yes,' I say, and then follow him back into the office.

'You do realize that things are about to blow?' I tell him, under my breath so that no one will hear.

'What?' Stevenson starts to rise from his chair. Perhaps I have been too dramatic.

'It'll not be sorted unless you get Sparks off the house,' I add and then get out of the office fast, feeling extremely uncomfortable.

Stevenson takes a look out of the office, but right then it starts: there is yelling and screaming from the TV room and the screws make a dash for it. Bernice and some others have fronted Sparks and her sidekicks. The screws take people off to the office: Sparks and Bernice and a few others. I feel sickened: I am a grass.

Half an hour later, I am called into the office. One of the screws from reception has come over with things that have been sent in for me: a couple of books, pads of paper, envelopes and, from my daughter, some slippers. I have been waiting for this stuff for ages. We usually wait weeks, sometimes months, for our parcels to get through. This drop is a special delivery, just for me. I am disgusted. The screws are inducting me into their system: rat on your fellows and we will make it worth your while. I resolve never to tell them anything again. Stevenson is not that different after all.

□ □ □

Mr Scott is a screw we see now and again. A short, slight man, he is usually pretty sarcastic and tends to treat us women with haughty disdain. Today his mood is worse than ever. I catch him in the office on my way in from gardens and ask for my *Guardian*.

'Here's your fucking paper,' he snarls. As ever, I ignore the offence and wander back to the room, to change and shower and overcome my weariness. We have had a particularly heavy session this afternoon.

At supper, Scott is at the servery.

'I only want just one of those,' I say, eyeing a tray of greasy fishcakes.

'You'll take what you're fucking given.' Scott throws two fishcakes on to my plate and looks pleased with himself. I am furious. This man keeps swearing in my face and I cannot swear back, for fear of getting nicked.

Half an hour later he is in the office giving out the post. I go to collect mine and ask to have a word.

'What about?'

'About the way you keep swearing at me. We've spoken twice today and each time I've got fucking this or that from you. I thought we were supposed to be treated with respect in here.'

'Put in a request/complaint in the morning,' Scott says, studiously avoiding looking at me.

'I don't want to make a request/complaint. I want to do this one-to-one.'

'Can't you see I'm busy? Come back later.'

I do so, but am disappointed that Scott wants to talk in the main office, with two other screws around. He will show off to them. Scott invites me to begin.

'Well?'

'Each time you've spoken to me today you've sworn at me. When I came to this prison I was told we'd be treated with respect, but swearing at me isn't treating me with respect. Quite the opposite.'

'When I swear, I'm not swearing at you,' Scott says. 'I'm just swearing.'

'When you swear, it makes me feel bad.'

'Your feelings are your affair.' Scott flashes a look at his fellow screws, who are looking amused. So much for the prison's 'duty of care' and all that. I try a different tack.

'When you swear, I want to swear back at you. Now, I don't swear like that on the outside, so what good is this doing me?'

'This is prison,' he says. 'When I started here I didn't swear either.'

'The other day, I got a knock-back and said, "Fucking hell," and I was told by the officer in here not to swear.'

'People do things in different ways.'

'That's very confusing.'

'Prison is confusing. There's no logic to prison.' I give up.

In the morning I go early to get my milk from the stores. Scott is there.

'Fuck fuck fuck,' we go in unison, and we both have to laugh.

'Here's your fucking milk,' he says.

'I want some fucking washing-up liquid as well,' I say, somewhat pleased that our chat has stayed with him as well as with me.

A couple of weeks later, I go to the office to drop off a tape I want to send out, and see Scott looking cheerful for once. It is his last day here. He is moving over to the men's side and is looking forward to it.

'You know where you are in men's prisons,' he says, adding: 'Guess what? You stopped me swearing. I haven't sworn in here since our conversation. There now, you've done some good while you've been here.'

I do not trust him an inch, do not believe a word of it, and go off muttering: 'Patronizing bastard.' The power differential makes trust, and genuine communication, almost impossible.

□ □ □

Highpoint seems to have a staffing problem. We are constantly being given extra lock-up and usually we are told it is because they are short-staffed. Not surprising, really. Who in their right mind would want to work here? The conditions are dreadful and the system the staff have to run is downright heartbreaking, though some of them inevitably get a certain sadistic pleasure from doing it.

As time goes by and the screws get to know me better, they seem less anxious to assert their authority over me. I suppose they initially felt they had to show me who was boss, to make sure that I would toe the line. I was, after all, used to running organizations for clients who were not that dissimilar to my fellow inmates, and I had managed my own staff teams. 'It's a bit like running a night shelter,' I tell a young screw who is trying to arrange who sleeps where.

The way the screws work to defend themselves from the emotion around them also reminds me of my shelter work. They have to contain the fury, the anguish and the despair felt by the women they are incarcerating. Working for the homeless, I had to do that too, but to a lesser extent. People were free to come and go, and I was providing much-needed services to the clientele. Here the screws are running a system that, if any of them stops to think about it, is mostly causing damage to those who are, in many cases, already deeply damaged by their difficult lives. If they allowed their feelings to get in the way, they would not be able to do the job.

Resources: it is always resources. Our overcrowded prisons are starved of them and the situation is bound to get worse as we continue to incarcerate increasing numbers of people. Some extra money is coming in for offender programmes and drug treatment, but usually at the expense of general funding for the provision of the regime. Hardly effective, giving people a bit of input to help them face their problems, only to grind them down again when they get back into the system and its destructive regimes.

□ □ □

When I was on House 3, I put my name down for Listeners training. Listeners are prison inmates who act as onsite Samaritans. The training sessions start after I have been inside for about three months. Eight of us gather in the chapel for the first one. It proves to be good medicine. The four people who come in, all members of the local Samaritans branch, treat us with respect, as if we are normal human beings, which is an enormous relief after the day-to-day responses we get from the screws. Being a Listener will offer us a chance to contribute, and to be valued for ourselves. Though one of my fellow trainees admits to me: 'I'm only doing it for my parole.'

The course lasts for seven weeks, after which we can get going with the work, listening to fellow inmates in distress. The Samaritans tell us the scheme has been running for three years at Highpoint and has had its problems, particularly over the issue of confidentiality, a strict rule and one that the screws do not like. They want to feel in total control.

'Does the confidentiality apply to everything?' I ask.

'Yes,' say our trainers. 'Are you worried about anything in particular?'

'Well, is it even for drugs?' I venture.

'Of course,' they reply. 'Confidentiality is an absolute rule for Listeners.'

The irony does not escape me. A central reason for my conviction and imprisonment was that I kept to our confidentiality policy at the day centre, refusing to give the police the names of homeless people involved in drugs when they asked for them. Much was made in court about my unwillingness to give the police these names. The judge had said we could not 'hide behind confidentiality'; now, doing the five-year sentence he so thoughtfully delivered, I am being instructed in its use.

□ □ □

There is more irony to come. Peter Bottomley MP has been tabling questions in the House of Commons, asking for information about drug supply in prisons. There has been quite a lot of discussion about the position of prison governors since my conviction. After all, everyone knows there are illegal drugs in prisons, heroin more often than not, and by the very nature of the situation these drugs must have been supplied on prison premises. Peter Bottomley sends me copies of his parliamentary questions, along with the answers given.

MR PETER BOTTOMLEY (Worthing West): To ask the Secretary of State for the Home Department, if he will estimate the proportion of prisoners known to have taken illegal drugs who could only have taken the drugs while in prison. (107931)

MR PAUL BOATENG: In 1999, 84,911 mandatory drug tests [piss tests to us] were undertaken, and some 17,789 of those tests were positive for drugs. This figure includes results from both random and targeted tests. Provisional information indicates that, during 1999, there were 15,857 recorded offences of 'unauthorised use of a controlled drug', of which 13,409 were recorded as being proven at adjudication and punished under Prison Rules.

That is over 20 per cent positive results on the piss tests. The prison service is not being very effective, and on a scale that dwarfs the Wintercomfort situation. At my trial, Judge Haworth said that if measures to stop drug supply failed, an establishment had to be closed. When I relate this to Janis, she says: 'I'm packing my bags right now.' An admirably logical response.

MR PETER BOTTOMLEY (Worthing West): To ask the Secretary of State for the Home Department, if any prison establishment has been closed because of illegal drug use. (107930)
MR PAUL BOATENG: No.

Answering an earlier question, Boateng states that in 1999, 823 visitors to prison were arrested attempting to bring drugs into prisons. Now that just does not square: only 823 arrests when there were 17,789 positive piss tests. Again, not very effective. John and I were told in court that our drugs policy had to be implemented effectively for us to stay on the right side of the law. During an evening lock-up, I pen a letter to Jack Straw, the Home Secretary.

Dear Jack Straw,

I write to report to you the fact that Class A and B drugs are being supplied at this prison, HMP Highpoint, where I am currently being held.

As director of a charity, the number one as it were, I was convicted for allowing drug supply of which I was not aware. I therefore feel it is my duty, to ensure the safety of the Home Secretary, to make you aware of this supply as you are, of course, the number one as regards the prison service. After all, I do not want to see you doing a five-year stretch as I am.

I was charged under Section 8 of the Misuse of Drugs Act. At court, my judge directed that we were guilty if we 'were unwilling to use any reasonable means that were readily available to prevent the prohibited activity'. Those reasonable means included, accorded to Judge Haworth, closure of the project. The failure to adopt such a measure if other measures to stop the activity had failed would, according to the judge's directions, indicate an unwillingness to use a 'reasonable' step and as such be evidence of permitting drug supply.

You may also wish to note that in questions to Paul Boateng in the House of Commons (nos. 164–167), Peter Bottomley MP *was informed that in 1999, there were 17,789 positive drugs tests in prisons and 13,409 proven cases of unauthorized use of a controlled drug in prisons. Over the same period, 823 visitors were arrested for bringing drugs into prisons.*

In our case, Wintercomfort banned some people for dealing or drug use at its day centre, but there was additional dealing which could only be caught on a police surveillance camera. We were said to 'know' because we discussed our drug problems at the project with, among others, the police. The similarities are striking: you have caught some dealers but not the overwhelming majority in the prisons.

Your methods are clearly ineffective. As you live under the same laws as I do, I believe you are liable to arrest. Or would you like me to perform a citizen's arrest on the governor here?

I look forward to your reply.
Yours sincerely,

Ruth Wyner

I laboriously write it out in neat longhand with copies for Peter Bottomley, Anne Campbell, Alexander and my solicitor, keeping it all under my hat as regards my fellow inmates. I am terrified of being labelled a grass through this. About three weeks later, I get a reply from a minion in the government's Drug Strategy Unit, asking me to become just that: to grass on my fellow inmates by telling prison staff what I know, or by ringing Crimestoppers. Well, here is someone who does not know his way around prisons. Imagine trying to phone Crimestoppers from the unit's payphones! You would be slaughtered on the spot.

I write back, but the first letter made the real point. In my innocence, I did not expect the difficulty it subsequently caused me.

□ □ □

I have completed my Listeners training, and this morning I am due to go with the five other trainees to the chapel to pick up my certificate. Governor number one is coming over to present them. But as soon as we are unlocked, Mr McCafferty, the lanky Irish screw, takes me into the office and through to the room at the back. He shuts the door.

'You're not to go to the chapel this morning,' he says. 'You must go straight to education.'

'But I'm due to get my Listeners certificate,' I say.

'The governor got a call from the Samaritans late last night,' he says. 'They won't have you because you mentioned the Listeners in the press.'

I am mystified, and go back to my room to search my cuttings but can find nothing there. I feel quite upset. I have a fag and go to tell June, who has been doing the Listeners training with me.

Bernice is in there too.

'Go to the chapel anyway,' she says. 'Say you're going to see the Sister. Then you can speak to the Samaritans when they arrive.'

I take Bernice's advice and sneak into the chapel when we are let out for work. The Sister has someone with her, so I sit and wait. Two minutes later, she pops her head round the door.

'Is Ruth Wyner here?' I get up slowly, playing for time.

'I'm sorry,' she says. 'The officers have rung to say you're to go straight to education.'

'They're not supposed to do that,' say my fellow prospective Listeners. 'Sister's not supposed to tell you where to go. Anyway, it's roll-check, no one's supposed to go anywhere during roll-check. That never happens. What's going on?'

I take my time, and as I go out of the door hear the Sister complain: 'I've never, ever had to ask someone to leave this chapel before.'

I walk slowly down the path to education and catch the Samaritans as they make their way up it. The main trainer stops and so does another woman, who is, I discover, director of the local Samaritans branch. She is smartly turned out, in her best.

'You mentioned the Listeners in the press,' she accuses, somewhat aggressively. 'You used it to advance your cause.'

I tell her I do not know what she is referring to and ask to see the press cutting that she has in her hand. It is from the *Cambridge Evening News*: a story about how I am being trained to be a Listener and to work with complete confidentiality; the reporter comments that in prison I am being trained in the practice that got me convicted in the first place. I wonder how the press got hold of the story. Probably through Alexander. I remember writing to him, thinking he would be as tickled as I was about it.

The cutting goes on to mention my letter to Jack Straw, where I offered to make a citizen's arrest on the governor. Ah, that's the source of the paranoia: the governor is due to present the certificates. Perhaps they imagine that I will jump up and try to arrest him.

I ignore the rudeness of the Samaritans director and turn to the trainer, who I got to like very much.

'I'm sorry,' I say. 'I enjoyed the course.'

'I'm sorry too,' she says. 'You'd have made a good Listener.'

But she is being hustled away. I grab her hand to shake it.

'Good luck with the Listeners,' I say.

'You're a powerful woman,' she whispers as she is rushed off. I do not feel the slightest bit powerful, but her comment gives me some strength and I meander on, doing my slow walk to the education block where the screws hurriedly lock me in.

Back on the unit for lunch, Bernice grabs me.

'They were going nuts in the office about you,' she says. 'When McCafferty heard you was in the chapel, he went ballistic. You should've heard him. "Ruth Wyner, where's Ruth Wyner?" Then he rang Miss Stratford and told her not to let you out of education under any circumstances. I tell you, babe, he was looping the loop.' June is less cheery.

'They'll ship you out. The Samaritans woman thinks they will too.' That does worry me: the thoughts of being whisked away out of reach of Gordon and Rachel.

'More like ghosted out,' says Glenda menacingly. I ask her what that means.

'They come and get you in the dead of night and put you in the seg [segregation, also known as the block] so you can't talk to anyone. Then first thing the next morning they take you off to goodness knows where and there's fuck-all that you can do about it.'

It all adds to the stress, the constant feeling of insecurity. I write a letter to the governor saying that I would not really attempt to citizen's-arrest him, that I was trying to make a point, tongue-in-cheek. Though I know I am writing the letter because I feel threatened. These people have a great deal of power over me.

□ □ □

Stevenson is sympathetic. He is walking me across to medication because Nurse No-No refused me during the first run. I had forgotten my ID card; all inmates have one. It has your photo and prison number on it, and you have to present it at medication to get what you are prescribed. Very understandable, except that Stevenson vouched for me, saying: 'That's definitely Miss Wyner,' and Nurse No-No defied even him. As usual, it upsets me, cuts through my protective layers. The stress in here makes us super-sensitive to the smallest slights.

Stevenson is a reassuring figure as he walks me back to the medication block. I have my ID card clutched in my hot hand. We chat a little on the way.

'I wouldn't really citizen's-arrest the governor,' I say. 'I just wanted to make a point.'

'I know,' he says. 'You have one.'

Highpoint is full of heroin addicts, but I have yet to see anyone actually using the stuff. That experience is still to come. I usually know when there is some about; we all do, can pick up on the urgency of people desperate to hustle some gear for themselves. Most of the addicts are in for petty thieving, trying to make a few quid to fund their habit. Some are small-time dealers. I discover that the police do quite a lot of undercover work and that the standard punishment is the four-year sentence for selling £10 worth to one of them unawares. It does not seem to do people much good. Few get the level of rehab that they need while in prison and most carry on from where they left off when they get out.

Then there are the drug importers.

'We're the forgotten ones,' Bernice once said to me. 'Lots of the women here are doing long sentences for importation, but you never hear about it on the news. You get statistics for thefts, assaults, an' all that, but importation is the biggest crime. And why don't we hear about it? Because it keeps everyone in a job.' Bernice was convinced that the system was crooked. 'Why don't they stop it all? Why don't they stop and search everyone who comes in? I'll tell you why. You know these politicians, the police, these judges? They all like a snort, believe me. I know it. You should meet some of my customers.'

I am sure it would be impractical to search everyone entering the country but did not feel quite able to say so. Bernice was on a roll.

'I'll tell you something else. My trial, now, I brought in 5 kilos. At each hearing the amount went down, till it was only 3 keys at the end. They said it was due to shrinkage, but, I tell you, that powder was dry when it came in.'

I have heard this before, from other women who say that the amount of drugs they brought in was reduced by the time they got to trial. It is not something that any defendant would want to make a fuss about. When you are in court, the smaller the amount the better. But the plight of the drug importers is dreadful.

'They're victims, really,' one of the governors told me, and he is right. These are not the real dealers, but are mostly impoverished women, Jamaicans and South Americans, with a smattering from Europe and the United States and some from Africa too. A percentage have done their crime under duress, suffering threats against their families. Alicia from Colombia lost her grandchild to the drug barons: she brought the stuff in successfully, but when she got caught her husband told her story and the child was kidnapped and killed. Anyway, we all know the system; they even know it at Customs: send someone through who looks obviously dodgy and she becomes a decoy for the main cargo.

The only Britain these women know is the airport, the police station and the prisons, and they are incarcerated thousands of miles from their families and their homes, doing anything from seven to twelve years. Many apply to be deported, to serve their sentences in their home countries, but they usually have to wait years for everything to be finalized. A terrible punishment, and the cost to the British taxpayer must run into millions of pounds every year. Still the drugs pour in. Surely there is a better way to stifle this black market.

□ □ □

We have another new face on Skid Row: Marina is of Asian descent, and is as skinny as Nancy is fat. The emptiness of her face alerts me straightaway. I say to Viv that I think Marina is one to watch. One of the screws tells us that she is dangerous and that we should have nothing to do with her. Marina is in for harassing and attacking unsuspecting males. She gets people to ring her prey and pass on messages.

True to form, Marina tries to persuade inmates to make her phone calls, and she asks me to write a letter. We all refuse, dare not risk getting involved in her ploys.

'She's weird,' June comments, which is true – Marina's behaviour is very strange. She mixes with no one and has a haunted look. She also eats very little, hovering at the servery during mealtimes, very pernickety, taking little of anything and then trying to sneak it into her room, which is not allowed.

'I do feel sorry for her, but it makes the room unhygienic,' says Lulu, who shares with her.

'She looks unwell to me,' I say. It must be obvious to any doctor that this woman is paranoid, obsessive, needs treatment and proper care and should not be in prison at all.

□ □ □

Marina becomes increasingly isolated. She has a way of sneaking around the unit trying to cadge things from other people, mainly food or phone cards, and is thoroughly disliked. Some people on Skid Row call her 'the coolie' and 'Paki', even when she is within earshot. She complains to the screws, but several of the inmates cannot see anything wrong in it.

'The shop down the road from us was always called the "Paki shop" and no one minded,' someone says.

Marina becomes more unwell. She eats virtually nothing, says she is a vegan but the screws do not believe her, and she still stores food in her room. Tonight things come to a head shortly before lock-up. Perfume has been stolen from Karen's room – you can buy it on the canteen but it is expensive, is a luxury – and Karen saw Marina sneaking about earlier on. She confronts her, demanding to look in her locker. Marina refuses. Karen gets the officers and asks them to look for her.

'Have you looked in everyone else's locker?' they ask.

'Yes,' we say, lying in unison.

So Marina's locker is searched and three bottles of perfume are found, along with other toiletries, none of which Marina could afford as she is still on the basic regime and getting only £2.50 spending money a week. The screws look through the rest of her stuff and find clothes that do not belong to her as well. I manage to grab a pair of my socks before the stuff gets taken to the office.

Once we are locked up, the abuse starts. Thankfully it is only verbal, but Marina gets very scared. People yell and curse at her through their open doors so that they can be sure she will hear it. I try to stick up for Marina, saying she is mentally unwell and that her behaviour is compulsive, but get shouted down.

'That fucking coon needs a good lesson.'

'Teach her to fucking thieve off her own.'

'She knows what she's doing all right, there's nothing wrong with that bitch.'

It is a typical scapegoating situation: Marina the outsider is the target for the desperate pent-up anger of all these women. But I fear for her safety. Marina does too and at 11 p.m. she presses the alarm button. She asks the screws for paracetamol for a headache. Of course they refuse, and she does not tell them the real reason for her call. When they have gone, the abuse continues.

First thing in the morning I bump into Stevenson and, despite my vow to tell the screws nothing, say: 'Marina was terrified last night, and I don't blame her. You'll have to move her off the spur, she's not safe.' He gets her into the office and, presumably having been told the same by her, sends her across to House 2.

At lunch, though she is off the house, there are more angry words about Marina. Perhaps unwisely, I come to her defence.

'Marina is not well,' I say. 'The woman has a condition, she's obsessive and very depressed. She'll have a harder time in prison than any of us.' I am shouted down and wonder if I have put myself in a difficult position.

□ □ □

I get good news and bad news through the post. The good news is that Michael Mansfield QC has agreed to represent us *pro bono* for our appeal, which means that he will only take a fee if we have costs awarded. He is a well-known and very capable barrister, and has defended many miscarriage of justice cases. I feel I am in good hands.

The bad news is about Wintercomfort. They are having difficulty with the statutory funders and the trustees are under pressure to get rid of John and me. They have taken on a new 'temporary director', were determined not to fill the post permanently until after our appeal, and the deputy manager on the Bus is filling John's shoes for the time being. But, facing threats of money being withdrawn, the trustees cannot wait.

'What shall we do?' they write. 'Our first priority has to be the charity.'

My instinct is to resign. Perhaps I should have done it earlier, but the trustees wanted me to hang on. I phone one or two people, who tell me not to be hasty, to get advice from my union or from an employment solicitor.

'After all,' someone reminds me, 'your contract of employment from Wintercomfort states that you're not allowed to give out confidential information.' It is a pertinent point. The major reason for our conviction was our refusal to hand the ban book over to the police. But it brings me down. Losing Wintercomfort is another loss on top of all the others. I get very depressed and retreat inside myself, cannot join in with the activity on the spur, hold on to my sadness and keep to my routine: eat, sleep, read, write, walk the compound, go to gardens and the gym.

Meanwhile, everyone seems to be pairing up.

'It must be something in the water,' says Viv. The unit is full of sex-starved women, most of them young and all looking for a little comfort. Viv, full of mischief as ever, puts a note on our door.

'It's all about Room 2 [that is June and me]. They've switched.' We retaliate by pouring water into Viv's room through the gap at the bottom of the door. It is a big mistake: Viv pays us back by catching us in the corridor and hurling bucketloads at us. I lose my rag and, once I am changed and dry, furiously bundle all Viv's bedding out through the bars of her window to where she cannot get at it. Viv persuades one of the Kainos co-ordinators to fetch the bedding for her and she spends the rest of the day sneaking me kisses, seeking forgiveness. How could I refuse her? The next day she strews toilet roll all over my bed, around my noticeboard, in my wardrobe, in my shoes, everywhere. I take it as a peace offering.

But the situation at Wintercomfort continues to bring me down. It eats into the equilibrium I have achieved. There is no point in fighting with the trustees; they have supported me as much as they can. I write my letter of resignation and withdraw into myself again. I am in mourning.

On top of that I have drawn the wrath of Kainos down upon me. A friend sent me a copy of questions Lord Avebury has tabled in the House of Lords about Kainos, and I wrote to him in return letting him know about my experiences on the community and during the Journey. Lord Avebury wrote back, saying he thinks Kainos is contrary to the Human Rights Act, because the only way to get better conditions in Highpoint prison is to join Kainos. As it is a Christian community, some people would feel debarred due to their religious beliefs. I suspect that he objects to the evangelism as much as I do.

Now the prison has got wind of it through one of the letters I have received. It was marked 'Rule 39', which means it was a solicitor's letter and should not be opened by prison staff. But they open it anyway and find out it is from an academic lawyer rather than my solicitor, which apparently means it is not a real Rule 39 letter. The letter contains extracts from the lawyer's research about the activities of Kainos, along with a copy of the write-up, which is not supportive of the organization.

I get called into the office to see a senior officer I have never met before. He hands me the letter and says he has two messages from the governor: first, that I should consider going back to the main prison because I am 'undermining Kainos', and second, that I am being designated a security risk. That is a shock: a security risk. It heightens my fear of being transferred to another prison, miles away from home. I come away feeling shaken.

Even the co-ordinators are giving me grief. One of them calls me into her office.

'Some of the prisoners have complained about your attitude on the Journey,' she says angrily. 'You're undermining Kainos. Perhaps you should move off it.' She has obviously had information about my letter. I wonder which prisoners complained, if any.

I hassle one of the governors to find out what has been written on my P16, and she comes back a week later to tell me that no, I am not seen as a security risk, and the SO never said I was.

'Oh, I must have misheard,' I say, getting the hang of it: prison double-speak. I am determined to stay on Kainos, to hold on to my soft-bottomed chair. I write to Lord Avebury about what has happened: he could be a protection for me. He helpfully speaks to a governor, which must make the prison more wary about pushing me around.

'Don't move unless they force you to,' says Karen. 'In a way you've warned the prison – they should be thanking you. You're looking after people's human rights.'

She is the only one on the spur who seems to be talking to me right now. My roommate June has gone very cool; even Viv and Jan hardly acknowledge me. In the mornings they come in to greet June with a 'Good morning, Mother, how are you?' June responds in a similar tone, but all three of them ignore me pointedly.

'And how's Ruth?' I pipe up, but get blanked.

'I'm fine,' I say out loud myself, and wonder what I have done to offend. Perhaps I should not have spoken up for Marina.

□ □ □

Like a lot of the prisoners, June tries to sleep through most of the lock-ups, lying on her side on the hard bed and snoring lightly. She sleeps badly at night, eats little, and looks utterly worn out from her period of incarceration. I move around quietly while she slumbers and stay off the typewriter when she is in the room.

'We like the typewriter,' some of the women tell me. 'You can hear it all over the unit but we don't mind. It's a non-prison sound.'

Even so, I know it annoys June. It is only a small old typewriter that belonged to my uncle, but like most manuals it is noisy.

Despite my care and consideration, June now spends most of her time when she is awake in with Viv and Jan, with anyone other than me. It is hard to cope with such rejection, along with all the other pressures of being in prison. I decide to tackle her about it.

'I'm uncomfortable in my own room,' June says. 'The atmosphere is terrible.'

'I feel uncomfortable too,' I say. 'But it's something between us, it's not just me.'

'It's not me, it's you,' June says. 'You've stopped speaking, everyone has noticed.'

I tell her I have had some bad news from Wintercomfort and that it has probably made me go more inside myself. 'Why didn't you ask me if you felt something was wrong, instead of freezing me out?'

June gets annoyed. 'I was OK until you came in. There's no point in talking about it. I'll move.' That would be disastrous. She has been in this room for months and if people feel I have pushed her out of it, my life on the spur would be hell.

'No, I'll move,' I say.

'Do what you want,' sniffs June, and she goes off to talk to Viv and Jan.

I go to the office to negotiate a move upstairs. Miss Turney is on duty, which is bad luck for me. In the light of previous experience, I do not expect much help from her.

'Why do you want to move?' she asks tartly.

'Because people are blanking me.'

'Do you want to put in a bullying complaint?'

'God, no. My life wouldn't be worth living.'

Turney offers me one choice of the rooms upstairs: going in with Mary, the large middle-aged woman who self-harms.

'But there are other spaces up there,' I protest.

'Not for you,' Turney says.

I have to take the only option and start to pack my stuff. Karen comes by.

'I heard what June said to you,' she says. 'I didn't agree with you about Marina, but it's wrong, you know. They shouldn't treat you like that.' The support is heartening.

Leah and Franny have heard the news and race down to help me carry my things upstairs.

'Well, you'll be all right up here,' Franny says.

'Yeah,' says Leah. 'We all just get along.' The two of them share a room up the spur and I welcome their friendship.

Mary will be hard to share with. The room smells of piss; she must be a bit incontinent. I curse Turney, open the window wide and sort out my stuff. Everyone wants to know why I have moved, and I tell them I was frozen out.

'June did that to me as well,' says Mary. 'I know what it's like.'

Despite her difficulties, Mary is a kindly woman. I stretch out on my bed and feel more relaxed than I have for a long time. People have told me that there is a lot going on up here. I wonder what I will find.

□ □ □

There are over thirty of us women on the three different spurs upstairs, and we can get to each others' rooms during the lock-ups. Life definitely feels more easy-going here. People constantly pop in and out of the room. Allie comes in to show off a photo of her prison pen-pal. He is tall and muscular, and we all admire him. Allie is in for robbery.

'I didn't rob the guy,' she says. 'I just hit him. My co-defendant took all the stuff.' She likes to hang around Mary and me. Allie's day-to-day cheeriness hides a deep insecurity, her drug taking and criminality a symptom of what lies beneath. She likes my typewriter, especially the 'ding' it makes when it reaches the end of the line, and she gets me to do it over and over again.

Franny and Leah are both jangles of nervous energy. They pop in and out, looking for reassurance. Franny's words come out of her in a torrent, like the hair that springs wildly from her head.

'I can't have my kids visit me, the youngest screams when he has to leave. The next time I see them I want to be there, y'know, and not have to go away again. They'll be all right with my mum. I just can't stand the visits. When they go, it does my head in. I'll do my bird this way. I'll get back to my kids, it's only another month to my tagging, eight more weeks on top if I don't get the tag. When I get back we'll be together properly, oh, oh, oh . . .' and the words still bounce off her as she walks out.

If you have a problem, Leah will sort it for you. It's her own problems that she has trouble with. She is only doing a short sentence but has a dark shadow over her: the police are trying to make a charge of dealing heroin stick – 'serving up', Leah calls it – and if they do, she reckons she will get another six years.

'How can I do six years?' she asks me.

'Face that when and if the time comes,' I say.

'You're right,' says Leah, grinning her toothless grin. She tells me about her family: they are all travellers, and she tries to teach me some of their language.

'Yer "yoks" are yer eyes, "knocker" is nose and "mooey" is mouth,' she says. ' "Gorgers" is non-gypsies and "gavvers" is, well, like, "Don't pukka nicksies in front of that gavver 'cos he's a proper bawlo." Got that, my liddy?' Well, no I have not, but it is fascinating and I ask her to tell me some more.

Next door are two young Jamaicans: Shula, the one who fancied Viv, and Cal, who looks fearsome and blasts us with furious jungle music every now and again. I generally keep out of Cal's way, until I see her poem up on the noticeboard at education. It is sensitively written and I tell her that I liked it. However fearsome she seems, her pain is similar to mine.

Lola, the religious black woman, is upstairs now as well, in the room opposite mine on her own. I wish I could have gone in with her; I could have endured her praying better than this fusty-smelling pad. Most days I mop our floor with lashings of bleach and disinfectant, as much of the stuff as I can get hold of. Mary helps out and does her best with her hygiene. I have known worse in the night shelters I have worked in. The window stays wide open. Thankfully, we both like fresh air.

Mary is a good-hearted woman. We go through the days quietly together, sticking to our routines and chatting occasionally. She is hugely depressed and her emotional defences are shot to pieces. If anyone has a go at her, inmate or screw, or even challenges her just a little, her eyes fill and overflow with hot tears. Mary should not be in prison at all. I become fiercely protective of her.

Mary's friends visit us, mostly Hester and little, quiet Naomi who lets herself be mothered. Mary has teenage daughters at home. Gabrielle is on our spur too. The argument about June and Glenda's *Sun* newspaper is forgotten, and she regularly comes in for a chat. We have a contingent of Jamaicans up here. They tend to do their own thing. And then there are the South Americans. Many speak little English and they all congregate in Alicia's room as she has one of the half-dozen much-coveted singles. They show me photographs of their kids. These women are living with unbearable sadness.

□ □ □

As always, I wake early and am usually first in the showers. They are not as good as the one downstairs. Afterwards I race back to the room and get under my covers to warm up. It is May and the prison heating has been turned off until the autumn, though the weather is not warm at all. We freeze in the evenings especially. I sleep fully clothed, with my coat over the blankets, and still feel the cold. An added difficulty is the open window, but I cannot bear to close it.

I have my own flask now, having saved up on my canteen for a month. At £7.99, it is an expensive outlay. We fill our flasks with hot water before lock-up. Now I am privileged: I can drink tea during the lock-ups and I have a coffee after my shower. Mary still sleeps. I light my first fag of the day. Opening the curtains a little, I can see the birds on our windowsill. Like me, Mary encourages them and we feed them old bread and cereal. We occasionally see pretty goldfinches, but it is mostly sparrows on this side of the house. There is a flock that is doing well and we watch the parents feed their fledglings. One of them is particularly aggressive. Gabrielle has named him Charlie.

I get dressed in time for unlock and take my half-dozen letters to the postbox, unsealed as usual so that the screws can check them.

Then, when people are off at work or education, I do a little yoga and start to write. Now the typewriter has been brought in, I am allowed to stay on the unit and write in the mornings instead of going to art, which is a great relief. Today the wind is up, whistling across these flat lands and blustering through the prison. From somewhere across the other side of the unit, the sound of a song cuts through, a woman's voice pure and plaintive. She is singing in Spanish. I imagine her by a country stream, brushing her long black hair as she gives us her refrain.

The sound of jangling keys breaks into my reverie: here come the screws doing their daily bar checks of the rooms.

□ □ □

The evening is routine, with Gabrielle asking me to spell words for her every few minutes for a letter she is writing. Franny comes to 'borrow' a couple of stamps, Leah tries to teach me a few more gypsy words and Mary is snoring by 10 p.m.

'One more day up the judge's arse,' says Leah.

Next day we have another security scare and the whole prison is on lock-down. Mary goes back to bed. No typing, and probably no gardens. Thankfully, I have had time to fill the flask and I make myself another coffee. Leah comes in doing a jokey flouncy walk and introduces me to a woman right behind her: 'This is my mate Carmen.'

I know Carmen just a little. She is very pretty, has deep-auburn wavy hair right down her back and large, doleful green eyes.

'Fucking lock-up,' she says. They scrounge a fag from me to share and sit on my bed to smoke it. I am at the table. We talk quietly to avoid waking Mary.

'Well, at least I don't have to go to gardens,' says Leah. 'Pete always gives me the worst jobs.'

'We've got the first after-Journey meeting after tea,' Carmen reminds her, and she is right. For the next six Monday evenings we're due to be holed up with the evangelicals for more of the same.

'I hope we're locked up all evening, then,' Leah says.

'I tell you,' Carmen continues, 'prison is like a secret society, and

Kainos is like a cult. A prison within a prison. A cult within a cult.' I have heard that before, on Skid Row.

As it turns out, we are locked up all day and only let out to collect our lunch, which we have to eat in our rooms. The rumour is that someone has reported a gun on the men's side. We feel annoyed that us women have to suffer for it as well. At teatime we are unlocked, feeling pretty bedraggled after the long hours of incarceration. We do not think any gun has been found.

'Oh, now we have to go to that damned after-Journey stuff,' Carmen complains.

We get the usual formula: singing, praying and preaching, and then time to discuss things at our tables. In between stuffing ourselves from the trays of biscuits that appear, we are asked to talk about occasions during the past week when we have been able to pass God's love on to someone else. Everyone on my table is dumbstruck as usual, so I say: 'We all look out for each other in here most of the time.'

'Yeah,' says Allie. 'And I don't feel like saying I did this or that. It's like boasting.'

Irene is at our table and looks despairing. Afterwards, Allie tells me that she heard Irene advising Lola and Georgette to pray for me. Praying for my soul, as if I am lesser than them.

'Don't fret,' says Allie, 'they're just idiots.'

'I believe in God, but this all too much,' says Carmen. 'I pray when I want, thank you very much, not when some old biddy tells me to.' I am again getting tempted to ask to come off Kainos, but my friends are here and I know the rest of the prison is worse. Stevenson confirmed that for me. Anyway, Kainos is on my sentence plan and leaving before I have finished the programme would not look good for my parole.

There is a group of black women on our landing, including Lola and Georgette, who have prayer meetings every evening. Kainos is ideal for them. We hear them down the other end of the corridor, fervently singing and praying. Carmen is in the room opposite and often seeks refuge with me.

'They're so bloody noisy that I can't hear myself think,' she complains. Carmen tells me about her life, how her mother died of AIDS and now her father is in prison, doing ten years.

'I went off the rails,' she says. I tell her it is hardly surprising.

We suffer the six after-Journey sessions. Sometimes they clash with the evening outside exercise, when we can walk the compound. I complain about it to Turney, but she is not sympathetic.

'Go and take your medicine,' she says, with obvious pleasure.

Some of the women are still puzzled by my Jewishness.

'The Jews killed Jesus,' Mary says.

'No, the Romans did,' I say. 'They crucified hundreds, maybe thousands of Jews. Jesus was a Jew himself.'

'Oh,' says Franny. 'I didn't know that. I suppose he does look kind of Jewish, with the dark hair and the beard and all that.'

'He probably had similar colouring to you,' I tell her. Franny is mixed race. As she wanders off down the corridor, I hear her tell someone: 'Guess what? Jesus had the same colour skin as me.'

□ □ □

I now know for sure how you can tell when there is heroin on the house. I was not so canny before, but, with my current knowledge, I know that it has been around all the while. The screws know as well. They just cannot catch it. They rarely, if ever, find anything but occasionally get enough proof of suspicion to get someone moved to another house or to another prison. The situation is reminiscent of mine at the day centre: we banned people and we too knew we could not catch everything. Similar problem, similar response. They have their job to do, just like I did at Wintercomfort. They might make some progress but will never completely stop the drugs coming in, despite having a lot more power over their clientele than I ever did.

Carmen is a key person in the drugs scene on our wing, though there are others as well. I am coming out from visiting Allie in her room when Carmen pops her head round a door.

'Have you got any foil?' she asks, looking anxious.

'Foil?'

'Yeah, you got some tobacco?'

'Yes.'

'Come in.'

She pulls me into her room, takes the wrapping from my tobacco and gives me the tobacco back into my hand.

'Sit down, it's OK,' she says.

There are a few other women in there and I watch one hold a lighter to the tobacco wrapping, burning off the colouring so that only the foil is left. Carmen gets out the heroin. It is wrapped in cling film. They put a little on the foil and roll up a bit of paper to make it into a straw. Then they burn the heroin from underneath the foil and suck the smoke through the paper straw: chasing the dragon, that much I do know. The doings are passed around.

Carmen looks at me. 'You want some?'

I have never before been tempted by heroin; it has always horrified and frightened me, and I have not had the slightest desire to touch the stuff. But this time, this time, it is a chance to escape from the misery, to block it for a while. To get some time out from the prison.

'No, no, but thanks all the same,' I say and hurry out, leaving them to it. I have scared myself, that it had felt like a possibility, that I could have so easily said 'yes' to smack.

□ □ □

Various journalists have been trying to get into the prison to see me. One day a screw tells me: 'We've had a request from two journalists, from *Panorama* and the *Guardian*. You're only allowed to see one, so you have to choose.' I choose *Panorama*, which is a mistake. When *Panorama* find out they will not be allowed to film me, that they can only tape an audio interview, they are not interested anymore. That is how I hear it. I send a letter about it to a lawyer friend. In reply she sends me a copy of a 1999 judgement from the House of Lords, which allows prisoners access to journalists who are investigating miscarriages of justice. There is nothing about allowing only one visit. I make a written complaint to the prison, quoting the judgement from the Lords and asking why my rights are being limited by the prison service. I also write to the *Guardian* to explain what has happened.

One person who does get in to see me is the prison's rabbi. He comes during Passover, a major Jewish festival, and does me a little *seder* [a special symbolic Passover meal] in a room off the chapel. The rabbi has to explain it all; I am exceedingly ignorant of these matters, but find it quite fascinating. Passover is about the Jews' escape from captivity in Egypt. Very apt. I am also fascinated, in a different way, by the chopped herring and grape juice the rabbi has brought me: absolutely delicious. Then he explains that he has arranged for me to have kosher food through Passover week. That is a real treat. I get pre-packed microwave airline meals for lunch and supper, plus boxes of matzos with kosher margarine and strawberry jam. It makes a welcome change from the prison food. I share the matzos and jam, but some of the other women are rather suspicious about me getting the special food. I worry that it singles me out, especially here on this Christian community.

□ □ □

I am noticing more now how the addicts communicate and work together. One week someone gets something in and shares it, and so they get a hit of what comes in the next week from another source. But it is a constant hassle: the supplies are not regular and there are constant rows about what is owed to whom. I come across one woman who got her move to Kainos because her roommates had threatened to 'de-crotch' her. They thought she had smack hidden in her fanny and wanted to take a look.

'I can't be bothered with it,' a friend tells me. 'You only get a touch in here and it's more like a tease than a hit. I'll wait till I get out, when I can go for it proper.'

That is another problem: ex-prisoners overdosing because they do not realize on release that their tolerance to heroin is down. Or they just cannot hold back. There are leaflets in healthcare warning people about it. If the police had found one of those on the Bus, they would, no doubt, have used it as evidence against us.

□ □ □

During an afternoon lock-up, I am visited by Carmen and a couple of others.

'Got anything to make me sick?' Carmen asks.

'Put your fingers down your throat,' Mary suggests.

They have already tried that, and various other things. Carmen has had a visit and she swallowed some heroin that she was passed.

'How much?' I ask.

'About nine hits,' she says.

'Was it well wrapped?'

'I think so.'

It will kill her if it comes open inside.

The next morning I start a new routine. Because I am always up first thing, I have been given the job of waking people early so that they can get into their own rooms before the 7.30 a.m roll-check. We are not allowed to sleep anywhere other than in our own beds, but there is all sorts of pairing-up going on. Women squash together in the single beds, cuddling up like frightened children in this big bad place. My poor little bunnies. Mischievous little bunnies. I am relieved when Carmen wakes up with the rest of them.

'I don't do nothing,' Leah soulfully insists before padding back to her own room. 'It's just that I can't sleep on my own in here.'

□ □ □

During the night, I wake at 4 a.m. with severe gut ache. I lie on my hard bed for an hour, groaning and getting the sweats. It does not get any better. I haul myself up and drape myself over the back of the chair. That helps a little, but it wakes Mary.

'Shall I call the kangas?' she asks (kangaroo: screw). I am getting worried: the words 'twisted gut' and 'twisted bowel' slip into my head from nowhere.

Mary presses the call button and speaks to the screw at the spur gate; the screws are not allowed to come in to the cells on their own for fear of attack. He rings healthcare and comes back with a message.

'They asked if you could hang on till 7 a.m. when the day staff come on,' Mary says.

I do not have any choice and continue to groan. Mary gets an old squash bottle and fills it with hot water from the tap. I get back into bed and lay it over the bad spot. Gradually the pain eases and I drop off to sleep. When I awake at 7.25 a.m., the pain is thankfully gone and I race around just in time to wake up my sleeping brood.

I am tired all morning and doze through the lunchtime lock-up. Afterwards, at gardens, I take it as easy as I can, and by the evening I feel more like myself again. As usual, I collect my post, ring home and then head out into the compound for my brisk daily walk, round and round under the razor wire. The weather is getting better and more people are coming out. Viv is talking through the fence to someone from House 2. Leah joins her, and so do Ingrid and Gerrit, bringing a radio with them. Allie is on the bench outside the unit's front gate, with Hester and one or two others. Evelyn is exercising her arthritic legs; little Naomi walks beside her. Lola and Georgette are also walking, the two big women going very, very slowly. I pass them several times.

Carmen is inside. She still has not managed to shit out the heroin and everyone is getting increasingly jumpy.

'Don't worry,' she says gamely. 'I know people who've held on to it for days and days.'

Fizz is at one corner of the compound making a lot of noise, chatting animatedly to a group of black women on the other side of the wire. She is white herself, with short bleached hair, but sounds more black than her friends, working herself up into frenzies and jumping up and down, unable keep still. Eventually the group splits up and Fizz makes her way back to the unit, ending up walking beside me.

'It's the crack, you know,' she says unashamedly. 'It's totally done my head in. I'll never be the same again.'

□ □ □

Carmen has shat out the heroin at last, after three very tense days. We get the usual requests on the spur.

'Got any foil?'

'Can I borrow your lighter?'

Carmen had swallowed a piece of cannabis as well as the heroin, but she uses most of that to trade for tobacco and phone cards.

'Dope stays in the system for a month,' Carmen reminds me. 'You're more likely to be caught on the piss test. Smack's washed out in three days max. That's why people prefer it in nick.'

Quite understandable, but hardly sensible, that heroin should be safer to use in prison than cannabis.

As Mr Scott told me before he left: 'There's no logic to prison.'

□ □ □

This morning our family of goldfinches visits the windowsill together: dad, with his colourful plumage; mum, who looks much more ordinary; and junior being shown the ropes. Charlie, our aggressive little sparrow, does not let them stay long. The other sparrows seem much better socialized than he is. I wonder what went wrong with our Charlie.

Mary and I put muesli out on the windowsill to feed the birds – we all get it allocated in our food bags on Sunday night for Monday morning. No one likes the stuff much, so everybody on the landing brings their muesli to us, even people I do not speak to at all. It has become a Sunday routine, special to our landing.

We also get a cold supper in the bags on Sunday: sandwiches, crisps, a packet of biscuits, a yogurt and a piece of fruit. I give my crisps and biscuits away. The sandwiches are pretty basic, filled with a slice of cheese or ham or a scrape of tuna. Working in gardens, I can take an onion now and again, when they are around, and I like to slice one up to add zest to the sandwich. Occasionally I get a head of garlic as well and I load it all in, waking up my taste buds after months of plain prison fare.

The baby goldfinch opens his beak wide for its parents to fill with the bits of muesli. Sometimes I feel surrounded by open mouths, people in and out of the room after a stamp, a sheet of paper, an envelope, the spelling of a word, food, a fag, or just a little company. I give what I can; most of us do. In quieter times, I can at last focus enough to read interesting novels. The prison library is quick at getting the books we order. I have just read *Anil's Ghost* and *Beloved*.

□ □ □

Carmen sticks her head round the door of my room.

'Got any sugar?' she asks. I have lots. We get issued with it weekly, along with tea-bags and whitener, but I do not use much. I give her a pile of the sachets. I have learnt that in prison you never throw anything away.

'Right then, Ruth,' Carmen says. 'You're in on this one, then.'

A couple of weeks later I find out what I am in on: it is a bucket of hooch. We are an eager but paranoid bunch, sitting on the floor of Carmen's room downing mugful after mugful of the stuff in our determination to get tanked up. The taste is revolting. Then we wait. After fifteen minutes I can feel my body relaxing and a smile attaches itself to my face. As before, the warmth centres on my stomach and then it spreads out from there. Ten minutes on and we are collapsed with the giggles. This stuff really does work. Frantically we clean up every trace of it, sneaking bits and pieces out to the rubbish, washing our mugs and the bucket extra thoroughly. Then we make our way downstairs. I have to hang on to Carmen to get my bearings. The giggles take us over again, but we straighten up to walk sedately past the screws' office and into the compound outside.

We all sit on the ground against the far fence. Someone has brought out a radio and people start dancing. It is a lovely evening and I watch the colours of the sunset. The world is the same as always; whatever they do to me, it cannot be taken away. I study the unit before me, squat and flat-roofed with bars at all the windows. This small building is where sixty-odd of us women are herded into to live. It all seems ridiculous. Plain stupidity. In my drunken state, I have to laugh.

□ □ □

No drugs have come in for a while and the addicts are getting edgy, watching each other like hawks to see if anyone is holding out.

Carmen makes another bucket of hooch but it is drunk too early, well before it is ready. All it gives us is bad stomach aches the next day.

'I'm waiting on debts to be paid,' Carmen says. 'And they'd better pay them, I tell you.' One woman suggests I get some heroin in for them.

'You get regular visits,' she says, 'and you live locally.' This is alarming. I have heard of people being beaten up for refusing to help out, but I will not have it, will not risk my family – and know that anyway Gordon would not agree.

'Leave her alone,' says Carmen, adding to reassure me: 'They don't mean it, Ruth.'

'Nah, I'm just trying it on,' the woman concedes. 'I know you can't.'

□ □ □

I have taken to playing patience with Ingrid during the evening lock-ups. She has a single room. We play competitively, but Lady Luck does not smile on me: I mostly lose and Ingrid makes the most of her triumphs, teasing me mercilessly. She is now a qualified Listener and is enjoying a welcome break. She shows me her rota and explains that there are not enough Listeners in the prison to share all the work. Recently her days and nights have been constantly interrupted.

'Well,' I say, vindicated. 'I would have helped out but got dropped.'

Mary is not happy with me being out of the room. On three occasions when I am with Ingrid she harms herself, first by scrubbing her skin with a scourer and then by bashing her hand against the wall. She damages the hand quite badly and on the second time it swells up like a balloon. Healthcare is called at midnight and I am sent out of the room. I go to see Carmen. There are several women in there flaked out over the beds. They have been having a 'toot'. The sickly-sweet smell of heroin smoke pervades the place. Carmen's debts must have been paid.

I cannot help feeling angry with Mary; she always looks so satisfied after she has done herself damage. It gives her relief, to get out some of the pain rather than holding it all internally.

'I don't know how you stand it,' says Carmen. 'Now you're banished from your room.' I have to wait for nearly an hour, and when I get back I can hardly look at Mary, just go straight to bed.

In the morning I run around the landing doing my usual wake-up calls. At lunchtime lock-up I take time to talk to Mary, explaining how upsetting it is for me when she self-harms and urging her to talk when she feels like doing it. I get nowhere. She does it again. There are many people who self-harm in this prison, because it is the only way they can find to let out some of the anguish. Others take overdoses, and some people become physically ill as a result of their distress, even those who outwardly appear quite tough. Jules, the armed robber I met at Holloway when she had the flu, is now at Highpoint. She seems to have a permanent bed in healthcare. I saw her recently: she looked unbelievably pale and drawn.

□ □ □

On Sunday morning three screws come on to the landing and cart three people off for urine tests. Carmen is relieved that she has not been taken. I have a quandary. The sun is out and they will be opening the gate to the compound. Should I walk outside or go to the gym?

The sun wins. I put my shorts on and, ignoring Stevenson's ribald comments about me needing 'a licence for those legs', walk briskly for forty minutes. Afterwards I sit by the fence with card-player Ingrid and gardening partner Gerrit. Gypsy-girl Leah is jumping around from one group of people to another. Franny is indoors, trying to shut the prison out by hiding under the covers of her bed. All you can see is her Afro hair bursting out from the top of the blanket. Fizz is still fizzing at the fence, and old Evelyn sits with Janis, who tells me she has finally had her transfer to a prison with a drug rehab approved.

A group of people come in from chapel where they have been to the Sunday service, but everyone is waiting for the three that have gone for their urine tests.

'I could have given them more,' says Stevenson, 'but they only allowed us to send three.' Perhaps they did not want more, I think to myself. It might look bad on the prison.

In the afternoon I have my family visit. Impatient as ever, I am ready way before time. Because it is hot, the screws have opened the doors at the end of the unit to let in some air. I peer through the bars to the car park and manage to make out Gordon and Rachel arriving.

'Gordon!' I yell. He doesn't hear. Others take up the shout.

'Gordon! GORDON! GORRRDDOOONN!' Something hits home and he looks vaguely around but does not see me frantically waving. At last we are let out and escorted through the sun to the visits hall.

'No funny business on the visits, now,' says the screw. 'Remember those strip-searches we can do afterwards.' And she adds as an afterthought: 'Though we know you lot swallow it before we can get there.'

'That's knowingly allowing,' I respond.

'Well, it is very difficult, Ruth,' she replies.

The next afternoon I have a visit of a different sort. Sally Weale, a *Guardian* journalist, has finally got in to see me. I am told to go to the block instead of the visits hall. I find the place, get the most polite frisking I have ever had, and am now sat down at a table opposite the journalist. Cockburn, the pillow-pinching screw, comes up to where we are sitting.

'I'll be down the corridor, and don't worry, I won't disturb you. I just have to be sitting there,' he says, ever so nicely. I have never heard him talk the least bit politely before, and have to laugh. Sally asks me what is so funny and I do my best to explain, *sotto voce* of course. Then another screw comes up and offers her a coffee. Sally says she would be glad of one, that she takes it black, and then because there is no way out of it, the screw offers me one as well. I have never had a screw make me a coffee before.

'Thank you,' I say, amused. 'That's very kind. I take mine black as well.'

The interview goes well, though I am a bit out of practice and find it quite hard to concentrate. At one point, Sally wants to know my opinion about drugs.

'Come on,' she says. 'Fifty per cent of our friends smoke cannabis.' It is difficult to talk about it, with a screw just down the way.

'I think cannabis should be legalized in some form,' I say. 'If nothing else, it would separate it out from the hard drugs. They do the real damage.'

Although this is not a controversial view, I worry that I have gone too far, do not want to appear soft on drugs. Even so, I am sometimes surprised by the kind of people, often very respectable, who think that all drugs should be legalized. It is not something that I would necessarily subscribe to, though being in prison has made me very aware that what we are doing at the moment is not working. Prison does not seem to cure addicts. If anything, it brutalizes them and makes them worse. The prescription of some hard drugs seems to be the answer for those not ready for rehab, to replace black-market supplies and reduce criminality. In the event, Sally does a great piece and it appears in the *Guardian* the day before our appeal.

Before I am led away, a screw asks me whether I would like to represent House 1 in discussions about changes to the canteen list. I accept the offer but am puzzled as to why they are asking me here and now. Later, I figure out that it is for Sally's benefit, as they asked me while she was in earshot. They want to demonstrate that I am being treated with respect. I hear nothing more about it subsequently.

When I get back to the unit, Stevenson asks how I got on.

'Fine. Mr Cockburn deserves an Oscar: I've never heard him speak politely before.'

'Neither have I,' says Stevenson, laughing.

□ □ □

The wild Irish woman I met at healthcare has been moved into the room opposite me, with Lola. She is not on Kainos but they have put her up here to keep her out of trouble. She continues to act out the fights she has been in and gabbles away non-stop. I feed her fags, having decided it is not worth resisting her requests.

'Leave it to me,' says Leah. 'I can handle her. We're both travellers; she's an Irish one but we're travellers all the same.' This time, Leah has taken on more than she can handle. The Irish woman grapples with her in a friendly kind of way. Leah extricates herself and suggests a different game. We are all wary. This woman is not in control, and, sure enough, she ends up back in the block a few days later.

□ □ □

I am on tenterhooks. I have been phoning the appeal court to hustle them for a date and at last we have one: 11 July. At first I was ecstatic, but now I feel unsettled and am getting increasing edgy. I want to pick up the phone and speak to people all the while; I want to get outside, get out of here, the frustration is driving me frantic. It is known as gate fever. I do not dare expect anything from the appeal; all I know is that it is on the way. I struggle to keep my feelings down but they boil up again and again. A caged animal, that is what I am, and I will get no relief until I am freed.

It is a strange thing, ringing the outside world when you are in prison, particularly speaking to staff in official places. The people at the appeal court are totally courteous, which feels odd. I have got used to a very different sort of treatment. I also ring the Prison Reform Trust. A lawyer friend has sent me their new report about women's prisons, *Justice for Women: the need for reform*, and she suggests I write something about it for their newsletter.

The report is substantial but I read most of it in one sitting, engrossed. I know first-hand how dreadful prison is; that it is a negative and damaging experience; that most of the women I have met inside are victims; that many have been badly and repeatedly let down by life, and are now being made worse by their incarceration. *Justice for Women* says it all for me, for us, with facts and statistics to back it up. It comes up with constructive suggestions: that more women should be punished in the community; and that for those who need to be held in secure accommodation, smaller community prisons are the answer. Just like community care, I think, when they closed down the large Victorian psychiatric hospitals and got people into smaller units or into their own places. More humane, same principle, same need.

I write my piece for the newsletter and send it off after showing it to the screws. A week later I ring the Trust to see if they have got it and again feel the strangeness of talking as a prisoner to ordinary people at their offices outside. The article has not got through. I type it out a second time and try the post again, telling the screws what has happened, that I have telephoned the Prison Reform Trust and that they are expecting it. This time the article arrives at its destination and I am delighted when it gets used:

A second report on prisons comes out, entitled *A Joint Manifesto for Penal Reform 2000*. This one is issued by the Penal Affairs Consortium, which is made up of forty different organizations, including the Prison Reform Trust. The manifesto makes the case for less use of prison, because imprisonment is so costly and is largely ineffective, disgorging hurt and often embittered people. I am getting to see prison as a form of institutional abuse, based on vengeance rather than sensible approaches to rehabilitation. Most ex-prisoners reoffend.

It seems that neither of these reports gets much response from government, if any at all. It strikes me as an arrogance. The public need to know, are pretty ignorant about the situation in our prisons. So are most of our politicians. I was ignorant too, before I got jailed. Prison is a hidden world. It is as if by throwing people into jail, some kind of justice has been served and we can all feel better and forget about it. What this attitude overlooks is that prisoners have to be released, and that they are real people too. Only about twenty-five of the 70,000 people we incarcerate at any one time are doing whole-life terms.

I have to send off a letter to get the manifesto, and see Stevenson in the office and tell him about it. He expresses interest. I give him the address to write to.

'We get frustrated with running these regimes too, you know,' Stevenson says. This time, I believe him.

□ □ □

My appeal is on Tuesday, but the day before I have to travel down and stay overnight at Holloway to be ready for the hearing in the morning. First I have to pack my things and deposit them at the prison reception on Sunday, all except for an overnight bag and what I want to wear in court.

'They've still got my writing,' I complain to Carmen.

'Listen, girl,' she says. 'When you leave this prison, you have to take all your possessions with you. Tell them you won't get on the bus unless you have the writing. Then they'll have to give it to you.'

I do as she says and tell reception on Sunday: 'I won't get on the bus without my writing.'

'What?' say the screws.

'The governor took it,' I explain. 'And I'm not going without it. A box file and a ring binder.'

'Don't you want to go to your appeal, then?'

'Of course I do, but I have to take all my possessions. I have the right. You have a duty to get me there.' Carmen has tutored me well.

The next morning I am up early and cannot wait to get unlocked. I chat to one of the Colombians. She cannot sleep either and shows me photos of her two young children. She has lost them now, to their father, because of her imprisonment. I tell her that they are beautiful.

In reception, after I have been strip-searched and processed, I re-iterate my message: that I will not go without my writing. Without replying, they shut me in a small room with another woman who is coming with us. We will be dropping her at Ipswich on our way. She is up in court for soliciting and, to pass the time, tells me about her life: prostitution in Leicester, Norwich, anywhere, and how it pays for her crack and heroin.

'I used to live in Norwich,' I say. 'I worked at the night shelter there.'

'Oh, I know Norwich Night Shelter,' she says. 'You can get anything you want in there.'

The sweatbox has arrived. We are unlocked and let out of the room. Five privileged prisoners, including Ingrid, who go to work outside in the prison's conference centre, are lined up waiting for their daily strip-search. Several screws are there. I have to go first. The Group 4 guard frisks me and opens the door to head for the bus.

'My writing?' I say.

'It's on the bus,' says a screw.

'How do I know?'

'You'll have to trust us.'

'Is there anyone else on the bus?'

'Yes,' says the guard. 'A chap called Brock.'

My spirits lift. I embrace Ingrid and am straight out of that door, waving to some women waiting at healthcare. They shout out messages of good luck.

'I'll be back,' I say, and expect to be.

In the sweatbox I see my writing. It is wrapped up and labelled: 'Not to be given out at court'. And there is John, locked in one of the cubicles. I am put opposite him and we can communicate a little, mainly with hand signals. He is surprised to see me smoking. Though the journey is uncomfortable as usual, it's a thrill to be in the outside world. Unfortunately, I cannot see much through the smoked-glass windows. We make the drop at Ipswich, and when we hit London I can just make out places I recognize. Part of the route is one I take when I drive from Cambridge with the family to visit my mother. John is dropped off first, at Pentonville, and then we head for Holloway. The journey has taken three-and-a-half hours.

It is a strange feeling to be back where I started, at HMP Holloway. I am put in a room with two other women who are in custody for the first time. They have been waiting two hours and are very wound up. One is only sixteen, the other is close to tears. Unlike them, I am prepared. I have my Walkman, a book, an apple, chocolate, peanuts, a tin of mackerel and a bottle of squash. I'm exhausted after the sweatbox journey, and call the screws to demand lunch. I get the usual barely edible microwave meal. Then I ask for some water and add squash to it. The other women want some and I would oblige except they cannot get the water, have yet to acquire the knack. They ask me what it is like in prison and I tell them what I can.

Another woman is put in with us for five minutes or so. She wants to know our stories. When I tell her I have been at Highpoint, she has lots of questions about people she knows there. In prison, you make firm friends fast.

'Give them my love when you get back,' she says. I promise that I will.

I have to wait, and wait; one hour, two. At last I am called out and leave the other two behind. A screw takes me up to D3, where I was before. It has not changed. Everyone is locked up.

'Do you want a single room?' they ask at the office.

'I would love one,' I say, and am delighted to be locked in it. A single at last. My head is pounding, but I have brought two pain-killers out with me, pleading period pains, and I swallow them with some more squash, using the top of my flask as a cup. Then I put my stuff away and relax on the bed, listening to my Walkman. It feels great to be on my own.

We are unlocked for supper at 5 p.m. and I take my flask out to be filled with hot water. The screws and inmate workers accept me as a prisoner who knows the score, is into a sentence. Most of the others on this wing are remands. The food is as terrible as ever and I can manage little of it. I get two slices of bread and take them back to my room, eating them with the tinned mackerel I have brought. Holloway is a whole lot easier when you are on top of things.

We are allowed out of the cells for evening association after tea. I ring home, and my mother and my sister, and manage to sidestep requests for phone-card units from people who see me at it. Then, after some hustling, I manage to find a copy of the *Independent* – they always have it in here. There is a good big bit about John and me, which I tear out and keep. The shower is just across the way. I hide my Walkman and my phone cards and go off to clean up. When I get back, my chocolate is gone. Typical. Thankfully, every-thing else is safe. I nibble some peanuts, and drink cups of tea. At 7.30 p.m. I am happy to be locked up again in my single cell, enjoy the evening and sleep pretty easily, but am awake at 5 a.m. It does not matter. I have my own space and spend the time relishing the privacy. At Highpoint I will be back to sharing.

My breakfast is given to me early: cereal and a couple of slices of bread. I drink more tea, and when they come to get me at 7.30 a.m. I am ready, and very wound up. This is it. I am escorted downstairs and put into a holding room with about fifteen other women, including the two I met yesterday. Everyone is going to court. They are all young enough to be my daughters and I make myself as invisible as I can. We have to strip down to our underwear and put on dressing gowns that we have been given. Then we wait to be strip-searched one by one and to have our stuff checked and packed away for the transports.

At last I am taken through and submit to the search. My stuff is sorted out. I am allowed to dress again and shown into yet another room.

'Where's my tobacco for court?' I ask. I know I am allowed to have some: baccy, fag papers, but not a lighter.

'You didn't give us any,' says the screw.

'Yes I did, it was in a little pot.'

'Oh, we thought that was make-up.'

'Well, I want my tobacco.'

'It's been sealed up now, you can't. Just go in there and we'll see what we can do.' I have no choice, but they are true to their word. Ten minutes later, another screw opens the door and calls me over.

''Ere y'are love: we've got some spare,' and she thrusts a small pouch of tobacco and cigarette papers into my hand. I pocket it quickly and mutter my thanks, glad to have the poisonous stuff and to have the feeling reinforced: I know how to get what I am entitled to; this old lag can cope fine with prison.

We have yet another wait, fifteen of us banged up in this room with nothing but some tables and hard chairs and two toilets. People chat to keep their spirits up, but I am quiet, sitting on one chair with my feet up on another, engrossed in what lies ahead. One by one we are called out for our respective transports. While we're waiting, a couple of women bring out their goodies: a bit of brown (heroin), some foil and a lighter. They got it past the strip-search and now go off to smoke it in one of the toilets. It is the last thing I see before I leave the prison. The irony is inescapable.

The ride to the appeal court is relatively comfortable. For the first time I am in a Securicor sweatbox, which is superior to my usual Group 4 models. The plastic seat is moulded in such a way that you can sit into it without sliding about all the while, and I can see out of the windows: lovely, familiar London. We drive through the morning traffic and I am dropped off first, into the back of the High Court, handcuffed only briefly. I am deposited into a small cell. John is there already, locked up elsewhere. We are let out for a quick conference with the legal team. Michael Mansfield is worried that the Lord Chief Justice, Lord Woolf, who was to have heard the appeal, has pulled out at the last minute. We have been allocated Lord Justice Rose instead, and he will be sitting with two other judges.

The wait is interminable. At last we are called, taken up a long and winding wooden staircase and sat in the dock, high up by the side of the judges' bench. A Securicor guard sits with us. The public gallery is packed, upstairs and downstairs, with our families, friends and supporters, and I can pick out several policemen from Cambridge, on a day's jaunt to London. Journalists squeeze on to the press bench. This is a grand courtroom: the carved stonework and tall ceiling give it the appearance of a church, with the lawyers' wooden benches set out like pews. Our three judges enter and everyone stands. The lawyers bow their heads deferentially and the proceedings begin.

Michael Mansfield has already told us that in his opinion the case should never have been brought and that it was subsequently handled wrongly. He takes the court through the arguments, dropping in first this and then that to see what the judges will pick up. They seem to be sympathetic, nod and smile occasionally, even look quite friendly.

'Weren't the defendants put on notice?' asks Judge Moses, who is sitting with Rose, meaning: weren't we warned that we risked a criminal prosecution? Ah, Moses: lead us to the Promised Land.

'No,' says Mansfield, 'they weren't,' and now he gets to it: the question of subjectivity. What was in the minds of the defendants? Shouldn't the confidentiality policy have been taken into account as affecting our decisions, and anyway, wouldn't it be hard for Wintercomfort to fulfil its objectives without one? Also, shouldn't our awareness about the level of dealing, the level of knowledge, have been an issue as well? How could we be convicted of something we were not aware of? The criticism here is of Judge Haworth's legal rulings and his summing-up at the trial.

'Talk more about subjectivity,' say the judges. I catch my breath.
Are we finally being understood? These judges seem to be interested
in what our barrister is saying – a new courtroom experience for me.
Mansfield has been going through the very same arguments that my
barrister Karim put forward on more than one occasion during our
seven-week trial. Each time, his views were dismissed. At last we are
being heard.

I glance down to Karim, sitting behind Mansfield. He looks impassive, but I can sense the frustration he must feel. My frustration is
building too. There in the public gallery are Gordon, Joel and Rachel,
my mother and sister, personal friends, work colleagues and campaign supporters. I can see them but not touch them; I am held apart.
I cannot even wave to them for fear of antagonizing the judges. And
of course, I cannot speak, am never allowed to speak at these hear-
ings. My only chance was when I gave evidence at our trial and was
bullied and sneered at for nearly three days by the prosecution. Judge
Haworth unceremoniously waved away Karim's anxious objections.
Now, I remain silent. What I, as a criminal, have to say is of no import
at all. Mansfield can speak for me but does not have the intimate
knowledge of the case that I do. I have no choice but to rely on him.

One hour, two hours pass. Mansfield covers the ground, trying to
draw the judges in. There is a stillness in the courtroom, as if everyone is holding their breath, hoping. I dare not allow myself to hope,
or even to wish for the freedom I so urgently desire. In prison I have
become used to containing my feelings, but here they insistently
push against the barriers I have built up. With effort, I maintain my
equilibrium. I have been let down by the courts too often. If I
hope for nothing, I cannot be disappointed.

I look again at the family and wonder if I will get a chance to speak
to them in the cells afterwards. Can I at least hope for that small
comfort? Probably not. I suspect they will not allow it. Nothing is
given to the prisoner unless it is unavoidable.

Mansfield winds up his submission. The judges have no more
questions and he sits down. I had expected the prosecution to follow
him, but this time they are the ones who cannot speak. The three

appeal judges put their heads together to confer, staying on the bench. They do not even go outside to discuss their decision. Sitting in the dock with John, I am close to where they are huddling, can hear their whispers but cannot make out the words. I try not to look at them for fear of being intrusive. My muscles are locked rigid with the tension. Don't hope, don't dare to hope, that these whispers are for us.

The judges separate and Rose speaks.

'Leave to appeal against conviction is granted.'

The words drop so easily, so lightly, giving us the decision we have been working towards for months. A wave of relief passes through the courtroom, a sprinkle of hushed talk rises from the public gallery. Unable to remain impassive, I nudge John hard in the ribs: we've got it, we're over the first hurdle.

Lord Justice Rose seems keen to get on to the next phase of the proceedings and invites the prosecution to present their arguments. Their bully of a barrister rises, looking uncertain, his face grey now that he has lost the confidence he possessed when supported by Haworth, our trial judge. He says he is not ready, needs time to consider the issues Mansfield has raised, and asks for an adjournment. The small hope I had allowed myself to feel crumbles to dust and drifts away. I try to prepare myself for the return to Highpoint, tell myself that I will be no worse off than I was before.

'An adjournment would take us into the next term,' says Rose, meaning the autumn. At least another three months' wait inside. Expect nothing. Do not allow disappointment. Protect yourself from the hurt.

Rose says he wants a date in weeks, rather than months, and then he smiles, looks almost playful.

'Would you like to make an application, Mr Mansfield?'

The urge for freedom charges through my system, overriding all my good intentions.

'Bail,' I hiss at the lawyers. 'Bail, BAIL!'

Mansfield draws breath, the silence of anticipation fills the court-room, and then he makes the request: for bail pending the next hearing. The judges confer briefly again. Still I cannot look at them and, try as I might, cannot make sense of their whispers. I would wish them to be quick but a quick decision is of no use to us if it is the wrong one. I fight to contain the emotion, to expect nothing. At last, they go back to their places and Rose speaks.

'We will grant unconditional bail.'

Bail, BAIL! WE'RE OUT! I grab John and plant a huge wet kiss on his forehead. The public gallery erupts joyously with cheers and applause and I wave frantically at Gordon and the kids. Rose demands silence, and sternly tells John and me that we may yet go back to prison if our appeals fail. Somehow I know we will not.

There is more applause as the guard escorts John and me back to the cells. I stand at the door of mine and, strengthened by my new situation, protest at the proffered indignity.

'You can't lock me up. I am a free woman.' It feels wonderful to say it.

'Just for a little while. We have to do the documentation.'

I reluctantly acquiesce, sit on the bench and alternately laugh and weep with relief. My body sings with the expectation of freedom. But I have an hour's wait, a long hour. I smoke and drink tea. Then we have to go back into court. Someone has said that we cannot have unconditional bail.

'Since when has this court not been allowed to grant unconditional bail if it so wishes?' demands Lord Justice Rose. Minor officials look sheepish. I presume that this is yet another attempt by the police and prosecution to made it hard for us. We go down again and get processed, the bureaucracy of custody taking control of us for one last time. Our possessions are issued in polythene HMP bags. I make sure my writing is with them and harass the staff to speed things up. At last, the door is opened and we walk through.

There they are, my family and friends, waiting to greet us in the entrance hall. There they are, my reasons for living. There: I have my life back again. Gordon sweeps me off my feet, I embrace my Joel and whisper to Rachel: 'Darling, it's over.' May I never have to abandon my family again. We jubilantly face the phalanx of media outside the court and I manage a few coherent words. Someone pulls me into a pub over the road and a schooner of wine is set before me. I down it fast and instantly am drunk and misbehaving. Gordon piles me into a taxi and I urge it on: faster, faster.

Freedom. At last I can go home.

eight

Back at home, after a week of pure happiness, my energy levels became erratic and I often felt very tired. On the first morning, Gordon and I took the dog for a long walk. I was overwhelmed: countryside, sun and sky – all too much to take in after the restricted views of prison. I could not adjust my perspective and the most distant trees seemed to be looming in on me, as if I was on an LSD trip or having a psychotic episode. I was alarmed, but not surprised. Months of sensory deprivation made this inevitable.

It was a shock too that the summer was so well advanced. I had missed seven months of seasons: a block of time snatched from my life. I was determined to make up for it. I enjoyed special togetherness with my family and gorged myself on real, good food. Everything was suffused with the joy of novelty. I wanted to do it all at once and it was difficult to decide what to do first. My major failure was that I could not give up the fags: I was truly addicted, and coughing well. It was nine months before I could lose the habit, to the righteous and vocal disgust of my daughter.

Everywhere I went in Cambridge, people recognized me, saying: 'I'm glad you're out.' They really did know what had gone on – that my conviction had been unjust. But their support could not completely counteract the acute shame I felt whenever I ventured into the world. My confidence was shot to pieces. I was a criminal, a jailbird; my badness was exposed and I wanted to slink around surreptitiously, to become invisible. Most of all, I just wanted to be at home. The dog was ecstatic about my return. Even the cats deigned to give me a welcome.

It was hard to leave the prison behind. Every time I looked at my watch, I automatically thought about what they would be doing at Highpoint. I did not have my own time proscribed anymore, was freed from the endless drudgery of fixed routine, able to walk outside whenever I chose, to pick up the phone and speak to people as I wanted. I was imbued with sadness for the women I had left behind who continued to endure those agonies of prison. I felt guilty that I had got away and left them to it.

At least I was hopeful about the full appeal hearing. I doubted that John and I would be incarcerated again and felt an urgency to get the convictions quashed. The issues were wider than Wyner and Brock. The way the law stood now, just about everyone running premises for homeless people was theoretically guilty under Section 8 of the Misuse of Drugs Act, which meant that the police had huge discretion about whether or not to charge people. 'Bad law leads to tyranny', a banner on one of the Cambridge Two marches had proclaimed. The campaign so far had been more active and effective than we could have dared to hope. The legal team wanted it to continue.

We decided to organize a second petition, calling for changes in Section 8 as recommended by the Police Federation's independent inquiry into the Misuse of Drugs Act, which brought out its report when I was in prison. It stated that Section 8, as it stood, was 'unclear and confusing' and a potential 'source of serious injustice'. Like Anne Campbell, my MP, they suggested that the word 'wilfully' be added and that 'a person is not to be regarded as acting wilfully merely by reason of his failure to disclose confidential records', which struck me as a resounding condemnation of my conviction.

Even so, there were those who would continue to believe we were guilty and if the convictions were quashed would think it was on a technicality. Some people even assumed I had been involved in the drug dealing. I knew these things were not true. We would just have to refute whatever we could.

The press coverage so far had been excellent in the national media and outside Cambridge, but the local papers were more restrained. The *Cambridge Evening News* had been keen to parade our guilt but not so enthusiastic about reporting the news of our release. The *Richmond Comet*, which was the local paper for the London area I grew up in, ran a 'Free Ruth Wyner Campaign' for weeks. And the *Eastern Daily Press*, the morning paper for Norfolk and Norwich, did me proud with a three-page interview and feature. It was a shame the *Evening News* could not be braver.

'Prison is a closed, secret society,' I told them, refusing to be bowed. 'The public doesn't really know what goes on. I've had a privileged glimpse.'

□ □ □

Rachel had booked a week away on an adventure holiday for herself, so Gordon and I took ourselves off to a cosy bed-and-breakfast by the sea in southern Brittany, France. It was like a second honeymoon. We were in love all over again. When we got back, I sorted out the house and garden and replied to letters. The family felt more whole again.

Then, reality crept up on me: I had no job, had lost my livelihood and had been wronged in a way that could never be put right, whatever the result of the appeal. I busied myself to escape the feelings but there they were, still bubbling away every time I stopped. And I had to stop often, got tired fast. My sleep was still disturbed by troubling dreams. A feeling of being robbed kept recurring.

Up and down, and down and down . . . a black shroud crept over me. I hit the wall, and then the floor. Gordon held me and I wept. I struggled to do anything, anything at all, other than this inertia. And I wanted to do so much. It was all ego, I told myself. Life was more than that, more than what you do. But I had lost my place in the world. Everything seemed futile. It is a cruel thing, imprisonment. The pain of it lingers long after it is over.

I cleaned the house some more, bought plants for the garden, cut back the growth, walked the dog, but still got tired quickly, and downhearted. I helped Alexander with some campaign stuff, but my head felt unclear, my thoughts were scrappy and unbounded, and my feelings insistent. It would take time. Time. But too much time had been taken already.

A couple of months later, I stayed away from home for a few days. It panicked me. In the middle of the night I opened the door so that I could come and go, inside and outside, smoking fags under gentle trees in the light of a full moon. I had heard that John had the same urge: to open doors and go through them, to wander his house freely, as if to reassure himself that this freedom was not an illusion. He was convinced that the courts were going to send us back to prison. There was no longer any safety in the world. He had reached his own Ground Zero.

Someone wanted an article, others wanted me to speak. I tried saying I could do nothing until September, but September was only two weeks away. The shroud crept up and over me again, and I was sleeping in the day when I wished I could write, get out, anything but sleep. I sent cards and letters and gifts to people in prison. But I could not give them this freedom, and if I did, would they want it? Of course they would. I was ungrateful.

Prison had locked itself inside me. I continued to dream about it: dreams of panic, restriction, fear and pain. And I visited Gerrit twice, with Gordon. The first time I became a bit manic, racing around the visits hall embracing old friends. Prisoners were not allowed to get up from their places, so I was taking every chance to exhibit and enjoy my new-found freedoms. Mary was there with her husband and kids, and so was Alicia. She had been granted a retrial but was having to wait for it to happen, still incarcerated and away from her family.

Gerrit was suffused with a prison weariness that was sharply reminiscent of my own, and I was shaken, feeling the place around me again. The second time we visited I found it easier, but Gerrit said it was too upsetting for her, seeing someone from the outside. She hated the visits hall anyway: it was noisy and impersonal, with the officers watching you constantly, staring at you. We continued to write to each other. Later, Gordon and I were able to take her out on monthly town visits; Gerrit was one of the few women in the prison privileged to have them. She greatly enjoyed walking the dog with us, going around the Cambridge shops and about the city, but found the assault on her senses exhausting and had to pace herself carefully.

When she had served her time, Gerrit was deported back to Germany, where she had to do a further six months for an additional offence. She looked forward to going home – we had heard that German prisons were better than ours – but Gerrit was quickly disappointed. Prison is prison wherever you go. Eventually, she got moved to more open conditions and life began to improve for her.

I was invited to the farewell party of a colleague and great supporter of the campaign, Professor David Brandon. A lifelong activist, he was moving up north, disappointed by Cambridge intransigence. The discussion got around to Zion Baptist Church, where I had helped to set up a local night shelter. David said that the view there was that I had led John astray. What was I supposed to have done? Said to him: 'Let the dealing continue'? The good guy pitched against the wicked witch, the woman who did not know her proper place: subservient behind the man. It was all very archaic, very primitive.

People still continually stopped me in the street: 'I'm glad you're out. It was terrible what they did to you.'

Helping me to heal.

Meanwhile, homelessness issues raged around me. The government announced plans to spend £124,000 on an advertising campaign for Christmas 2001 to urge people not to give money to beggars, presumably in the hope that it would push the homeless off the streets. On top of that, there would be no winter shelter in Cambridge for the first time in ten years: with me out of action, it seemed that no one else was willing to take it on. Anyway, the government actively discouraged winter-shelter provision in Cambridge, to the point that agencies had realistic fears about loss of grant funding should they set them up. People were now sleeping rough in the city throughout the year, in all weathers. Street counts went on. There were accusations about the results being fixed by the authorities, again anxious to hold on to their government grants by showing that efforts were having an effect. Numbers in Cambridge remained high nevertheless. The local police were reported to have said they were going to sweep the streets clean – as if the street homeless were just piles of garbage, as if poverty should be swept away from sight. They did manage to reduce aggressive begging, but the quieter, more unassuming beggars stayed with us, triggering vitriolic letters in the local press, totally out of proportion with the actual situation.

A local homelessness strategy was drawn up. Gordon had got the senior job at the hostel where he worked, and, ironically, it was designated to take in rough sleepers, most of whom were addicted to drugs or drink, or both. We worried about his safety. Surely the police would not attack us twice. But there was no knowing, no certainty, with the way the law stood. His employers were a large national housing association. We hoped they would offer him more protection than a small local charity like Wintercomfort could.

There I was on the outside, looking in, unable to contribute. I had to content myself with haranguing the appeal court for a date and eventually got one: 1 December. Five months after we got bailed. So much for Lord Justice Rose wanting a speedy hearing. Five months in limbo, trying to get myself righted. My mood was still unstable, but not as dramatically so. It was more down than up. It was hard to avoid attacking myself, hard to hold on to the belief that my punishment was undeserved. It subverted my sense of security in the world, that the authorities had got it so wrong.

I was home a lot; I wanted to be more active but there was nothing for me to do. I was on bail and could not work. No one would have me anyway. Meanwhile, the world continued on. Everyone else seemed to have somewhere to go, a place where they belonged. I did not.

I took to going swimming, and to a local gym. They had rowing machines there just like the one in prison. I watched daytime TV and caught the Commons Select Committee for Home Affairs discussing events from HMP Blantyre House, an enlightened resettlement prison. About eighty officers had undertaken a heavy-handed night-time raid and the media was given a story about contraband, drugs and money being found. As it turned out, this was a considerable exaggeration. A little cannabis was picked up, but the inmates tested negative on their piss tests – all except one who refused to do it. A result like that was exceptional for any prison. Most of the money that was found belonged to the chaplain and the 'contraband' appeared to be tools the prisoners took to work with them every day. This was a resettlement prison and people worked outside.

The MPs on the Select Committee gave the perpetrators of the raid a hard time and seemed surprised at the way things had been mis-construed. I was not surprised. That was jail all over, I fumed. The prison officials squirmed a little, but the real losers from what I could make out were the prison's outstanding governor (who had got moved out of his job the day before the raid), the staff at Blantyre House and, of course, its inmates. We must not forget about them.

□ □ □

In the House of Lords, Lord Thomas of Gresford tried to introduce the amendment to Section 8 that was originally put forward by Anne Campbell in the Commons.

'Is it in the public interest that a person who does his best for the community by taking homeless people off the streets and providing a roof over their heads takes a risk that they will use or consume drugs because that is their way of life?' he asked. 'Is it in the public interest that that person is committing a criminal offence simply because he knows that that is happening, or should not there be an additional element of wilfully consenting to it happening?'

His Lordship was backed up by Earl Russell.

It is a very high priority of this Government, and of the Prime Minister in particular, to get homeless people off the streets. We accept that priority, but it entails providing them with somewhere else to go. We have a situation where the use of drugs among large sections of the population is extremely common. We also have a situation where one cannot impose many sanctions against someone who has no home, no property and no regular source of income; that person has nothing on which any of the regular sanctions can purchase.

Therefore, people who are in charge of hostels for the homeless may be confronted by a situation in which either they must know that drugs will on occasion be consumed on the premises, although they may not know by whom, or, in order to prevent that, close the place down altogether.

What they said made eminent good sense, but of course the government was not for turning, although Section 8 was now unworkable and contained the two specific dangers: that the jury set the professional standard, despite being lay people with a limited understanding of the issues; and the level of discretion it gave to the police. Technically, as the law stood, every hostel manager could be liable to criminal charges, and also every prison governor, head teacher, publican and club owner, psychiatric charge nurses, landlords, parents and so on. And it was completely at odds with the government's stance on reducing rough sleeping. The majority of homeless people who were living on the streets actively used hard drugs, and if they were housed, were inevitably going to use on site.

I wondered if government ministers had decided that the only thing they could do now was turn a blind eye themselves.

□ □ □

Cambridgeshire Police were still pushing managers in the homelessness sector to become 'casual contacts' – that is, informers. It was one of those ongoing situations. When I was in jail, the acting manager of the Bus was repeatedly asked to become a casual contact. Wintercomfort's trustees had complained and they had got the heat taken off her; the police promised not to approach her again. It was of little consequence. Desperate to protect themselves, some other local projects were falling over each other to pass information to the police, mostly only about their suspicions of drugs rather than actual knowledge, which was hard to come by. The drug problem was driven further underground.

Christopher Cordess, a professor of forensic psychiatry who was honorary consultant and director of research at Rampton Hospital, mentioned the Wintercomfort case in a new book he had edited, *Confidentiality and Mental Health* (Jessica Kingsley, 2001). He wrote about how, in his view, if the criteria used in the case for drugs monitoring were generally extended, psychiatric units in metropolitan areas, where drug misuse was rife, would most certainly be at risk. The book expressed professionals' concern about how the tide had shifted away from offering, at root, a confidential service for clients to one where disclosure was the norm. After reading it, I resolved to be more careful about what I told my GP.

Managers of homelessness agencies around the country were reported to be running scared, some putting a blanket ban on people who used illicit drugs. A survey by Homeless Link, a national agency representing homeless organizations, found that a third of its members had experienced accommodation providers refusing to house drug users following the Wintercomfort trial. It was not surprising, after what had happened to John and me. Inevitably, anyone housing active drug addicts could be seen as turning a blind eye because they knew, through deduction if not direct observation, what would be going on. Different police forces responded in different ways: I was sent a copy of a letter from a chief constable in another part of the country who stated categorically that he would not have acted as the Cambridgeshire constabulary had done.

Meanwhile, Alexander and I headed up to Leeds with Stuart Shorter, a one-time homeless drug addict and campaign stalwart, to talk to the local TUC. Stuart captivated them all; he spoke from dire experience and eloquently from the heart. A woman from Bradford complained that the police in her patch were demanding, not just asking, for the names of local drug users. It sounded ominous. People would feel compelled to give out the information for their own safety.

A week before the 1 December appeal hearing, my mood lowered further. I got headaches, felt paralysed; I wondered if it was with terror. Everything was so painful that I just wanted to blot it all out, permanently. I wished I did not feel like this: slowly dying, not really living at all.

We had a comedy benefit gig fixed up at the Hackney Empire. It cheered me up enormously. Mark Thomas headlined, having

featured our case in his TV series, along with Robert Newman, who
had added a new joke to his website.

Cambridge Wintercomfort Homeless Shelter
TWO CARE ASSISTANTS WANTED

We have two vacancies since the departure of Ruth and John.

We are looking for people who can create a supportive, receptive,
nurturing environment, be a sounding-board so that our residents
will feel safe enough to open up about their drug problems.

And then you must be prepared, diligently, carefully and with
great compassion, to grass them up to the Old Bill so they get
banged up for ten years and guaranteed to become
smack addicts.

□ □ □

December the first arrived at last. On the way to court, Gordon, Joel,
Rachel and I stopped for a coffee at Charing Cross station. A woman
in there recognized me – the first time I had been spotted in
London – and she wished me luck. I hoped it was a good omen.

The appeal court was packed, mostly with our supporters, but five
police officers claimed a front row in the public gallery. Michael
Mansfield started the proceedings, initially outlining the case and
then concentrating on the issue of subjectivity – level of knowledge
and confidentiality – and the way the trial judge, Judge Haworth, had
handled this.

Then there was an address from the prosecution. They had a new
QC, William Clegg, and to our surprise he brought in traffic cases as
examples, which seemed totally irrelevant. But Clegg also conceded
on a major point: level of knowledge. He accepted that it was an
issue which had to be taken into account. Mansfield was triumphant
and rounded on this after the lunch break, in his second address.

'Do you realize that at the trial there was three days of legal argument over this point,' he said, waving a sheaf of papers, presumably

the transcript, at the bench. 'The judge ruled against us, but the prosecution has now given way on it.'

They gave way because they had to. No agency could act as if something was taking place when they were not aware of it. Being psychic is not in our job descriptions. Mansfield sensibly pointed out that our beat bobby, who had free access to the project and visited regularly, was not aware of drug dealing either. He described how those involved in the dealing had a system of lookouts and reiterated that they would not do any of it in front of John and me, or in front of our staff. At last: a bit of reality coming into the courtroom. As for confidentiality, there seemed to be disbelief among the judges about Haworth's attitude to it. Mansfield went through various points from Haworth's summing-up to the jury, in which he had seemed to us to be giving them no choice but to return a guilty verdict.

The relief came at the end. The appeal judges said they needed time to clarify and write up their decision. I thought it would finish there, but the judges asked to look briefly at the sentencing, and then it came out. They said that the sentences were 'far too long' and reassured John and me that we would not be going back to prison, whether or not the convictions were quashed.

'For once, my optimism has won out over your pessimism,' I said to John, who had brought a bag with him to court, expecting to get banged up again there and then.

The judges asked for the prosecution's response if a retrial was ordered. Clegg said they would not present any evidence upon a retrial, and several people thought they heard one of the judges say: 'I'm not surprised.' Surely that should give us some hope. Meanwhile, the five coppers sitting together at the front of the public gallery looked very dejected indeed.

I dared to think that the juggernaut of British justice was turning at last, that we were finally being properly heard. Three weeks later, the verdict came through and shattered my optimism. The appeal against conviction was refused. Despite the accepted failings of Haworth's summing-up, the judges had ruled against us. Lord Justice Rose came into the court alone and grumpily read a couple of pages from the judgement. The ruling was that the convictions would stand, but the sentences would be cut to fourteen months to reflect the time we had already spent in prison. We had done seven months, and, unless you behave exceptionally badly, you get out halfway through if your sentence is under four years.

Rose said that, despite the misdirections by the trial judge, a jury would have found us guilty anyway. I wondered how he could be so certain. It did not seem right to second-guess a jury. Rose had not heard the evidence being given in court, could not have read it all, and if he had relied on Haworth's biased summing-up, he would have been badly led astray. The misdirections meant that our trial had not been a fair one. I wished I had brought in more defence witnesses; we had plenty lined up. But my legal team seemed to have been intimidated by the aggression of the prosecution and they had advised me not to. One of the solicitors who had been key to my defence was so depressed and disheartened after our case that he left the profession.

Continuing, Rose criticized us severely for not passing on the request for names from the police to the Wintercomfort trustees. As usual, our judge got it wrong: a trustee had been sitting right beside me when that request was made by our liaison inspector and she had heard every word for herself. As an afterthought, Rose added that there was no reason to give me a longer sentence than John. Then he seemed to want to get out of the courtroom as quickly as possible, standing up to go before all the business had been done.

This bad-tempered person was not the Lord Justice Rose we had got to know and like.

'He's been got at,' said a friend.

'They don't want him to give out wrong messages,' said another.

It seemed that all Rose had done was to maintain the status quo: we had done time, we would stay out, and no one, judge, police or prosecution, would pay for the injustice done to us.

□ □ □

I had a criminal record, was an 'ex-offender'. No, not an ex-offender, I told myself, but an ex-prisoner. After a wonderful family Christmas, I was left with the task of trying to earn a living. I sent my CV out to everyone I could think of, applied for jobs, but was met with a resounding silence. No one wanted to take on an ex-con.

The Prison Reform Trust came to my rescue and gave me some freelance work. It was enormously hard: my self-esteem was shattered and I did not have the same resilience as before. But I kept at it, gradually finding my feet, and the people there were friendly and helpful. I got a few additional titbits from NACRO, the National Association for the Care and Resettlement of Offenders.

Occasionally, I was invited to speak at conferences. One was a speak-out for homeless people in London, organized by Groundswell, a self-help group for homeless and ex-homeless people, along with the *Big Issue* magazine. I was asked to say a few words. What came out was a confused rant against homelessness policies, drug policies, prison policies, and a general plea for the underdog. My pain had become enmeshed with the pain of those who had been my clients, and I was infuriated.

I managed a slightly more focused presentation for the UK Harm Reduction Alliance, which sported a healthy display of professionals in the drugs field, ranging from frontline workers to university researchers and GPs. It was there that I met and was befriended by Eddie Ellison, retired detective chief superintendent, former operational head of the Metropolitan Police Central Drug Squad and a keen legalizer. He told me that the main problem with police drug squads was corruption; the temptation for officers was so great.

'Of course, if you don't have a drug squad, and drug crime is tackled along with everything else, you have a recipe for corruption. It's pretty much inevitable,' said Eddie.

'Cambridgeshire Police doesn't have a drug squad,' I told him.

As part of my work with the Prison Reform Trust, I spent one-and-a-half days at HMP Wandsworth, a tough London men's jail. The officer showing us around described it as a 'bang-up nick', which it was for sure: 1300 men in tiny cells, the spurs fanning out from a central area and rising up floor upon floor, everything caged in.

The cell doors lined each spur. Inside, each cell was tiny and cramped, more like a tunnel than a room, with the usual hard bed, a washbasin, toilet, desk and chair, and a window so high up that you could not look out of it. I reckoned I had been fortunate at Highpoint, though most of the Wandsworth inmates had single cells, something I had always craved. Perhaps having access to others had helped me maintain my sanity, to some degree at least.

□ □ □

I had been writing ever since I came out of prison. I worked on the material about homelessness that had come off my battered typewriter and developed new sections on the case of the Cambridge Two and my experiences in prison. I sat at home and the words spun out of me on to the computer, pages and pages of them as I tried to rid myself of the trauma locked inside me.

When I was on Highpoint's Kainos community, I was struck with how the community aspect of it helped many of the women, especially those who felt completely outside society, their sense of alienation reinforced by the general prison regime. Even those who disliked the evangelism on Kainos as much as I did would, for instance, volunteer to help run godparents' evenings, because it gave them a prized sense of being valued, of being included in the community outside as well as in the prison itself. I decided to develop my knowledge of group work and of therapeutic communities and got myself into some professional training.

I also made contact with David Parsons, a probation officer. Ten years previously, David had pioneered dialogue groups for prisoners, officers and community volunteers at HMP Whitemoor, a top-security prison in Cambridgeshire: fifteen or twenty people sitting together and talking on the level with no set agenda for a couple of hours each week.

'Walking a mile in each other's boots,' said David. The idea was to reduce the exclusion felt by prisoners, to help their personal development and to ease tension on the wings. It was a humanizing process for all concerned. I had been interested in using group work therapeutically in homelessness projects well before my arrest and had invited David to set up and run a weekly dialogue group at the Bus. Among our volunteers were local residents, a local councillor, a millionaire businessman and our two liaison police officers. One of them, the sector inspector, had used material from the dialogue group in his evidence against us, showing complete disregard for the confidentiality of the group, which David had repeatedly explained to all concerned. Yet another betrayal. The police seemed to have no understanding whatsoever of confidentiality. But if we ditched the concept completely, we risked moving towards a police state.

As well as working locally, David was involved with a charity in the West Country that was running dialogue groups at a prison in that area, HMP Blakenhurst. I attended some of the sessions and went on to fundraise three years' money for the charity to establish and run dialogue groups at another prison. We got the money and I was due to take on the new project, but then suffered another hammer blow: I was diagnosed with breast cancer. The work went elsewhere.

The first questions I asked my hospital consultant were about the timing of the cancer. Would the tumour have been there in May 1998 (when I was arrested)? He told me it would not have. Would it have been there in July 2000 (when I came out of prison)? Undoubtedly it would have, he said. I was under no illusions about what had caused my cancer: the stress of the arrest, trial and imprisonment – the shock of it, and the injustice. In prison I had feared that my self, my spirit, would be destroyed. Now I was facing complete annihilation. The cancer was well advanced. One of the nurses told me that I was on the edge.

Eight months previously, I had seen my GP because I thought I had felt a small lump in my breast. She had assured me that there was nothing there, that I need not worry, and she did not suggest further investigation. She was wrong and had let me down. Once again, the authorities had failed me.

I dropped everything out of my life to face this new threat. A week after my diagnosis, I was at Addenbrookes Hospital oncology out-patients in Cambridge getting my first dose of chemotherapy. I had six sessions over four-and-a-half months and each one made me feel

terribly ill. Every time it was as though I was fighting the bombard-
ment of poisonous toxins that had been sent flooding through my
body, fighting to stay alive. Which indeed I was. Chemotherapy can,
in itself, be a killer. I had finished the treatment by Christmas 2001,
and felt completely shattered but ready for my operation in the New
Year. I urged the surgeons to cut out every bit of the cancer: it had
come to represent the pain of my imprisonment. Then I had a few
weeks of radiotherapy.

Addenbrookes is a worthy hospital and I was thankful for the care
I got there, but I also determined to do everything to give myself the
best chance. This was not my time to die, it could not be. I developed
a regime that included yoga, chi gung (similar to tai chi, which I took
up later), relaxation, visualization, healing, shiatsu, a special diet,
vitamin and mineral supplements and carefully chosen herbs. I
walked the dog when I was able to, but there were days when I could
barely manage to walk around the house. Immobilized on the
sofa, I watched the events of 9/11 unfold.

It took me a year to attain 75 per cent recovery, my moods ranging
from the euphoria of survival to deep despair about my ability to
connect with the outside world ever again. At least I was alive. A
brush with death makes you focus on the real priorities: existence,
the people you love, and those who love you.

'Which was hardest, prison or cancer?' a friend asked me.

'Prison,' I replied without a moment's thought, astonishing
myself. Being locked up and treated like scum felt worse than having
a life-threatening disease.

There are always compensations. This book would not have been
published if I had not become ill. I would have been too busy with the
dialogue project to put the final and crucial touches to it. In the few
days between chemotherapy sessions, when I could think a little, I re-
organized my manuscripts. People who had read them found the
prison parts the most compelling. So I cut out the most of the sections about the court case and about homelessness to concentrate on
that. For me, too, it had been a shock and a revelation to discover
what prison was really like.

Perhaps young Pearl was right when she told me that everything has a reason and a purpose. Or maybe the task is to find for yourself a reason and a purpose for everything that happens to you.

□ □ □

I was gradually freeing myself from the hold prison had got over me. My dreams changed from being about entrapment and exclusion to situations in which I had got out of prison unlawfully and needed to sneak back in without being caught. Eventually, I hardly dreamed about prison at all.

My anger at being unjustly convicted and jailed started to emerge, usually unexpectedly and often causing me embarrassment. One day, when I was walking the dog, a woman with a little boy cheerily said: 'Hello.'

'Why isn't your child in school?' I snarled before I had a chance to restrain myself.

Eventually, the anger came out as an unstoppable torrent of murderous rage. Words poured from my mouth, colliding with the nearest available targets. For two days I raged, out of control. I longed to hurt people physically – the thought of it gave me immense pleasure – but managed to restrict myself to infuriated and totally inconsiderate verbal abuse, accompanied by streams of hot tears. Thankfully, I was among friends. I experienced huge relief afterwards and tried not to feel ashamed about my behaviour: I had good cause to be angry.

John was not doing so well. He put what little energy he had into home and family, but small things became huge mountains and any activity was difficult. He visited the police station on behalf of a member of his family, hoping that it would enable him to lay some old ghosts to rest. It had the opposite effect.

'I came out spitting blood,' he told me. 'They were all bastards. It reinforced how I felt. No therapy to be had there.'

Wintercomfort had, to its credit, survived, though in a different form. Two of its five projects, street outreach and a training scheme, had been dispersed to other agencies. The winter shelters had been discontinued, though agencies tried to replace the provision to an extent with a winter soup run. During the freezing weather of winter 2002–03, a street count found fifteen people sleeping rough; as usual, it was obvious that the count had not included everybody. Wintercomfort's fourth project, working to resettle people in rented housing, was retained in Ely but not in Cambridge, due to shortages of places to rent.

But the Bus project continued. Not long after John and I had been charged by the police, it was altered from an informal 'open door' operation to a 'closed door' project, with a heavy wooden gate, CCTV and a call system restricting entry, in order to protect the day centre and, crucially, its staff. In court, the prosecution had tried to use this against us, suggesting that such changes had only been possible with John and me out of the way. In fact, I had been very much involved in organizing them during my excommunication at St John's College.

The Wintercomfort trustees valorously resisted pressure to find a new name for the charity. The Bus was, however, redesignated as the Centre in 2002. Staff introduced yet more structure to the project, which protected them and increased the focus on rehabilitation but had inevitable repercussions for the clientele, a proportion of whom experienced Wintercomfort as less accessible. These further changes included a system of graded membership (using memberships cards that were, to us ex-cons, sharply reminiscent of prison ID), no longer allowing people to drink alcohol in the courtyard, and overall employing a much more structured approach. The GP surgery was moved out and it found a new home. Wintercomfort's original objective of getting the most alienated people off the streets by using an open-door policy had shifted in order to comply with local and national strategies and, essentially, to ensure the day centre's survival. While it continued to do tremendous and invaluable good work, in particular building on the sessional activities that John and I had originally introduced, its ethos had changed and it had, to an extent, gone upmarket. As a result, some of the old clientele disappeared into the underground and away from view. Partly with this in mind, the new policies were under continual review.

Towards the end of the year, Cambridge City Council admitted to the *Evening News* that its homelessness strategy had failed. A new strategy was drawn up, with much goodwill and good intentions from the various local agencies, but inevitably some people still festered on the streets. In October 2002 the *Evening News* reported that the strategy stated a need for 'somewhere for those unable to give up [drink or drug habits] to gather in the day, away from the public'. Just what the Bus used to provide – but who in their right minds would attempt a project like that in Cambridge after what had happened to John and me?

Accusations flew around that the street homeless were all drug addicts, and that lack of co-operation from homelessness agencies had caused the problem, as well as lack of co-operation from the drug addicts themselves because they refused to be cured. Organizations working with homeless drug users were particularly attacked, because this inevitably meant there were drugs on their projects, but they were doing the most difficult job of all. A colleague from Norwich, who was losing the battle to get a bit of humanity into the debate about homelessness there, said local people wanted to criminalize the homeless. I told her the same was happening in Cambridge.

John and I were sent invitations to the opening ceremony for Wintercomfort's newly designated Centre. I was anxious about the feelings that would be evoked, and we discussed it.

'I know what you're going through,' said John.

'I know you do.' He knew it better than anyone.

Neither of us went.

□ □ □

The problem of hard drugs in Cambridge continued to be as bad as ever, despite the removal of the Cambridge Two. The whole country was suffering in the same way. Journalists, politicians and practitioners called for a new approach, suggesting that illicit drugs should be legalized and regulated, with heroin given out on prescription to take it out of the hands of the criminal gangs.

'A grown-up approach to drugs,' said a *Guardian* reporter, who had telephoned to get my views.

Even the Home Secretary, David Blunkett, encouraged local agencies to prescribe more heroin to addicts, as we used to do in this country forty years ago. In December 2002 the Home Office produced an updated drugs strategy, stating that 'heroin should be available on prescription to all those who have a clinical need for it'. It also said that heroin should be provided in medically supervised safe areas with clean needles and with procedures in place to avert the risk of seepage into the wider community. The drug and alcohol services in Cambridge were reluctant to comply. Presumably they preferred to see heroin addicts begging, shoplifting, stealing and mugging people in order to get their supplies, to see them criminalized and imprisoned rather than treated, despite evidence from abroad that prescribing heroin considerably improved the situation for everyone – apart from those who controlled the illegal supplies.

With the homelessness situation in Cambridge as bad as ever, and local street counts consistently among the highest outside London, Cambridge City Council brought in a policy of offering longer-term services only for those homeless people with a local connection. It seemed to make no difference.

Meanwhile, Cambridgeshire Police had its own problems. One of its number, a Sergeant Paul Banfield, was sent to prison for eighteen years for raping a young woman in the police cells and assaulting others. Another police officer was convicted of arson and two more were charged with a string of offences relating to child pornography. The chief constable retired and the assistant chief constable moved on. Ian Negus, the detective who had led my prosecution, went into retirement as well. I discovered that I was not the only person who was glad to see the back of him.

I met a university lecturer who had spoken to a policeman about the Wintercomfort case when they had run adjoining stalls at a local fête. She had been told that yes, the police had been out to get me, and again, yes, I had been specifically targeted. Such abuse of power! Was it naïve of me to think that the police operated otherwise?

Some workers in the Cambridge homelessness and drugs fields reported a shift in attitude among their liaison police: there seemed to be greater understanding of these problems and more willingness to work in partnership. Could we believe it? As crack cocaine joined the influx of heroin into the city, one police officer made it absolutely clear that he and his colleagues never wanted another case like Wintercomfort. A section of the local force seemed to be deeply embarrassed about what had happened to John and me.

After all, taking us to court and then to prison must have cost us, taxpayers, well over a million pounds. And for what purpose? What had been gained?

□ □ □

I suppose it is harder doing a prison sentence if you feel it is not justified. The Portia Campaign estimates there are 3000 people in British prisons who have been wrongly convicted. I know of a prison officer who reckons that 7 per cent of his inmates are innocent of the crimes for which they have been convicted. That is equivalent to over 5000 people across a prison population of 72,000.

Miscarriages of Justice UK (MOJUK) supported John and me when we were in jail and added us to their list of hostages to injustice. The organization was started in 1996 by John O., one of the Birmingham Six, who served twenty long years of wrongful imprisonment. He had this to say about British justice, and it rang true for me:

Millions of people in the UK learn about the law from school, college, what they get from the media. The proper place to learn about the law is in a courtroom, where the proverbial shit hits the fan.

It is entirely possible to read numerous legal textbooks, go into a courtroom, see what's happening and be totally stunned by the differences between what the law says and what the law does, daily.

People observing the process of courts for the first time end up saying, again and again, 'They can't do that!', only to recognize that they are doing it, and they continue to do so.

Prison is hard, whether you are innocent or guilty, and as it stands it is largely a waste of money if, as a former Tory Home Secretary said, it makes 'bad people worse', though I would say it makes the badness in people worse. I did not see anyone in prison who was just bad, bad through and through. What I did see was plenty of people who had struggled with difficulty and disadvantage, and who had lost the struggle, their criminality often a natural reaction to their environment. As Deborah Orr wrote in the *Independent* early in 2002: 'Can we not see . . . that brutalizing the perpetrators of crime makes them more, not less, dangerous, more not less of a problem.'

A year later, in February 2003, Ian Burrell of the *Independent* reported on new Home Office research which showed community penalties to be more effective than incarceration.

'Prison does not work,' he wrote. 'Figures to be released to Parliament by the Home Office minister Hilary Benn will show that 44 per cent of criminals who are given community penalties are reconvicted within two years, compared with 56 per cent of those sent to jail.'

With the prison population in the UK the highest *per capita* in Europe, and government expectations that it would increase further, from 72,000 to a predicted 110,000 in 2009, such statistics seemed to fall on deaf ears. Martin Narey, speaking during the same month upon his promotion from director-general of the Prison Service to commissioner for the Correctional Services, accepted that 'we still have some staff who treat prisoners with scant respect'. But his fervour for imprisonment continued unabated.

'The challenge is to demonstrate we can change lives in greater numbers and that we can make prison the ultimate and successful social service,' he said. To designate the agonizing effects of a prison sentence as a 'social service' struck me as pure prison doublespeak – or had the man become completely desensitized by his work?

In his new role, Martin Narey would oversee the probation service as well as prisons. Harry Fletcher, assistant general secretary of the probation union NAPO, was quoted in Ian Burrell's article as saying that the government had failed to properly resource frontline probation staff.

'It flies in the face of economic sense,' he said. 'Probation is one-tenth the cost of prison and we now know it is more effective in reducing offending.' And a lot less damaging too.

I had a clearer perspective after hearing Professor Pat Carlen, from the University of Keele, talk at Cambridge University's Institute of Criminology on the very same day as Martin Narey's speech. She insisted that prisons were most definitely all about pain and punishment, which accorded with my experience, and that rehabilitative programmes simply did not work.

'Programmes can't change the material conditions under which people commit crimes,' she said. 'There is an executive dishonesty about what prisons can do. They try to legitimize it by saying they'll reduce crime through these programmes, but they don't work. Prisoners say how much they enjoy them and so forth, but that's only because it gets them out of their cells.'

Interestingly, Pat also quoted surveys that showed the public were far less keen to imprison people when they understood more about the offenders' background situations, using exactly the same information that magistrates and judges had on sentencing. Even victims of crime were less vengeful than we all assumed.

Meanwhile, a Home Office report predicted that forty new prisons would have to be built by 2010 to cope with demand, at a cost to the taxpayer of billions of pounds. The final word must go to Professor Nils Christie, speaking at the Prison Reform Trust's 2002 annual lecture. He said: 'Low prison population has some of the same qualities as absence of torture and absence of capital punishment.'

□ □ □

Some people do need to be punished with imprisonment and held in a secure environment, for their own and for society's safety. Far better to have a secure environment that humanizes rather than dehumanizes, that gives them chances for the future and thus protects society better. A few of our prisons do that, but far too few. Most of them are understaffed and under-resourced, and have to make continual cutbacks to the already strained prison environment because sentencing policies and practice lead to massive overcrowding, despite calls for restraint from Lord Woolf, the Lord Chief Justice. The outcome for the prisoner is more bang-up, more distress, more damage, more attempts at suicide and self-harm, and more stress for the prison staff.

In 2002 Lord Woolf described overcrowding as the cancer in our prisons and forcefully accused the present criminal justice system of being counterproductive 'because of the waste of public money, because of the effect it has on victims, witnesses and jurors who become caught up with the system and, most important of all, because it does not protect the public'. He called for a 'fundamentally different approach', a 'holistic' one, stating that heavy punishment did not solve crime. He maintained that his views were 'neither soft nor liberal, but realistic common sense'.

During his farewell address, on leaving his post as Chief Inspector of Prisons, Sir David Ramsbotham boldly called for an end to the imprisonment of women, children and asylum seekers. The issue of imprisoning the young is particularly poignant. Between January and December 2002, ninety-four prisoners committed suicide, the highest annual total since records began. These included a sixteen-year-old, a seventeen-year-old, and forty-five people aged thirty or under (sources: Inquest and the Howard League for Penal Reform). Prison is no place for young people.

There has been much talk about how prison affects women worse than it does men. In one major respect it does: family. Women feel the loss of their children acutely, biologically. Your kids are a part of you. Fathers are important too, but the relationship is a different one. An HM Inspectorate of Prisons Thematic Review of Women in Prison found that only 25 per cent of women could be assured that their children's father, or a spouse or partner, was caring for their children, while the children of 92 per cent of fathers were cared for by the children's mothers. Overall, 125,000 youngsters aged sixteen and under are affected by the imprisonment of a parent in Britain every year (source: Social Exclusion Unit).

Women are reputedly more in touch with their feelings than men, which suggests that they will feel the pains of imprisonment more intensely. Prison officers state openly that women's prisons are very different to men's, despite the similar regimes. However, we must not deny that men suffer too and that the outcome is predominantly unproductive: more than half ex-prisoners go on to get caught reoffending, and it is inevitable with the current system that many emerge from jail incapacitated and psychologically harmed. Far better to give people the chance to repay their debt to society in an honourable and meaningful way.

There is the potential for change. In July 2002 the Social Exclusion Unit came out with a hard-hitting report: *Reducing re-offending by ex-prisoners*, which came up with some interesting, if alarming, statistics. Regarding women prisoners, it states that at least a fifth were living as lone parents before imprisonment, 55 per cent had at least one child at home aged under sixteen, and a third had a child under five. Fifteen per cent of sentenced women prisoners had previously been admitted to a mental hospital, and a staggering 37 per cent had attempted suicide. Against this backdrop, the number of women prisoners has more than doubled in the past ten years.

The government seem to be taking on board some of the issues, though a huge amount of work is needed to alter politicians' attitudes and to educate the public in the realities of prison, to convince them that it is not in their interests to cause increased anti-social behaviour by incarcerating people in such great numbers. Bearing in mind the plans to vastly increase the prison population, I wonder if politicians will have the courage or even the intent to see it through.

Some of the prisons themselves have been able to move forward. After my release, HMP Highpoint set up a much-needed drug therapeutic community for the women. Kainos was removed, following an independent evaluation, and a Christian fellowship organization went in instead. Highpoint also got a new, purpose-built 'super-enhanced' block with single cells and in-cell TV. Ah, bliss. Work had started on it while I was still inside. I remembered Gerrit and I taking extended gardening breaks to ogle the workmen. Eventually, Gerrit got a room there for herself and reported back to me. Much better than the other units, she said, except that the windows in the cells were tiny and hardly opened at all. She roasted in the summer and, as in other UK jails, had to endure a whole lot more bang-up because of the overcrowding.

Britain: the prison capital of Europe. It was not something to be proud of.

□ □ □

As for me, I was proud of my children. Joel had completed his MA and was accepted for teacher training. Rachel, nearly three years after my release, had this to say: 'Now I can reflect on the experience (and on the most chocolate I ever ate in a seven-month period!), I know it has helped me gain a perspective. For starters, being the centre of attention is not always the best of things: fame is fickle and not everyone is on your side. I have learned not to be judgemental, and to treasure my friends, even if they are fleeting ones, which they often are at sixteen. I feel I have grown so much. When the subject of the police comes up, I can't really comment. How can you comment on a large body of people consisting of thousands of individuals? It would almost be racism. I'd like to say something positive but it's hard when I've seen such negativity. As for the campaign, it was such a support. I look back and think: "Did I deserve that?" At the moment I'm at university and aim to become a teacher. I hope I can help people as much as my parents and that I can make my children as proud of their mum and dad as I am of mine.'

□ □ □

I made contact with David Parsons again and together we set up the Dialogue Trust, to develop dialogue groups in prisons, with probation departments and for people in drug treatment, initially in the east of England. David was already working in HMP Whitemoor, running dialogue groups for two wings and training officers to lead some groups themselves. We enlisted support from people at Cambridge University's Institute of Criminology and Cambridge Group Work and worked to get some lifers' groups going at HMP Littlehey in Cambridgeshire. The hard part was getting hold of any funding.

In September 2002 I went as co-ordinator of the Dialogue Trust to HMP Wayland for the launch of the Ormiston Trust Eastern Region Families Partnership, the object of which was to retain family bonds for prisoners and their relatives. I was called over by one of the governors from HMP Highpoint. She had seen a book review I had done for the *Prison Service Journal*, a trade magazine for the prison service. She was in charge of the books section and asked if I would like to do some more for them.

'You did a good review.'

'Thanks. You know, I'm a different person now than I was when I was in prison.'

Having an on-the-level conversation with a 'screw', as an equal, was surprising enough. But this comment seemed to pop out by itself. I did become a different person in prison and it took me over two years to find myself again.

'Yes, you do look different, actually. Was it a coping mechanism?'

'It was the system that did it to me.'

What did it do? It took away my life, my loves, my hopes, and left me scared, despairing, hateful and angry; fighting to hold on to the last vestiges of my self as I became engulfed in the entrails of prison.

'Oh, I know. I'd be a nightmare if I was inside.'

As she went, I said: 'Say hello to everyone from me,' and immediately felt foolish. But she had expressed an interest in having a dialogue group at Highpoint and was keen for me to be involved. I was not so sure.

'It could be useful,' she insisted.

I met and spoke to a range of people at that meeting, from Hilary Benn MP, the new prisons minister, to Gary, a serving prisoner, and plenty in between: funders, voluntary sector workers, prison officers and governors. Perhaps this was a community to which I could contribute, and within which I could be accepted. Within which I could be restored. Perhaps not. It was difficult to get in and do the work. People were suspicious, especially of an ex-con, and resources were tight.

It had been a long road. As always, there was still a way to go on it.

postscript

A year after my release, the government brought in an amendment to Section 8(d) of the Misuse of Drugs Act, which was perfectly logical. It made it illegal to allow use of any illicit drugs on premises as well as dealing. The way the law had stood, it was permissible to allow use of heroin but not cannabis, though illegal to allow dealing of either or any other controlled drug.

At the time, it was agreed by Parliament to introduce some notes of guidance to 'help those who are carrying out important and legitimate harm reduction work with drug misusers'. In the autumn of 2002 the government began a period of quiet consultation over its proposals.

The Notes of Guidance stated:

> In deciding whether to charge a person under the amended legislation police officers must use discretion based on the public interest test to determine whether charging the suspect is appropriate and proportionate. If a person has been motivated by harm reduction factors when committing an offence under Section 8(d) of the Act these should be taken into account by the police.

Among the examples where harm-reduction factors might be taken into account were for those working with rough sleepers, along with parents, drug treatment workers, landlords and people working in the entertainment sector. No mention was made of schools, colleges, psychiatric departments and prisons.

The Notes went on to state:

> It is known that a high percentage of rough sleepers are chaotic drug misusers. Care workers provide shelter to stabilise the lifestyle so the causes of rough sleeping (such as drug misuse) can be tackled. In cases where drug misuse is an underlying cause there will be an interim stage where the person is in shelter and continuing to use drugs illegally. In

these circumstances harm reduction considerations should be a significant factor when deciding whether to bring a charge under Section 8(d).

I sent a copy of the Notes of Guidance to Nick Cohen at the *Observer*, and he wrote a great piece headlined 'The vindication of Ruth Wyner'. Could it be true? Apparently not. Kevin Flemen at Release, the national legal and drugs charity, was horrified at the limited protection that would be offered to workers, parents and others, and at the huge amount of discretion that the police would have about whether or not to prosecute.

'We are concerned that the definition and interpretation of "harm reduction" is not clear, and much activity may not fall under a strict "harm reduction" interpretation,' Release stated in their response. They thought the Notes of Guidance would criminalize families struggling with their children's drug use, result in an increase in homelessness among young drug users, and actually 'make it impossible to house and support people who use controlled drugs but can live independently with moderate levels of support.' They continued: 'We further believe that the implementation of the legislation without adequate legal safeguards will act as a substantial disincentive to landlords to house this vulnerable client group.'

Release also complained about the regional disparity that the Notes of Guidance would produce and declared they were 'deeply troubled' by the paragraph that stated that organizations should inform police at an early stage if they suspect drug misuse and that 'if the drug misuse continues, the failure to inform and co-operate with the police exposes individuals to prosecution'. Release responded:

> This obligation will make it impossible for organizations to work
> effectively with ongoing drug users. It will be impossible to maintain
> the trust of clients. It will be unworkable in practice, as organizations
> working with people who use drugs encounter situations on a very
> frequent basis and to report each new episode to the police would
> create an untenable amount of work for both agencies and the
> police.

In essence this guidance imposes a new duty on workers, and this is not a duty that exists in the legislation.

Release also made some highly pertinent general observations that were taken up by Dr Lynne Jones MP, who quoted them in a submission from a group of cross-bench MPs, including my own MP, Anne Campbell.

Working within the guidelines would mean that organizations would be working illegally, even if the police decided not to prosecute. This would:

a) have implications for the charitable status of organisations who are registered charities;

b) mean that managers instructing staff to work in such a manner would be inciting staff to commit a criminal act;

c) have implications for organizations' insurance both for building and liability.

It is not acceptable to create a situation that requires staff to work in a way that is illegal, even if the threat of prosecution is reduced. If, as the Guidance states, there is a recognition for this work to continue, it needs to be undertaken in a fully legal manner.

The problem for the government was that its policies on drugs collided head-on with its policies on harm minimization and reducing rough sleeping. If they went ahead with their Notes of Guidance, they would be the ones turning a blind eye, because they would know drugs were being used on premises throughout the UK but would be allowing it to continue on the basis of public interest. Where did public interest begin and end? Who decided? Who decided whether or not to prosecute? And who would protect those agencies who wanted to work 'eyes wide open'?

Bob Ainsworth MP, undersecretary at the Home Office, repeatedly told a conference held in October 2002 by Drugscope and Homeless Link that he did not understand what workers were worried about, as there had only been a few prosecutions. As one of those few, I wrote to him outlining the devastating effect of the prosecutions on John and me and our families, and on homeless provision in Cambridge. Mr Ainsworth did not reply.

Homeless Link took legal advice on the government's proposals, their substantive point being that it was unacceptable to expect agencies to operate illegally and rely on assurances that harm-minimization principles would be taken into account in deciding whether to prosecute. Specialist voluntary sector solicitors Sinclair Taylor & Martin agreed that the legislation created substantial legal problems for organizations, especially from charitable, employment and insurance perspectives. The advice also confirmed that the Notes of Guidance could offer no protection and were inadequate. Home Office lawyers did not agree.

These seemingly intractable problems about Section 8(d) do demonstrate the inconsistencies of the government's overall attitude to drugs. Should we criminalize people or protect them? Treat them or stigmatize them? The law demands zero tolerance on drugs, but that means you cannot work to minimize harm.

In March 2003 the government bowed to pressure and withdrew its proposed Notes of Guidance. Instead, ministers decided to wait for two years, in order to gauge the impact of measures in its new white paper on anti-social behaviour. They indicated that there would be specific sections to address the position of drugs and homelessness agencies. So, after a lengthy consultation with workers in agencies nationwide, it was back to square one.

John and I had stepped over an invisible line. That line had been rendered slightly more visible through our prosecutions, but what showed up was not in any way comforting to those in the field. In a sense, workers are all knowingly allowing: if you accommodate any-one actively using illicit drugs, you know that illegal activity will take place on your premises. Perhaps that gives people safety in numbers; perhaps not. Illicit drug use will never disappear from our society. The challenge is to ensure freedom from prosecution for everyone who works in good faith on these problems, carrying out govern-ment-approved harm-minimization policies for the benefit of us all.

Thanks

Thanks to all who helped with the Cambridge Two campaign, including:

Jo Abel
Marie Archer
Arco Iris Samba Band
Lord Avebury
Joan Baez
Helen Barnes
Lord Bassham
Francis Beadle
Prof. Dame Gillian Beer
Tom Behan
Linda Bendall
Alan Bennett
John Binns
Tom Binns
Adele Blakeborough
Rev. Martin Blakeborough
    from Kaleidescope
Peter Bottomley MP
Mary Braid
Jo Brand
David and Althea Brandon
Terry Braverman
Liz Brennan
Alfred and Ivy Brock
John, Louise, Lloyd and Dylan Brock
Sir Alec and Lady Mary Broers
Ian Burrell

Ruth Bush
Anne Campbell MP
Cardboard Citizens
Eliza Carthy
Martin Carthy
Rev. Prof. Owen Chadwick
Olivia Challens
Julie Christie
The many Churches that supported us
Nick Cohen
Caroline Coon
Julie Crocker
Graham Cuffley
Rhoda Dakar
Max Daly
Dido Davies and Wolf
Dodgy
Phil Drayton
Julian Dunne
John Durrant
Brian and Anthea Eno
Brian Farmer
Craig Fees
Jon Fitzmaurice
Kevin Flemen
Paul Flynn MP
Jean Gallyer
Anne Garvey
Martin Green
Groundswell
Andrew Grove

Philomena Guillebaud
Hackney Empire
Mary Hansford
Katie Hanson
Rev. Alan Hargrave
Rev. Ian Harker
Seth Harman
Jancis Harvey
Cathy Hembry
Boo Hewardine
John Hipkin
John Hollebon
Michelle and Robert Howard
Simon Hughes MP
Brian Iddon MP
Helen Jacobus
Hilary Johnys
Janet Jones
Nick Jordan
The Junction
Naz Kahn
David Kennard
Bruce Kent
Sharon Khazna
Bill Kirkman
Jane Langley
Ken Loach
Bob Lucas
Brent Ludwick
Juliet Lyon
Pat McCafferty
Chris Main
Michael Malone Lee
Judy Maude
Graham Mitchison
Emma Mount
Mo Mowlam

Robert Newman
'Not Guilty' musicians: Cath
    Coombs, Karl Ferre, Denis
    Hayes, Laurence Hobson, Andy
    Williamson and Gordon Bell
David O'Brien
Kevin Ovenden
James Paice MP
David Palfrey
Parity Internet
Drew Park
Amy Passa
Max Perutz
Greg Poulter
Prison Reform Trust
The Quakers
Eddi Reader
Release
Prof. Sir Martin Rees
Dr Robert
Daphne Roper
Alan Rusbridger
Diana Ruthven
Alexei Sayle
SchNEWS
Prof. Roger Scruton
Arthur Smith
Mel Smith
Jon Snow
Mark Steele
The Stockwell Project
Sir Tom Stoppard
Streetwise
Chris Taylor
Elizabeth Thoday
Mark Thomas
Transform

Unions:

CUSU

FBU, Scottish Region

MSF

NAPO, London and Manchester
   branches

NUS at APU

NUJ, Central and Magazine
   branches

PCS, Tax Credit Office

T&G, Housing Workers branch &
   ACTS

TGWU

UNISON

Unleash

The User's Voice – especially Andria
   Efthimidi-Mordaunt

Marianna Vintiadis

Terry Waite

Norma Waterson

Sally Weale

The Welsh Assembly

Matthew White

Prof. Sir David Williams

Michael Winner

Victoria Wood

Claire Woods McConville

Roy Woolford

Steve Wyler

and anyone else I may have forgotten